IMAGES
of America

Watermen of Reedville and the Chesapeake Bay

ON THE COVER: The local watermen of Reedville head out into the Chesapeake Bay into the early sunrise to begin another long day of fishing. It is a constant daily grind to provide for their families. The unique flat-bottomed deadrise boat is preferred by many because with its small draft, it is easy to maneuver in the shallow creeks that abound everywhere. (Courtesy of the Reedville Fishermen's Museum.)

IMAGES
of America

WATERMEN OF REEDVILLE AND THE CHESAPEAKE BAY

Shawn Hall

ARCADIA
PUBLISHING

ISBN 978-1-4671-1627-5

Published by Arcadia Publishing
Charleston, South Carolina

Printed in the United States of America

Library of Congress Control Number: 2015953481

For all general information, please contact Arcadia Publishing:
Telephone 843-853-2070
Fax 843-853-0044
E-mail sales@arcadiapublishing.com
For customer service and orders:
Toll-Free 1-888-313-2665

Visit us on the Internet at www.arcadiapublishing.com

To Donald George, who has dedicated much of his life compiling the most detailed guide and history of the menhaden boats and the men who served on them. Without his expertise, knowledge, and perseverance, all of this history would have faded away.

Contents

Acknowledgments

This book is only made possible by the wonderful photograph collection that is housed at the Reedville Fishermen's Museum. The museum boasts one of the most complete collection of historical records of the menhaden fishing boats that have plied the local waters. Our longtime curator of archives, Donald George, has spent a large portion of his life accumulating information and photographs on every known boat. All have been carefully compiled in multiple albums, alphabetically by name, and are available for researchers and family members looking for information. I want to deeply thank Don for his assistance with this project and proofreading the captions to make sure my terminology was correct.

I would also like to thank my staff at the museum, Karen Rogers and Wanda Hassler, for their help. Also, for sharing their experiences, memories, and/or history of Reedville and fishing on the Chesapeake Bay, I would like to thank the following: George Butler, Monty Deihl, George Frayne, Wendell Haynie, the late Somerville "Spud" Parker, Ray and Walter "Peale" Rogers, Charles Williams, and many other new friends in Reedville who have made me feel so welcome. I also greatly appreciate the support of the board of directors of the Greater Reedville Association, the parent organization of the Reedville Fishermen's Museum, for their support when this project was proposed to us by Arcadia.

I would also like to thank two of the very most important people in my life: my mother, Lorraine Hall, and my daughter, Heather Hall. Their love and support through the years as I have had to travel far away to continue following my museum career has made the extended periods apart bearable. Hopefully, we will be able to all be together in one place again soon.

Unless otherwise noted, all images are courtesy of the Reedville Fishermen's Museum. All royalties from this book go directly to the Reedville Fishermen's Museum.

INTRODUCTION

The Chesapeake is the largest bay in the United States and is probably the richest in both quality and variety of its marine life. "A Faire Bay," Capt. John Smith called it in his *General Historie of Virginia*, "compassed but at the mouth with fruitful and delightsome land." Nearly 200 miles long, it varies in width from less than 5 miles in Maryland to more than 30 in Virginia. Its average depth is only about 20 feet, although in some places it exceeds 150 feet. One can sail up the bay from the capes to the Delaware Canal and never vary one's compass heading by more than a few degrees from due north.

Its total shoreline is estimated to exceed 4,000 miles. The Susquehanna, James, York, Rappahannock, Potomac, and Patuxent Rivers, all on the western shore, were important commercial waterways until the early part of this century. Tributaries provide spawning and nursery sites for many of the important fish species, including menhaden. We are all "Keepers of the Bay," and our concentrated efforts must continue if this magnificent resource is to survive and flourish in the future.

The bay has provided many families their livelihood through various means, but fishing, oystering, and crabbing were the primary commercial products. With the arrival of Elijah Reed and the establishment of Reedville in the 1870s, a small fish called menhaden became the primary catch. The industry grew to immense proportions, and fishing fleets and huge factories sprang up in Reedville and many other areas of the bay. Initially, the primary use of the fish was a cheap alternative to whale oil.

Menhaden average about 12 to 15 inches and weigh two-thirds to one pound. They are silvery in upper air and more iridescent below the surface. Menhaden inhabit the Atlantic Seaboard from Maine to Florida and into the Gulf of Mexico. They favor rivers and bays as far inland as brackish waters. It is believed that they spawn in the ocean over the continental shelf in winter, and one female lays an estimated 22,000 eggs. The menhaden leave the bay in October and return in the spring.

One

Watermen of the Bay

The history of watermen on the Chesapeake goes back to the early days of Jamestown at the beginning of the 1600s. The term *watermen* denotes, whether male or female, someone who works in the fishing industry. There is a wide variety of fish, crabs, and oysters in the bay, and all have to be harvested by watermen before they can get to the hungry consumer. While the richness of the bay provides a bounty, it takes a strong and special attitude to do the dangerous work of the watermen. Most watermen earning a living for their family from the bay are completely independent fishermen who have purchased their own boat and equipment, risking it all in the hopes of having a good season to pay the bills and maybe have some left over to get the boat ready for the next season.

It is a tough and demanding life on the bay. A typical workday starts before dawn and ends long after sunset. While the Chesapeake Bay is a beautiful place, it can prove dangerous and deadly to the watermen. Sudden storms are known to turn the bay angry with large waves. The bay has claimed many lives over the centuries and continues to claim more. However, the watermen accept these risks as part of the job and head out again in the morning. The true watermen do not do this for glory but rather because it is a calling and a dedication to the traditions that have developed over the centuries. It is the freedom to be on the water, the thrill of a good catch, and the satisfaction of a job well done.

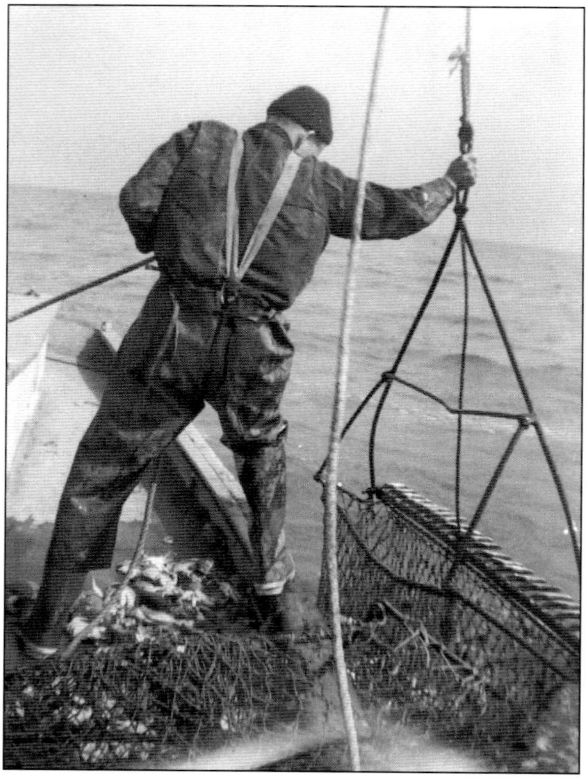

Back in the 1940s, watermen would harvest crab through the winter. Since the crabs would burrow into the bottom, a modified dredge was used to dig them out and place them into the netting. It was not a very efficient method, and many of the crabs were rendered useless. This practice is no longer allowed on the Chesapeake Bay.

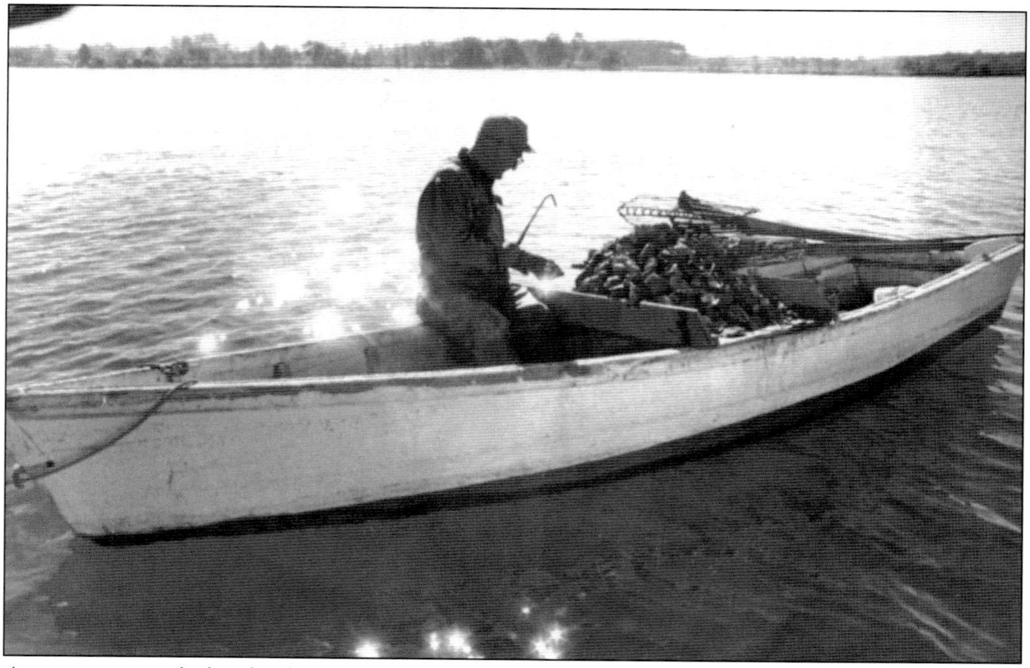

A waterman works hard to harvest a good day's worth of oysters from the waters around Reedville. He is using a flat-bottom wood skiff, a simple but versatile design. Unable to utilize the dredges of the bigger boats, oysters had to be harvested by long tongs. It was backbreaking work, but a good harvest made it worthwhile.

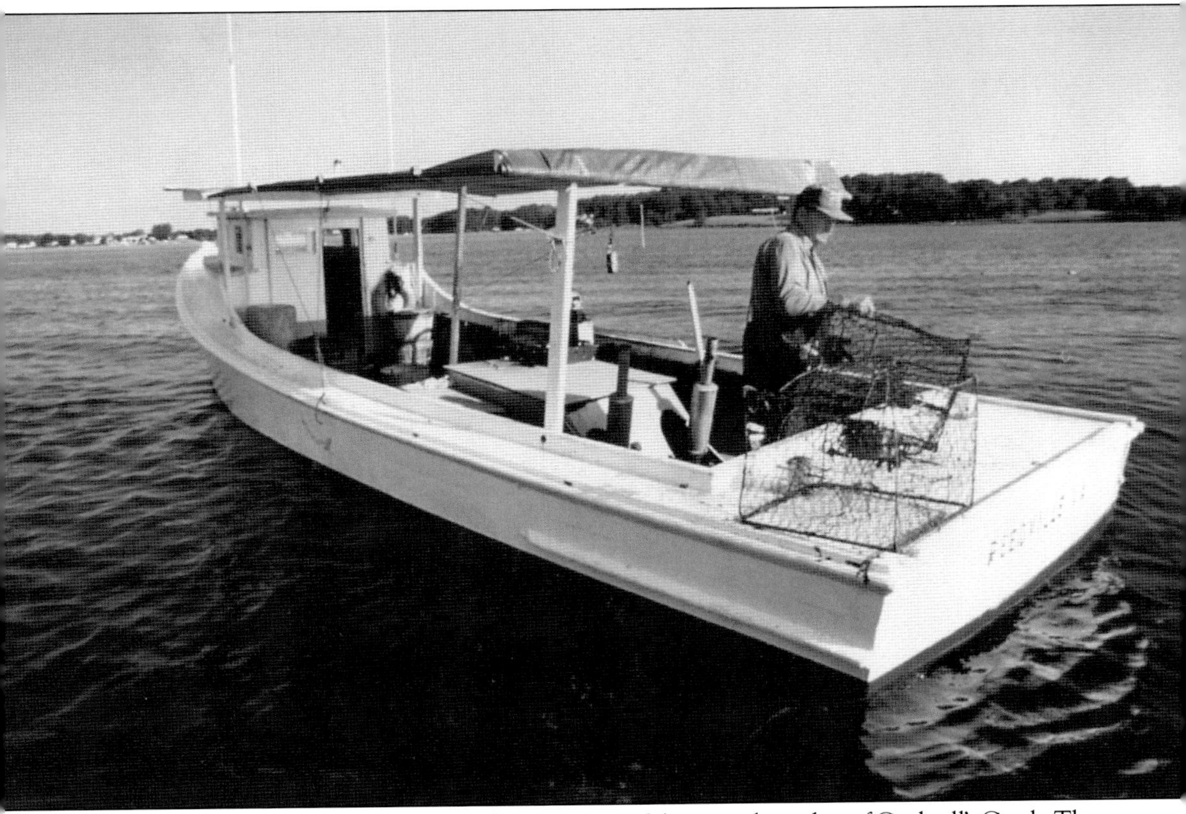

A local Reedville waterman tends his crab pots in one of the many branches of Cockrell's Creek. The area is known for the high quality of its blue crabs. This waterman is using a flat-bottomed deadrise boat, which helps provide easier access to shallow waters where the pots must be placed.

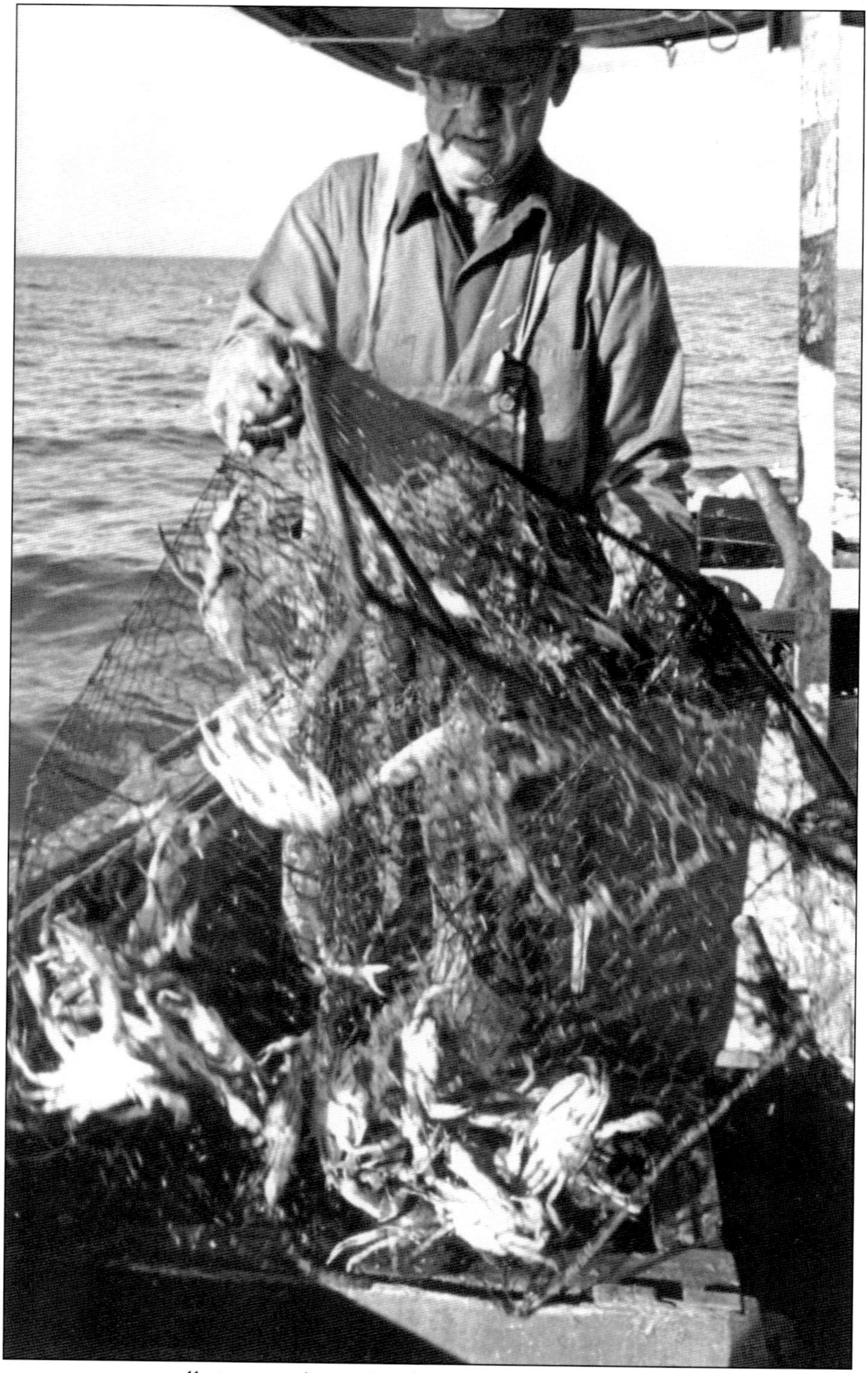

A veteran waterman pulls in a good pot of crabs up from the Chesapeake Bay during the 1950s. Many watermen of the area have family that have been here for many generations. The tradition is passed on, but as the years have passed, many families have stopped becoming watermen. It is a hard life with long hours and a lean year always looming.

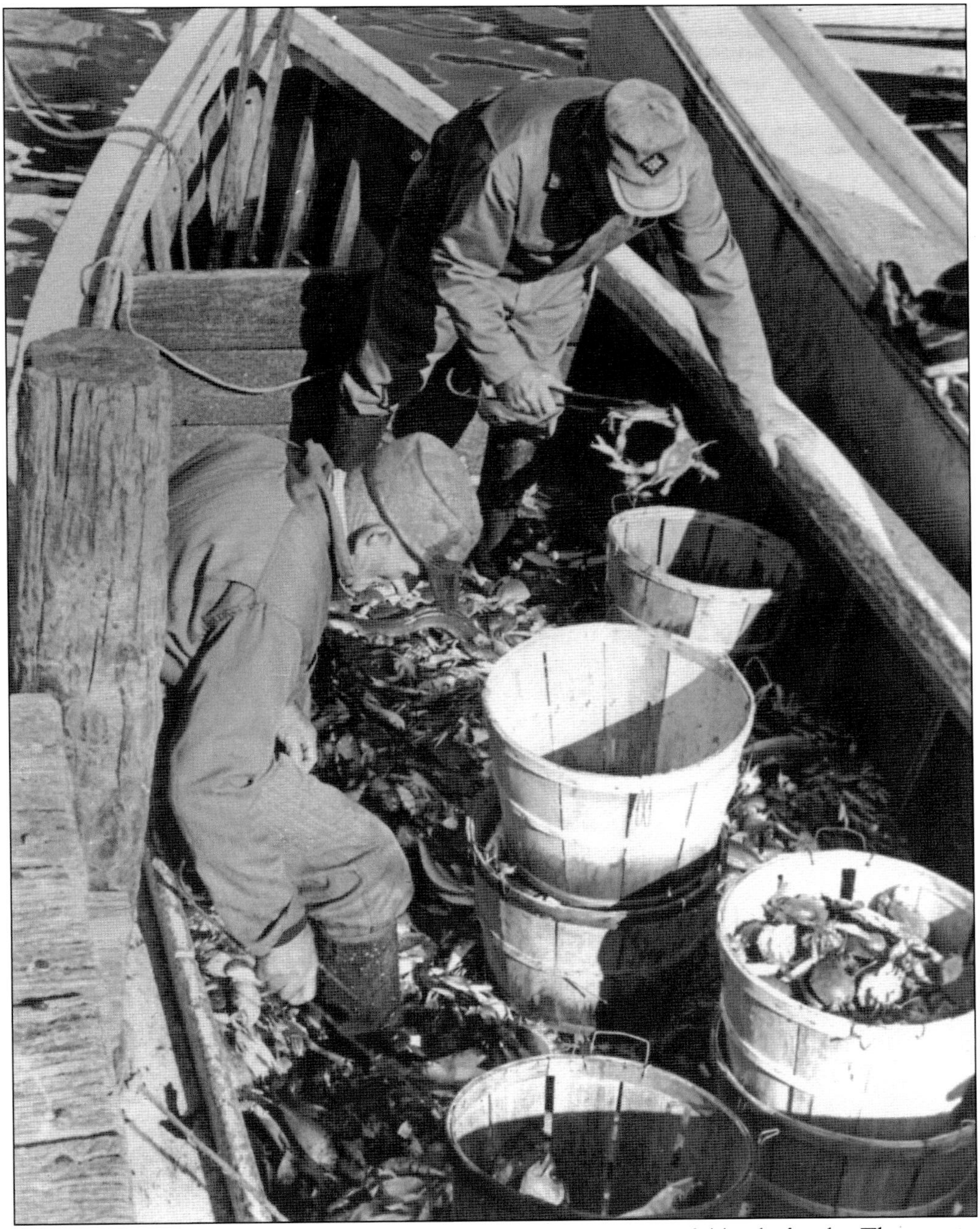

Back in the 1940s, these two old-timers have docked with a bountiful load of crabs. They are in the process of sorting the shellfish so they can sell the catch to the local fish market. A "buy" boat is adjacent and will receive the catch and haul it to market.

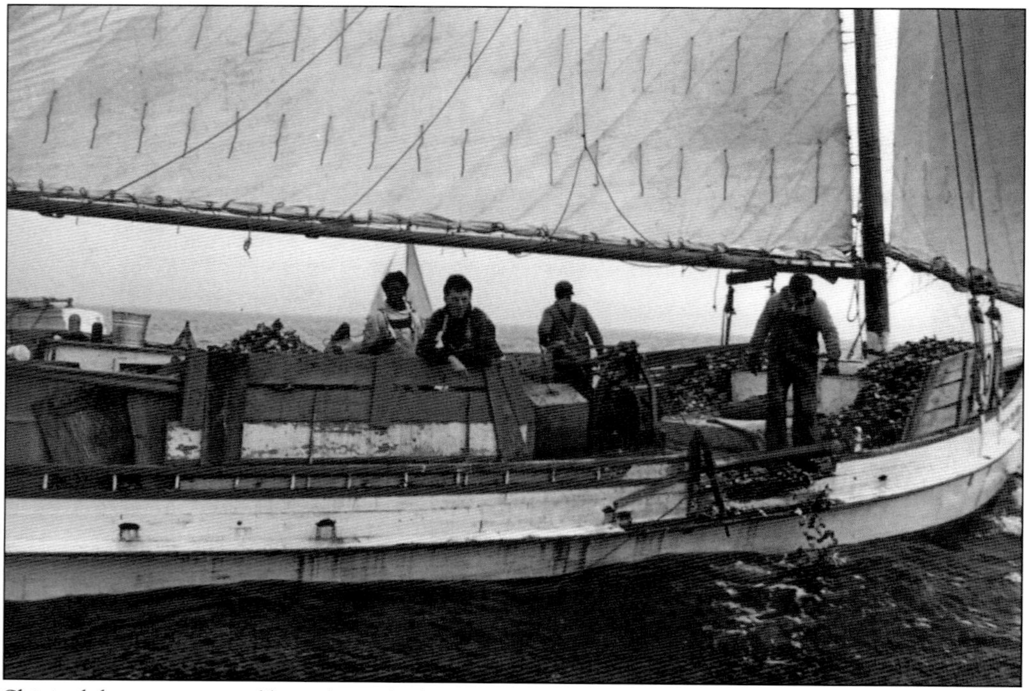

Skipjack boats were used heavily in the bay, particularly in the Maryland area. Dredges were used by dropping them on either side. During the peak of harvesting oysters, huge mountains of shells were prevalent at processing plants. Overfishing the supply led to more oversight, and the oyster numbers are once again climbing.

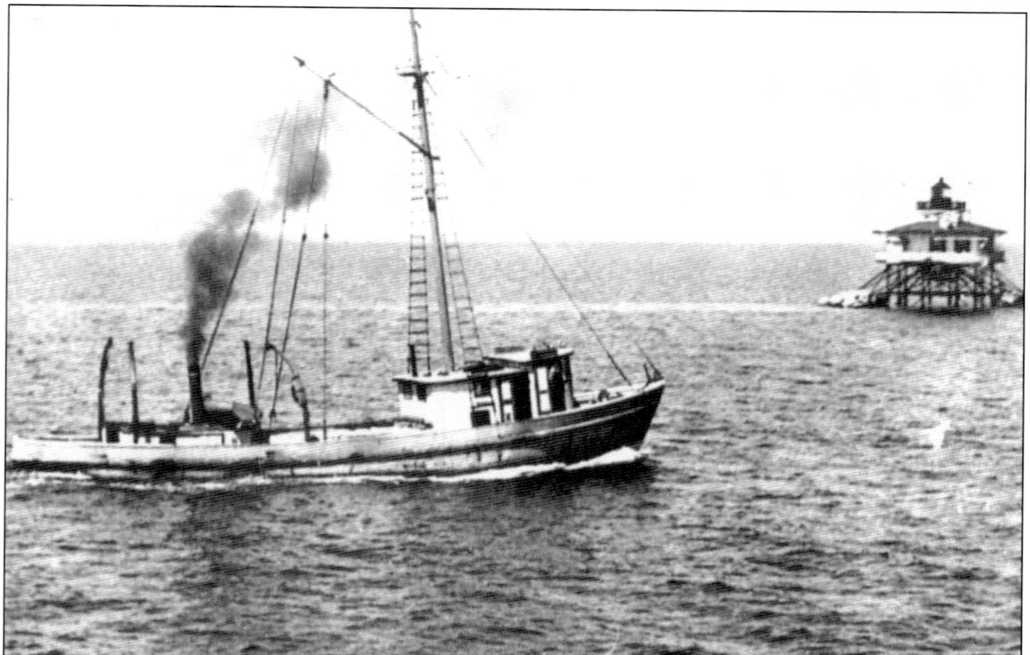

The fishing vessel *Colonel* passes the Windmill Point lighthouse at the mouth of the Rappahannock River around 1930. The lighthouse was originally built in 1869 but replaced in 1921 after ice swept it away. The structure was removed in 1965, and only an automated light is left.

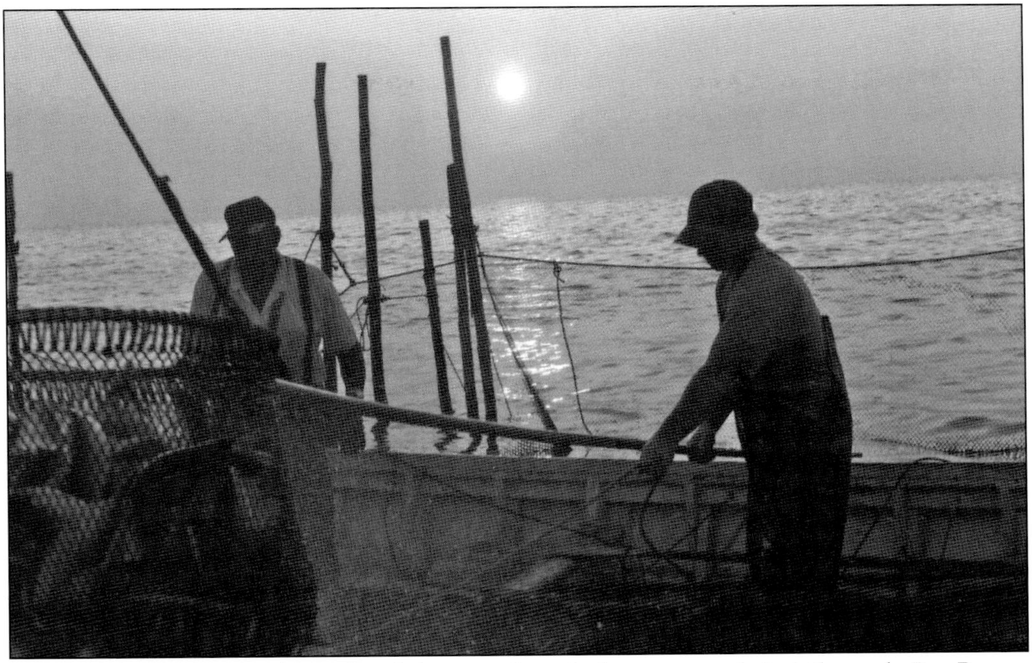

At sunrise, the watermen have already been working for hours to get their daily catch. Ray Rogers (left) and his son Peale are already out on the Great Wicomico River tending their pound net to see their catch for the day. It is a risky endeavor; one day, nets are full, but the next, they could be empty.

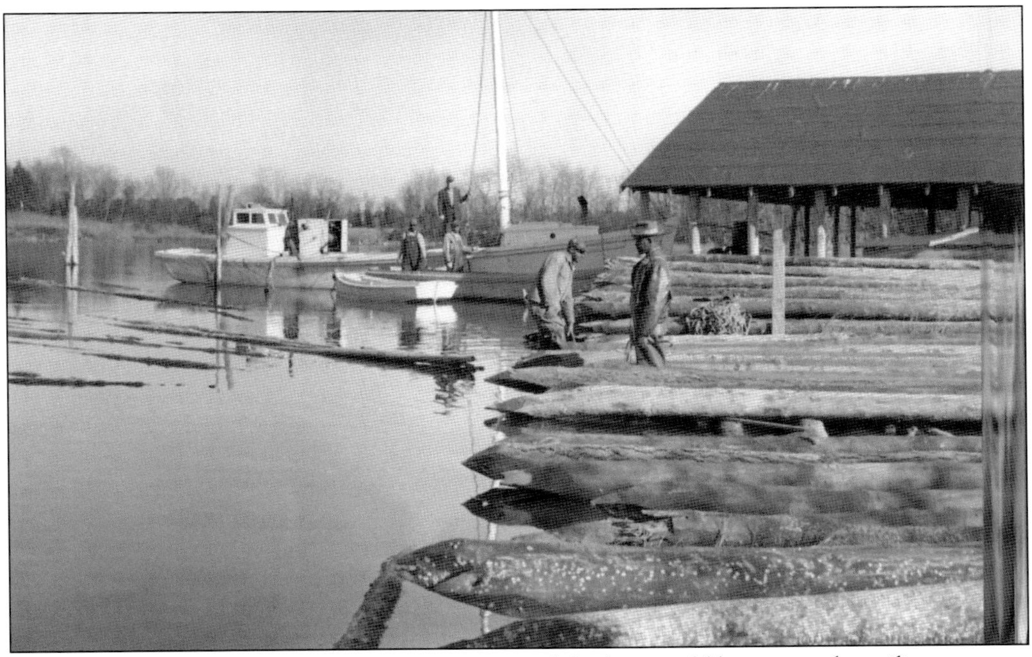

Every spring, watermen who ran pound nets around the bay would have to gather pilings to reset their nets, hopefully in a favorable spot. The dock pictured here is full of pilings in the process of being put in the water. The watermen tie them to the boat for the trip out to their fishing site.

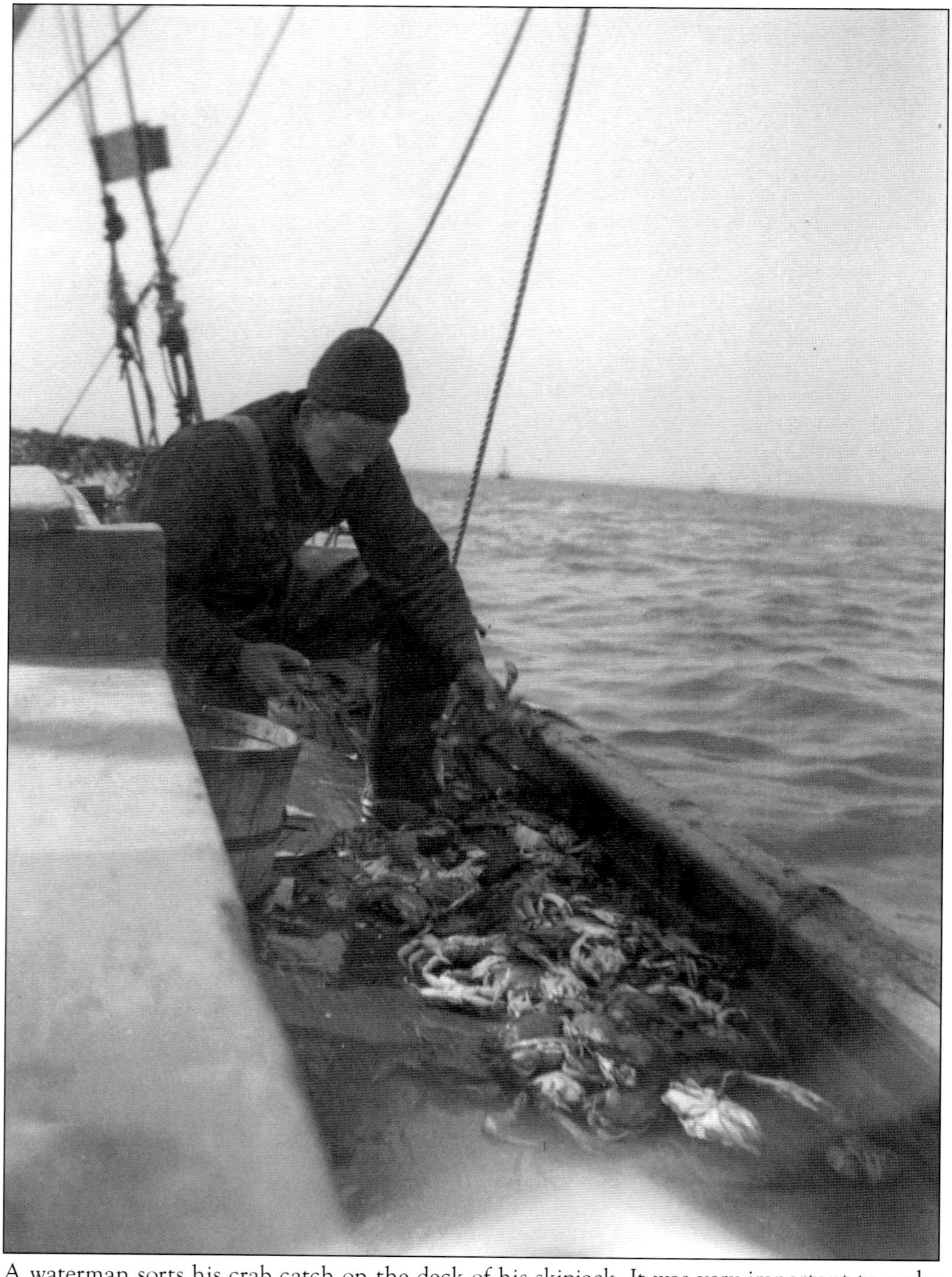

A waterman sorts his crab catch on the deck of his skipjack. It was very important to make sure that all the crabs were of legal size, since trying to sell undersized crabs would land him in big trouble. Throwing undersized crabs back into the bay helps to sustain their numbers in the Chesapeake Bay.

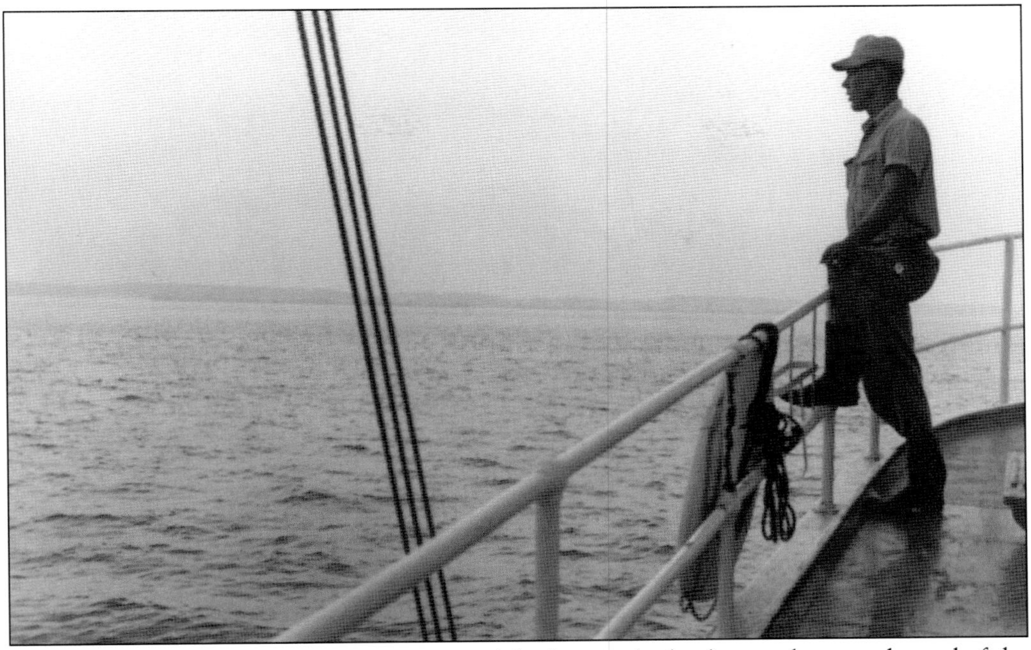

During the early 1960s, a waterman on one of the big menhaden boats relaxes at the end of the day as the sun sets. The days for the Chesapeake Bay's watermen normally start long before dawn and do not end after arriving at the docks near dark. Preparations for the next day's fishing have to be done before it is time to rest.

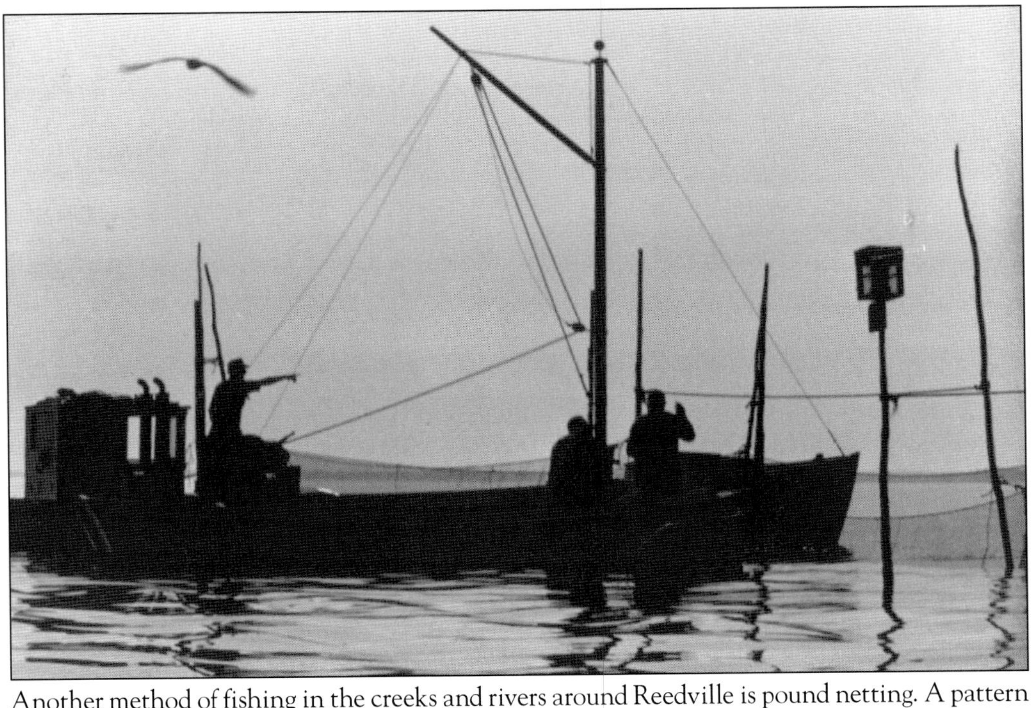

Another method of fishing in the creeks and rivers around Reedville is pound netting. A pattern of poles is set into the bottom and rigged with a series of nets. The fish end up at the end of the setup, unable to escape. Here, fourth-generation waterman Peale Rogers guides his boat, the *Glenna Fay*, into position to pull up the end net, which is hopefully full of fish.

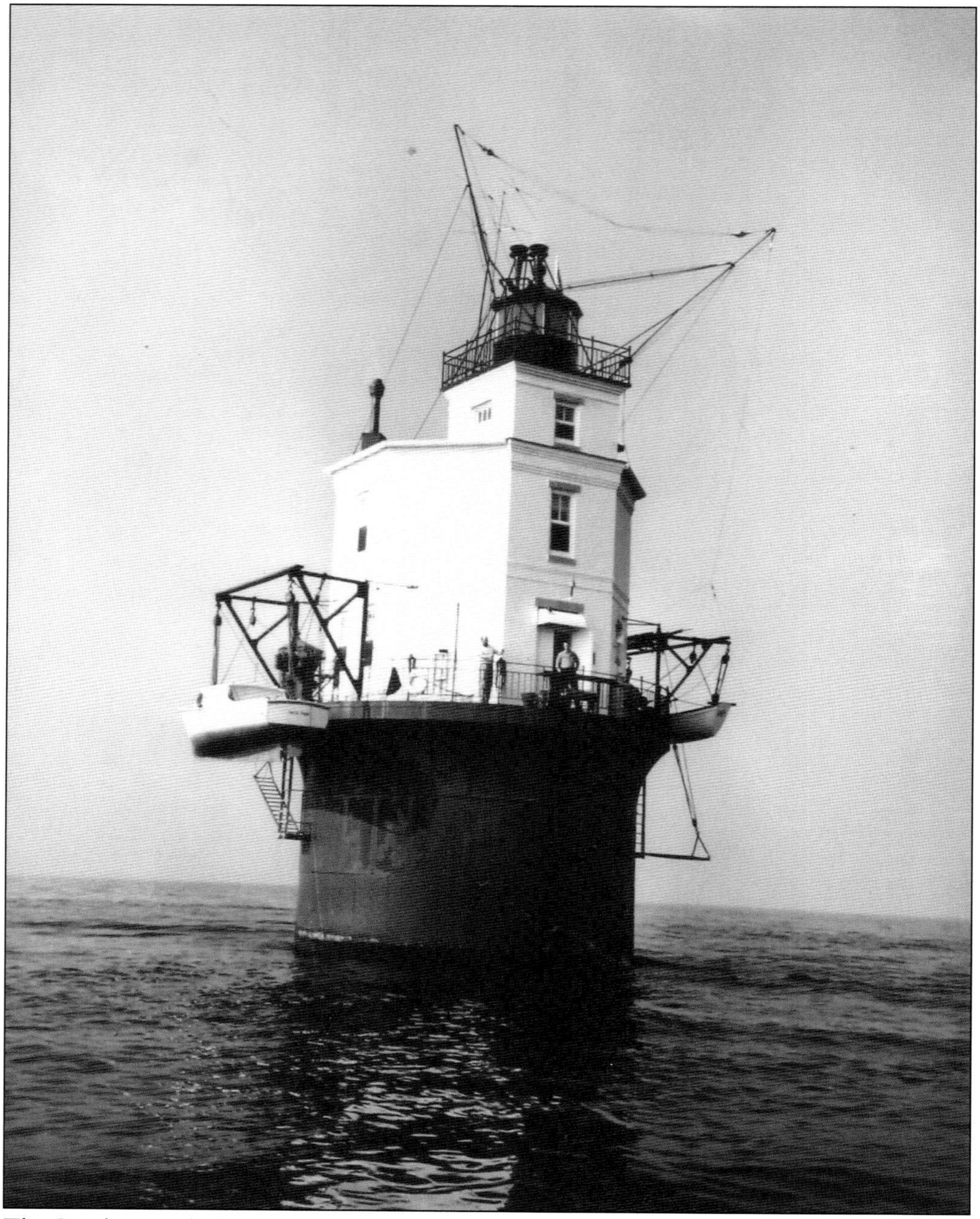

The Smith Point lighthouse was built in 1897 after the previous structure was swept away by ice. The lighthouse was the beacon at the mouth of the Potomac River and Chesapeake Bay. The house remained manned until 1971, when operations were made automatic. The lighthouse is in the National Historic Register, and while it is privately owned, the light is still used as a navigational aid.

Two

Menhaden Fishing

Menhaden fishing started in the 1879s and remains the major part of fish production for Reedville. The basic techniques of the catch are much the same as in earlier days, though diesel power has replaced steam and hoists are now hydraulically powered. As soon as a school of fish is spotted, the purse boats divide the seine between them and approach the school.

At the right moment, they separate and move around the school, paying out the seine as they go. Once the bottom of the seine is pursed up, it is drawn aboard the two boats. The "mother vessel" maneuvers into place to receive the catch. The fish are pumped into the refrigerated fishholds. The purse boats are then loaded onto the davits aboard the ship, which heads back to the dock to unload.

Finding the fish is the challenge. During the early days, spotters used crow's nests at the top of the mast to locate the tightly packed schools of fish. After World War II, planes began to be used for aerial spotting. With improved postwar communications equipment on both planes and fishing vessels, aerial spotting has become the accepted way to track the menhaden throughout the Chesapeake Bay.

The refrigerated fish are unloaded at the plant, where they are converted into fish meal and oil. The finished products made include Omega-3 fish oil supplements, fertilizers, paints, soaps, lubricants, and pet foods.

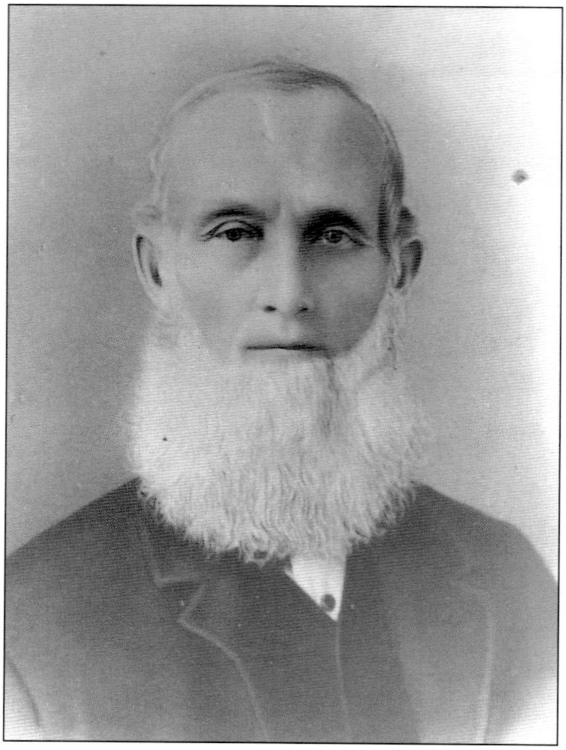

Capt. Elijah Reed, founder of Reedville, was a Maine menhaden fisherman who came to the future site of the town in 1874, looking for a winter fishing area. The abundance of the fish in the area led to a boom. The use of the fish oil as a replacement for the fading supply of whale oil made Reedville one of the most prosperous towns per capita on the Chesapeake Bay.

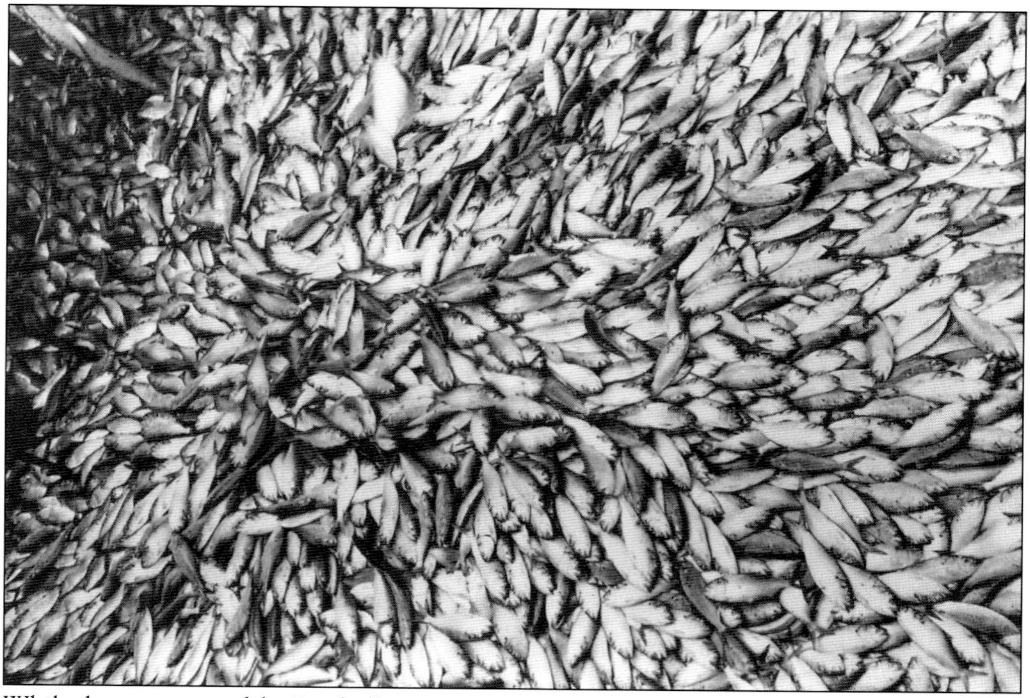

While the watermen of the Reedville area produced crabs, oysters, and fresh fish, it was always the fishing of menhaden that was the dominant moneymaker throughout Reedville's history. At one time, many fish factories lined the shore around the town. Although only Omega Protein Corporation remains, the port still has the second-highest production of all ports in the United States.

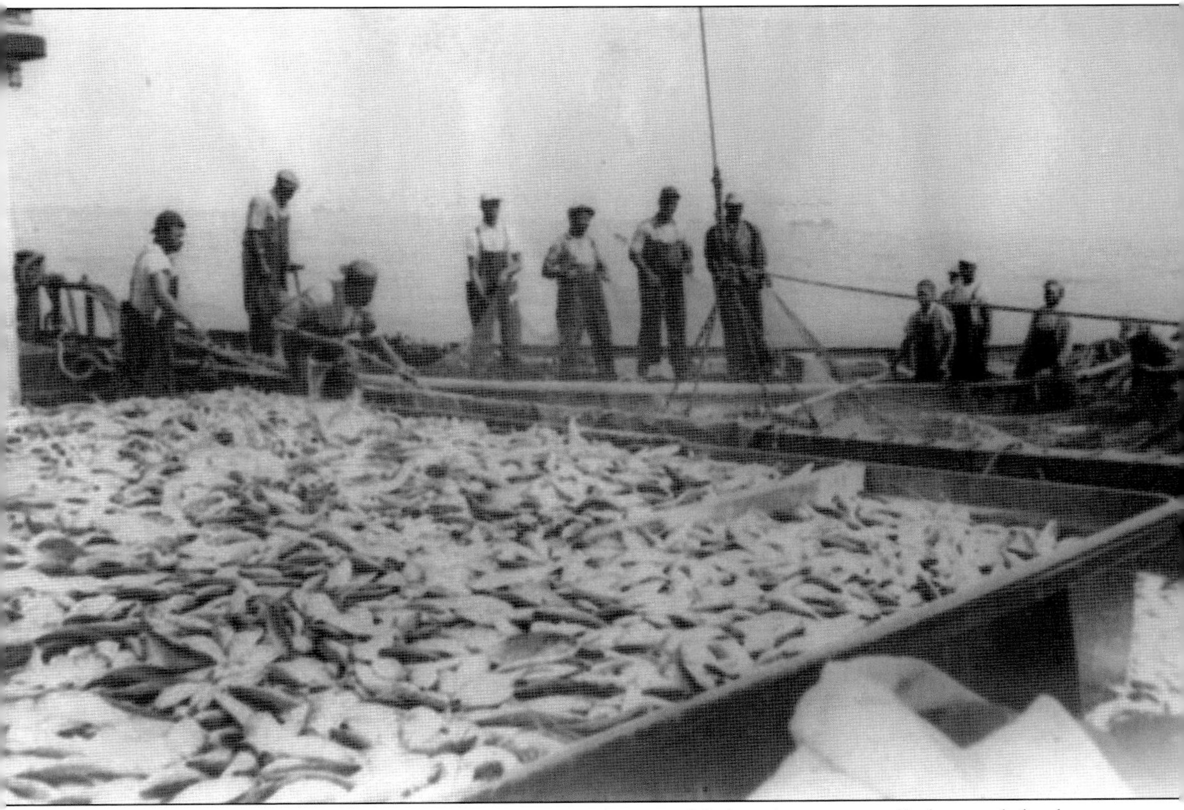

In the days before hydraulics, vacuum pumps, and powerful diesel engines, all the work had to be done by hand. Here, the purse boats have brought the nets full of menhaden to the fishing boat for unloading. The fish were then scooped out of the net between the boats and into the large trays in the foreground.

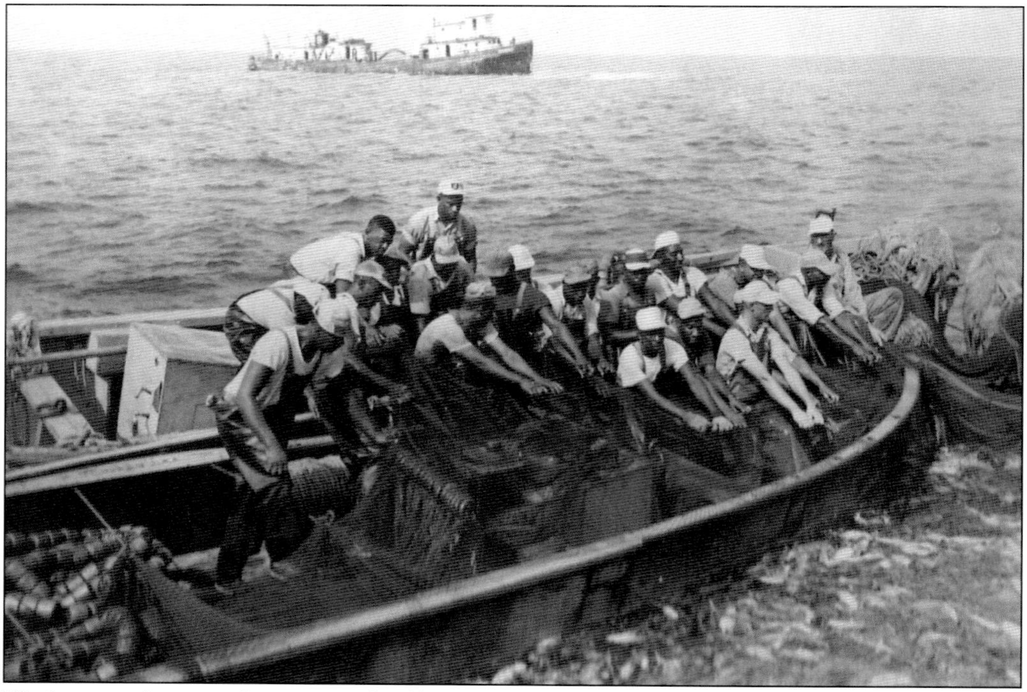

Working in the purse boats was a backbreaking job. After the two purse boats had trapped the school of menhaden with the large net, it took manpower to gradually pull the net back into the boat until only a small area of net, full of fish, was left. Then it was time to row to the main boat for unloading.

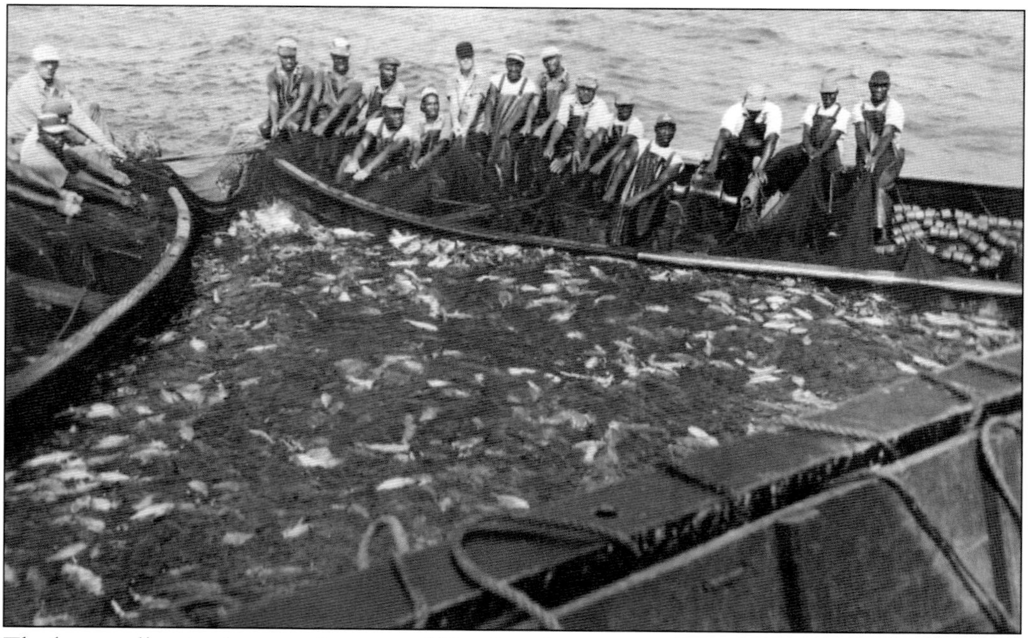

The bunt pullers in the purse boats would haul in the net, bunching up the fish. The menhaden steamer would come up port side to the purse boats and the crew would tighten, or harden, the net in order to concentrate the fish. Dip nets were then used to scoop up the fish into the boat's hold.

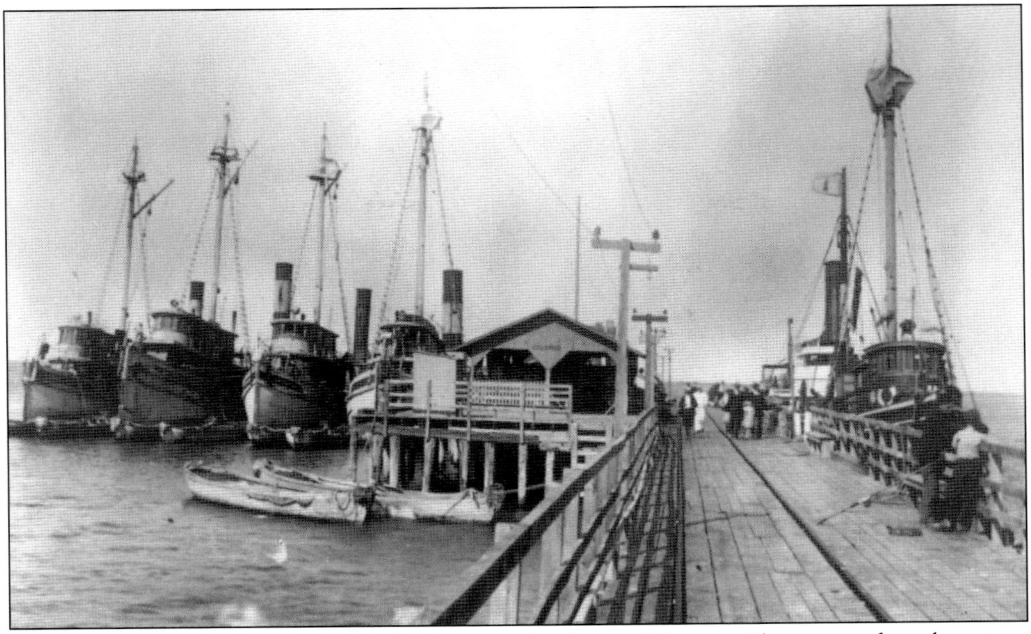

Not all of the fishing boats plying the Chesapeake Bay and Eastern Shore were from locations on the bay. Lewes, Delaware, served as the Atlantic Ocean port for a number of large menhaden companies. Here, a fleet of menhaden boats are moored along the steamship wharf in 1935 near the Hayes Factory. There were definitely some ill feelings about outsiders coming into the bay to catch the menhaden.

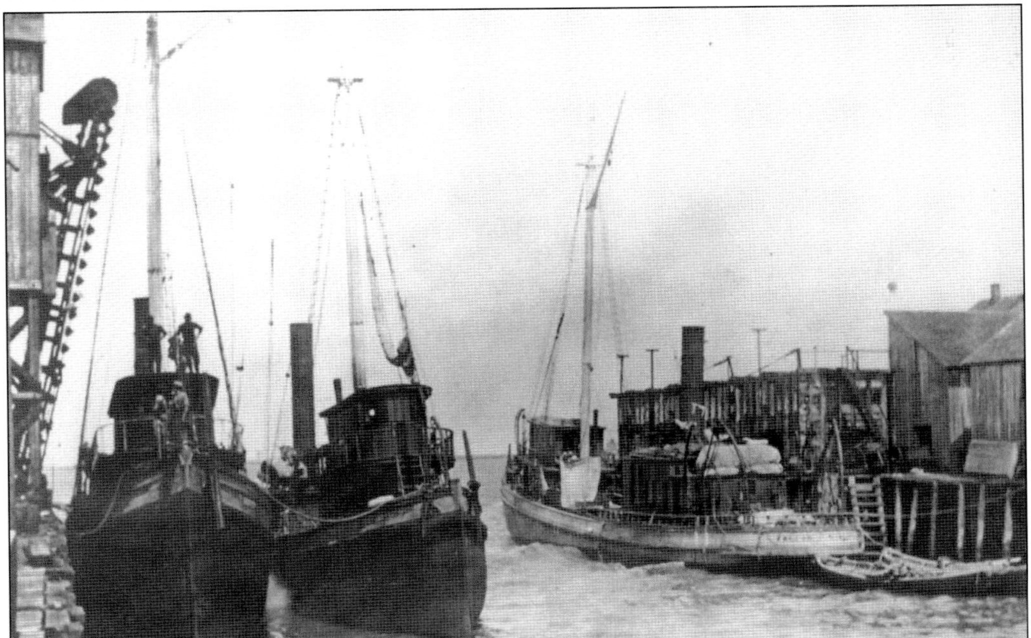

During the early years of the menhaden industry, the boats used were nothing like the huge steel ships used today. These boats date from around 1900 and bear witness to how dangerous it was to fish the bay during those days. The bay was known for sudden storms, which would arrive without warning, putting the small wooden boats at risk.

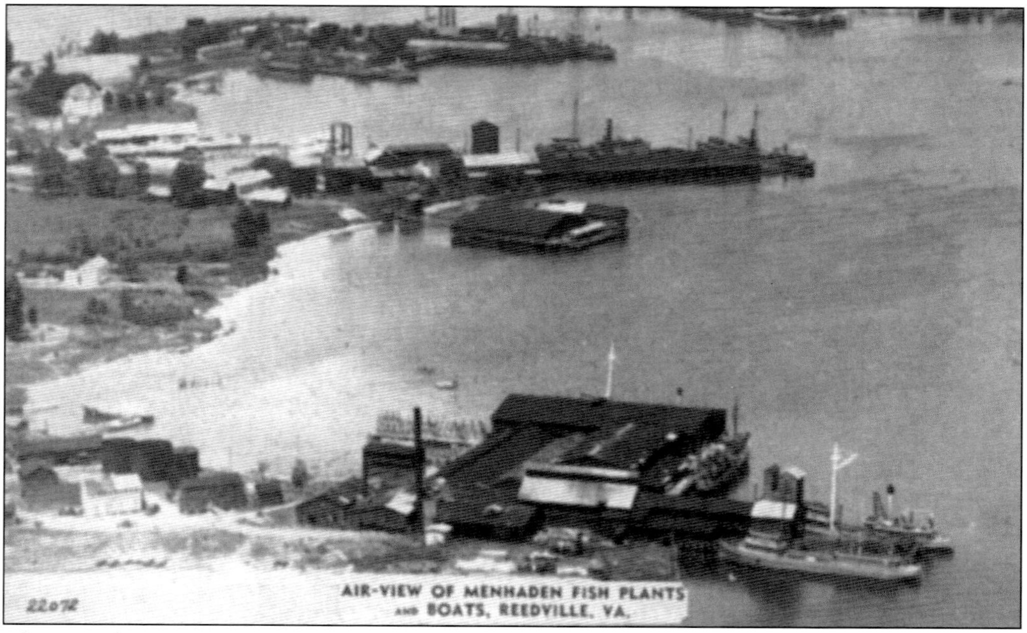

This aerial view from the 1940s shows some of the many fish factories that were in operation, working side by side. Each company had its own fleet of boats heading out every day. During the 1960s, the many fishing companies began a slow consolidation, the result of which was most of the factories closing down one by one.

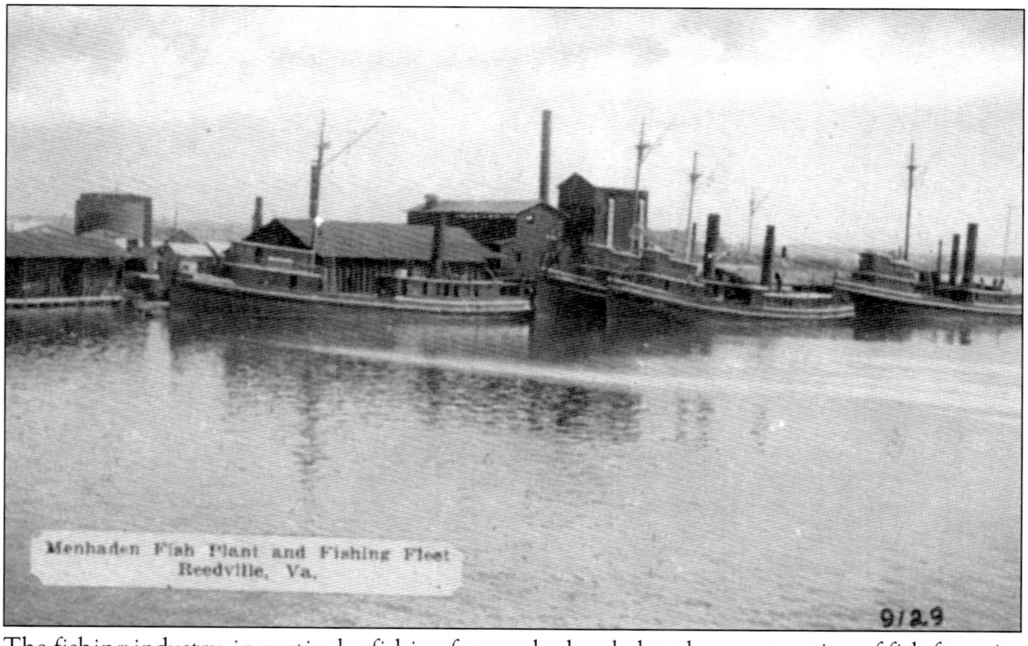

The fishing industry, in particular fishing for menhaden, led to the construction of fish factories all around Reedville. By the 1920s, more than 20 were in full operation. Seen here is the Edwards Company factory in Reedville, with a fleet of four fishing boats unloading the day's catch at the docks.

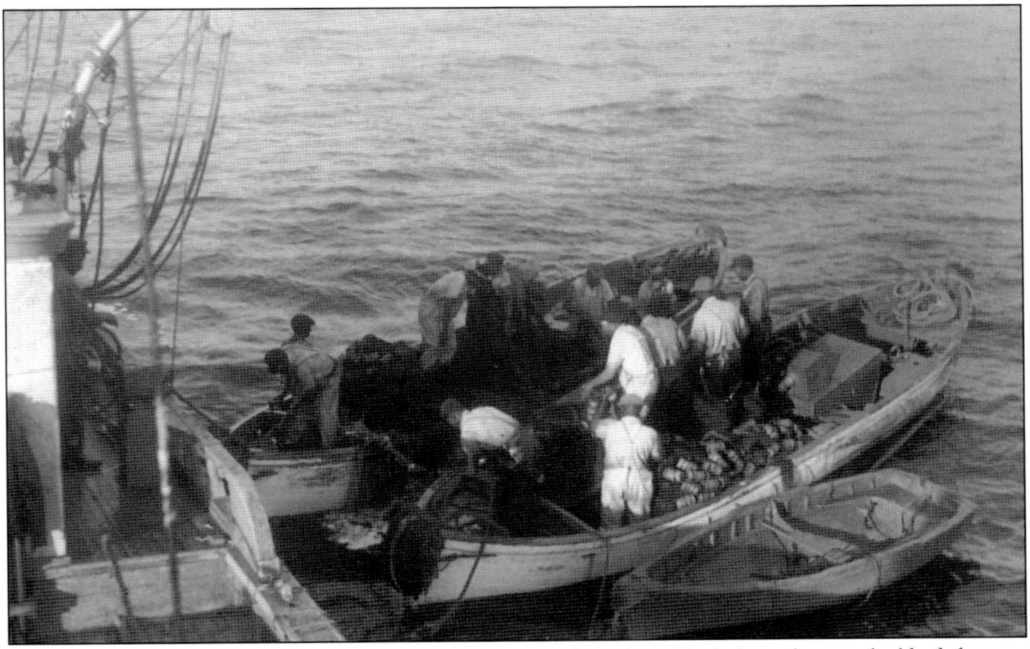

Two purse boats prepare to head out from their mother ship. Each boat has its half of the net used to capture the school of menhaden. These boats, from the 1950s, no longer have to be rowed—thanks to modern diesel engines. Note the striker boat tied to the purse boat.

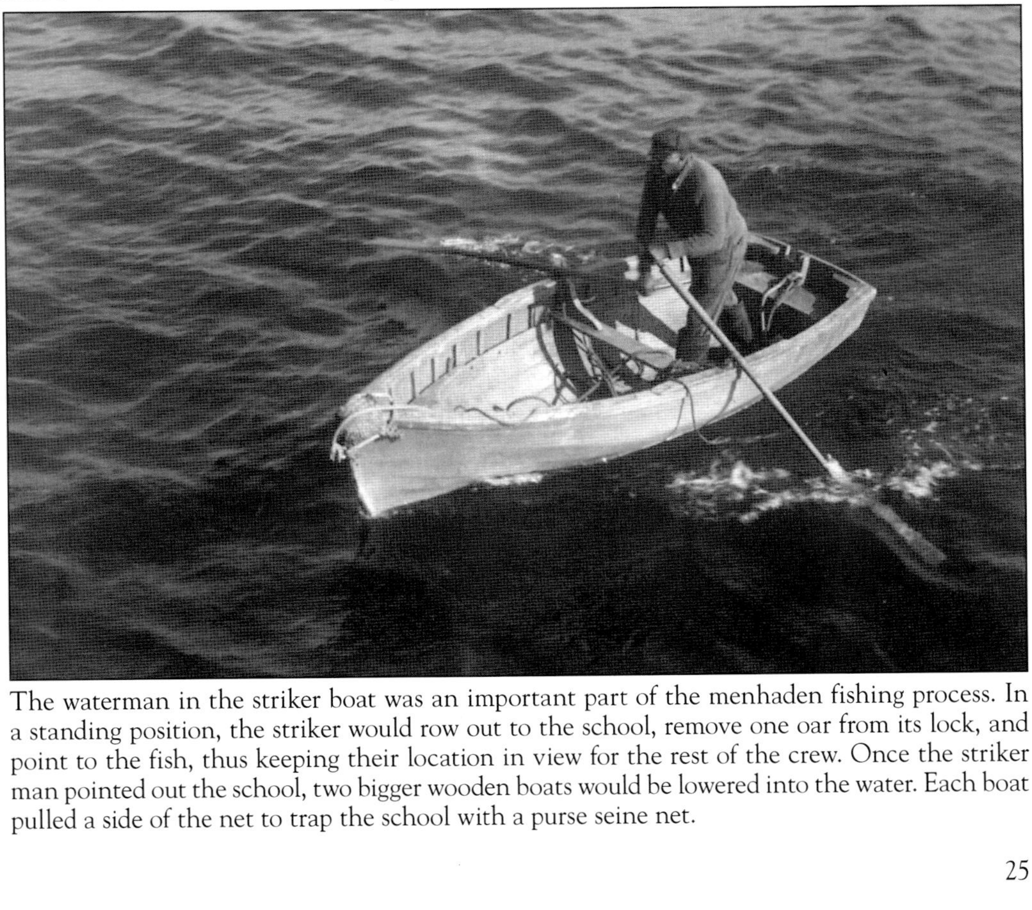

The waterman in the striker boat was an important part of the menhaden fishing process. In a standing position, the striker would row out to the school, remove one oar from its lock, and point to the fish, thus keeping their location in view for the rest of the crew. Once the striker man pointed out the school, two bigger wooden boats would be lowered into the water. Each boat pulled a side of the net to trap the school with a purse seine net.

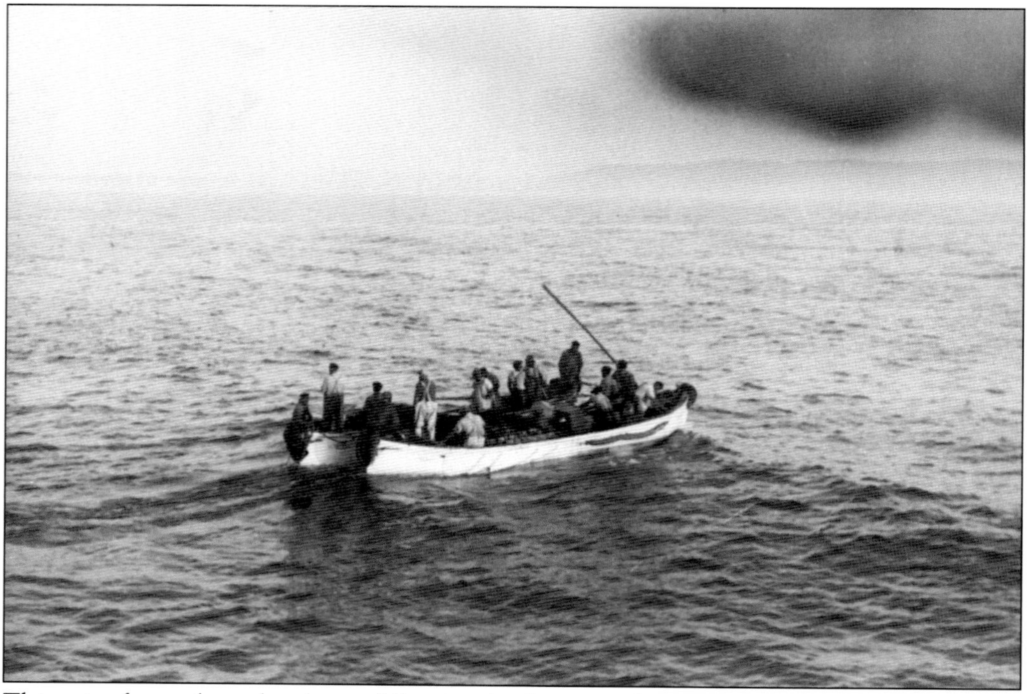

This pair of purse boats heads out, following the directions being given to them from the striker boat guide. Once the two crews began setting the seine, it was very important that they worked in unison to assure the net would be set properly. If a mistake was made, the school would have the opportunity to escape the trap.

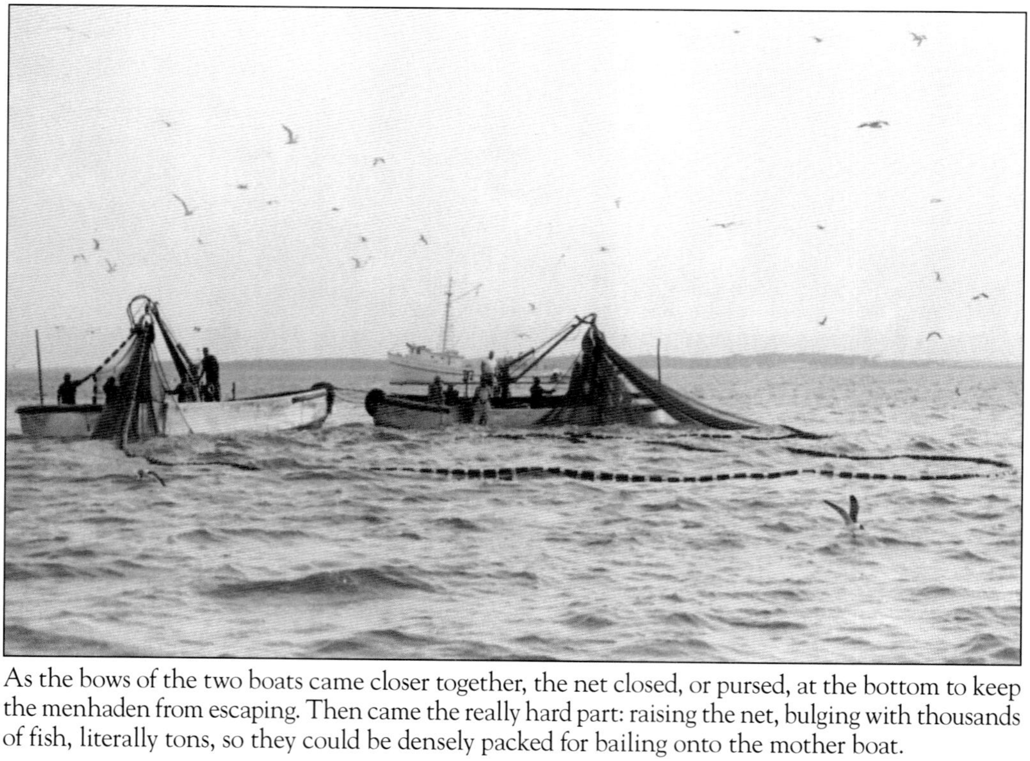

As the bows of the two boats came closer together, the net closed, or pursed, at the bottom to keep the menhaden from escaping. Then came the really hard part: raising the net, bulging with thousands of fish, literally tons, so they could be densely packed for bailing onto the mother boat.

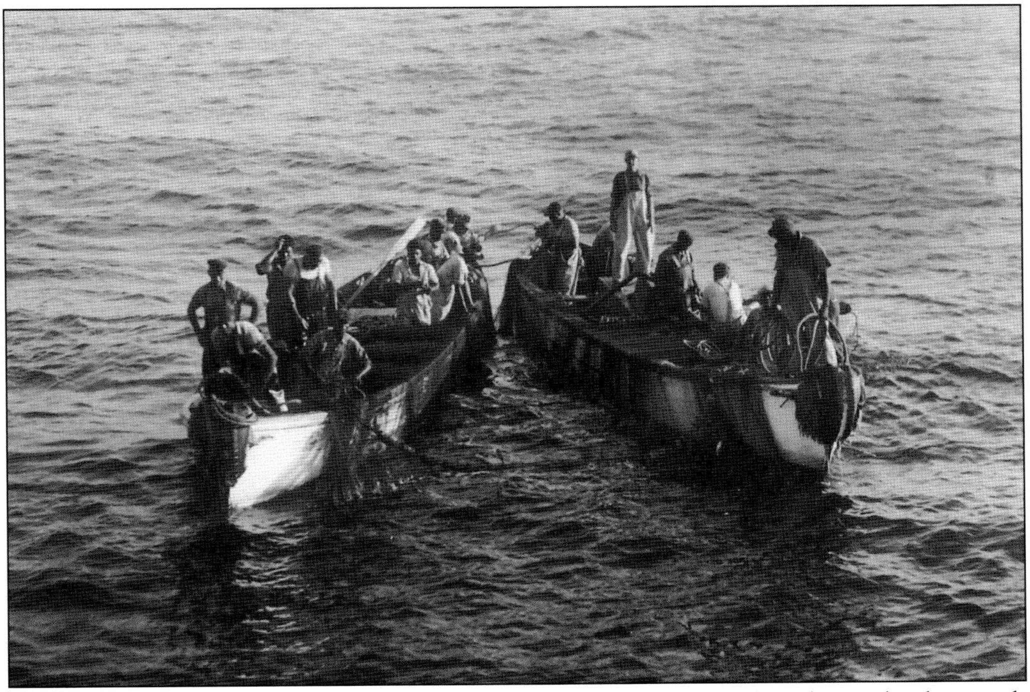

After a successful trip out into the bay, the purse boat crews arrive back at the mother boat with a seine of menhaden trapped between the two boats. Upon arriving at the boat, drip nets were then used to scoop up the fish into the boat's hold.

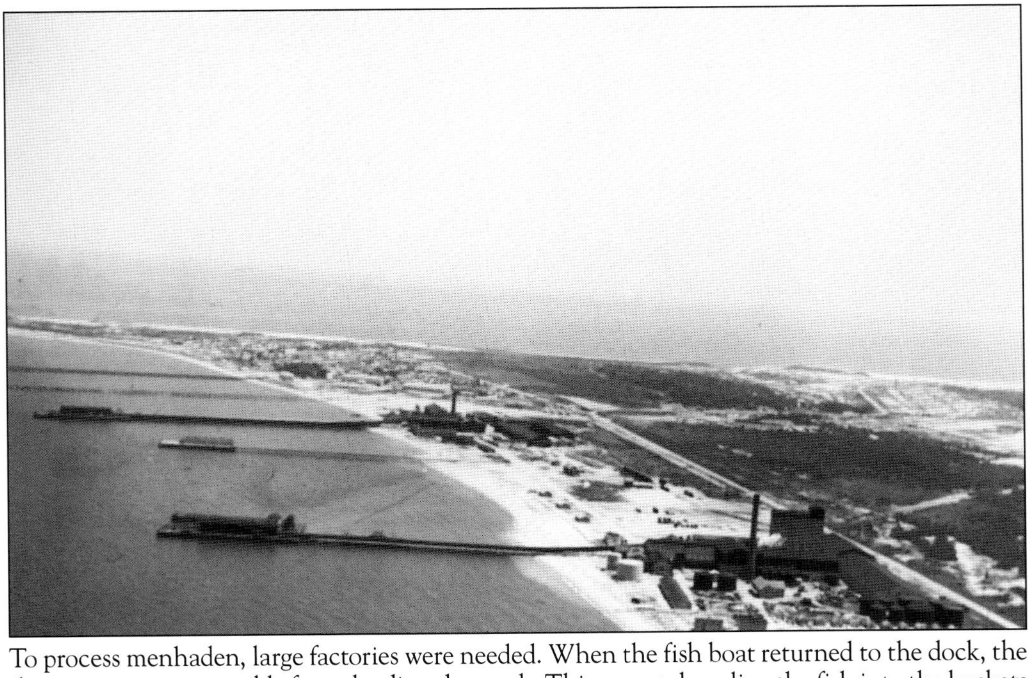

To process menhaden, large factories were needed. When the fish boat returned to the dock, the shore crew was responsible for unloading the catch. This meant shoveling the fish into the buckets of the conveyer belt to lift the fish into the elevation and then into the raw box.

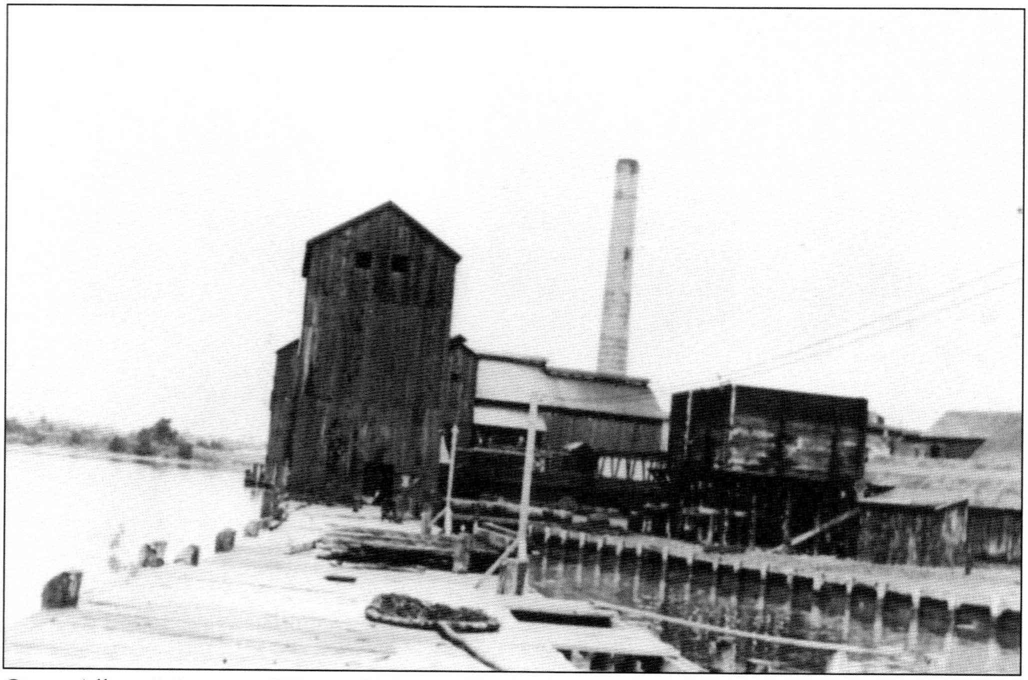

Capt. Albert Morris and James Fisher, Albert's brother-in-law, organized the Morris-Fisher Company, which was the largest menhaden factory in Reedville for many years. The large stack was built in 1902 and still remains today as the only remaining marker of the once-mighty Morris Fisher Company.

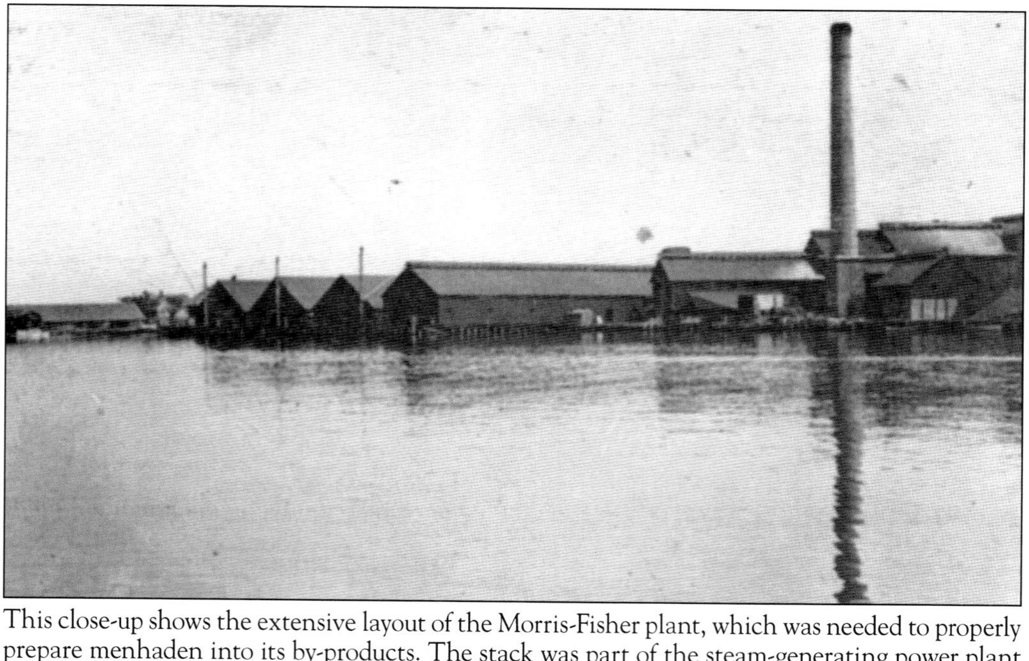

This close-up shows the extensive layout of the Morris-Fisher plant, which was needed to properly prepare menhaden into its by-products. The stack was part of the steam-generating power plant at the former Morris-Fisher menhaden factory. Bricklayers from Bordentown, New Jersey, built the stack because Reedville did not have enough skilled layers to do the job.

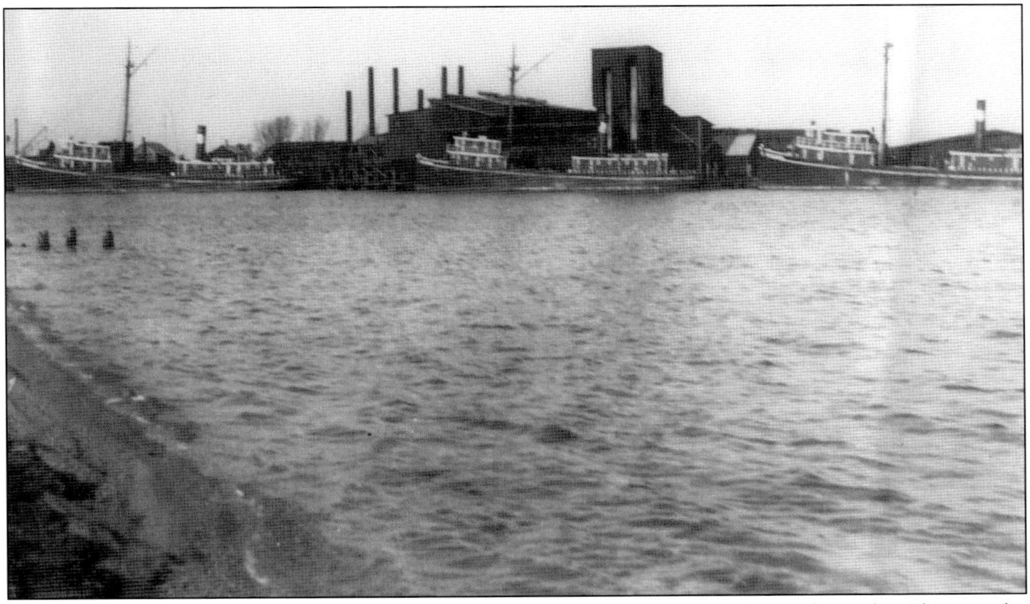

By the turn of the 20th century, fish factories were being built in many places along the Chesapeake Bay's shores. This was not only due to the proximity of the fish in the bay, but also because it was more sheltered than on the coast of the Atlantic Ocean. This is the Bellows Fishing Company factory in Ocran, Virginia, near White Stone. The boats moored in front are the *Margaret*, *Elizabeth Froelich*, and *Joseph Bellows*.

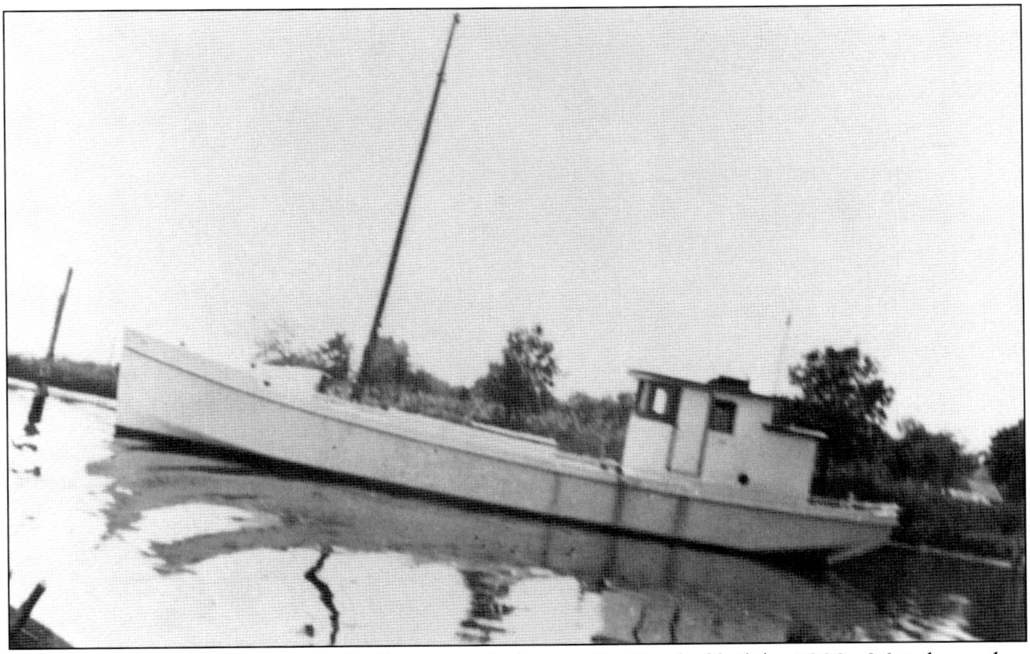

Buy, or deck, boats played a vital role primarily during the first half of the 1900s. Mainly used to buy oysters from watermen out on the bay and bring them to market, their service allowed more time to be spent fishing. A number were converted to be used for menhaden during the 1960s and 1970s, but their days of usefulness have faded. Many, like this one, ended up abandoned around the bay. There has been a big push to restore the remaining boats.

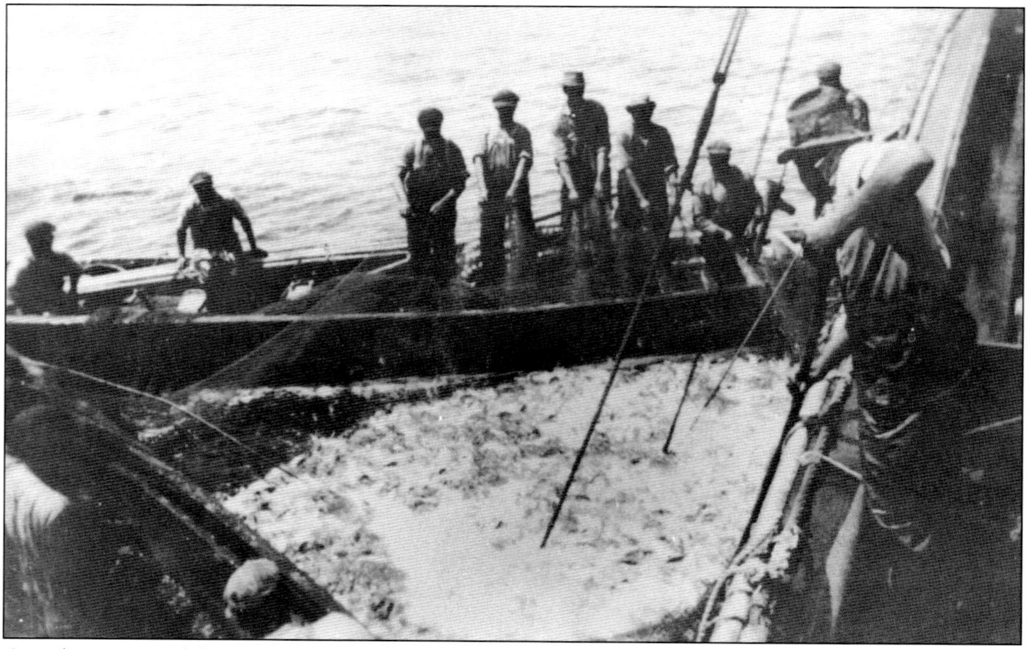

Another successful run comes to an end. The full net is a frothy white foam as the menhaden try to get away. The lines from the mother boat are attached to the bottom of the net to help raise the catch to the surface. Then, the catch will be loaded into the hold of the boat.

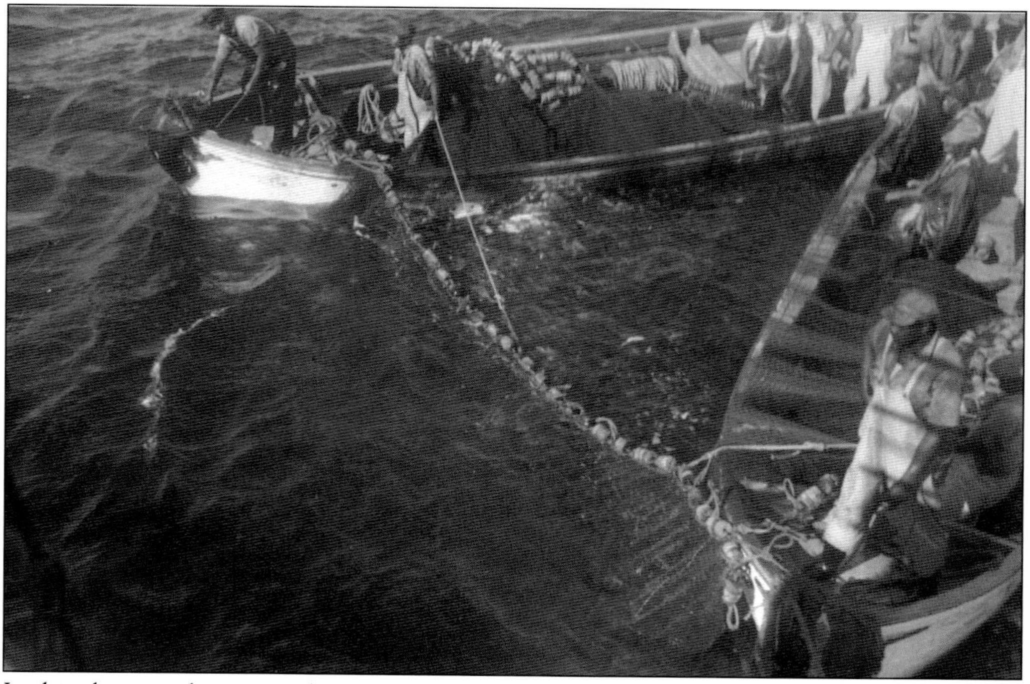

In this close-up, the net can be seen billowing out past the floats. The waterman pulling on the line is working to draw in the net tighter to consolidate the menhaden trapped inside. Before the days of hydraulics, this process was very labor intensive.

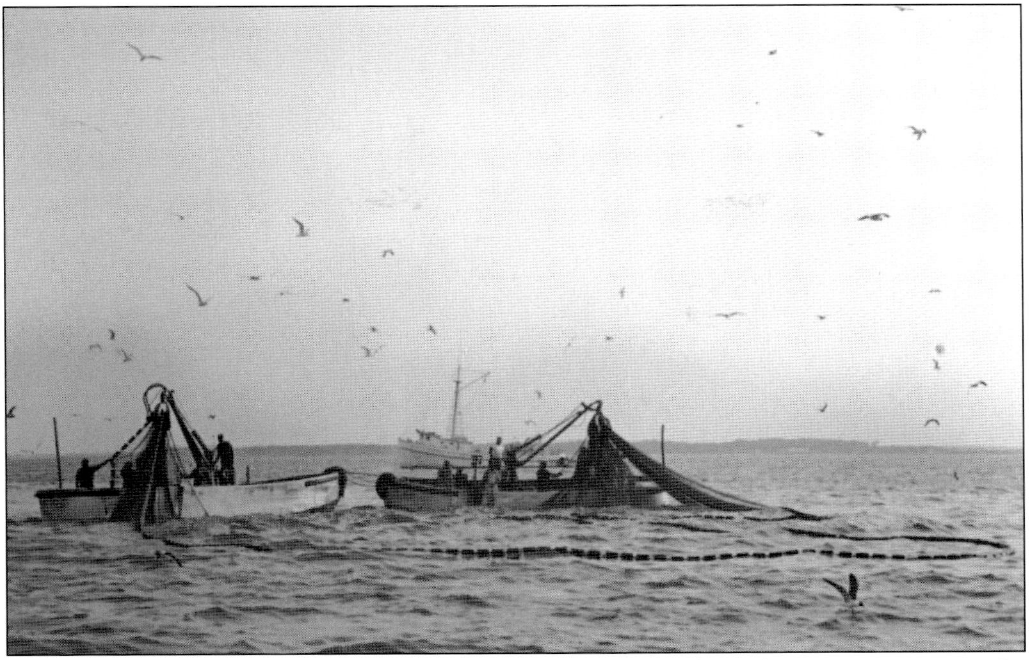

Two purse boats close the net. This photograph, from the 1950s, shows the newest innovation for menhaden fishing—the power block. A power block is a hydraulically powered winch mounted in the purse boat and used to pull up the purse net. It revolutionized the menhaden fishing industry.

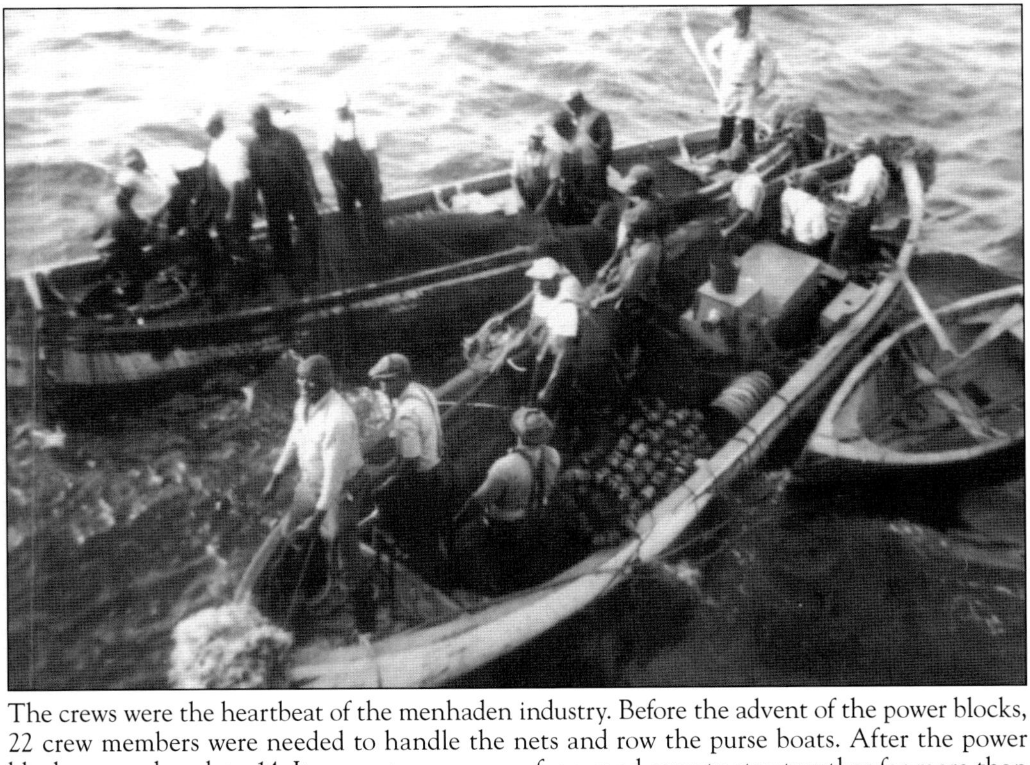

The crews were the heartbeat of the menhaden industry. Before the advent of the power blocks, 22 crew members were needed to handle the nets and row the purse boats. After the power block, crews shrank to 14. It was not uncommon for a good crew to stay together for more than 20 years.

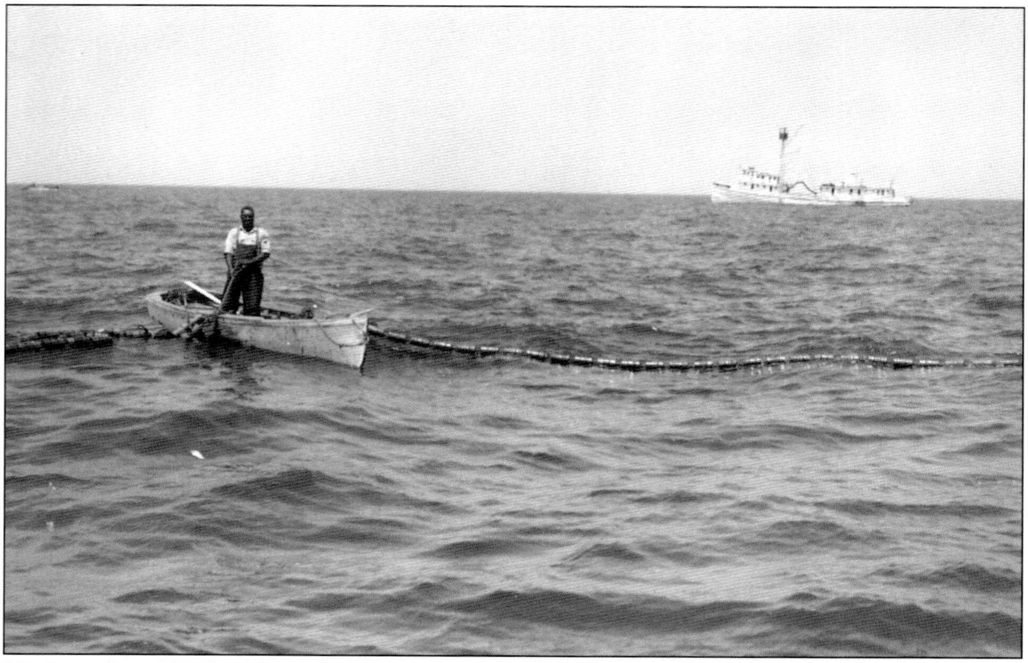

Working the striker boat for a menhaden crew was definitely a one-man job. Besides his responsibility to steer the purse boats to where the menhaden school was, he also kept a careful eye on the nets as the purse boats headed out to trap the school.

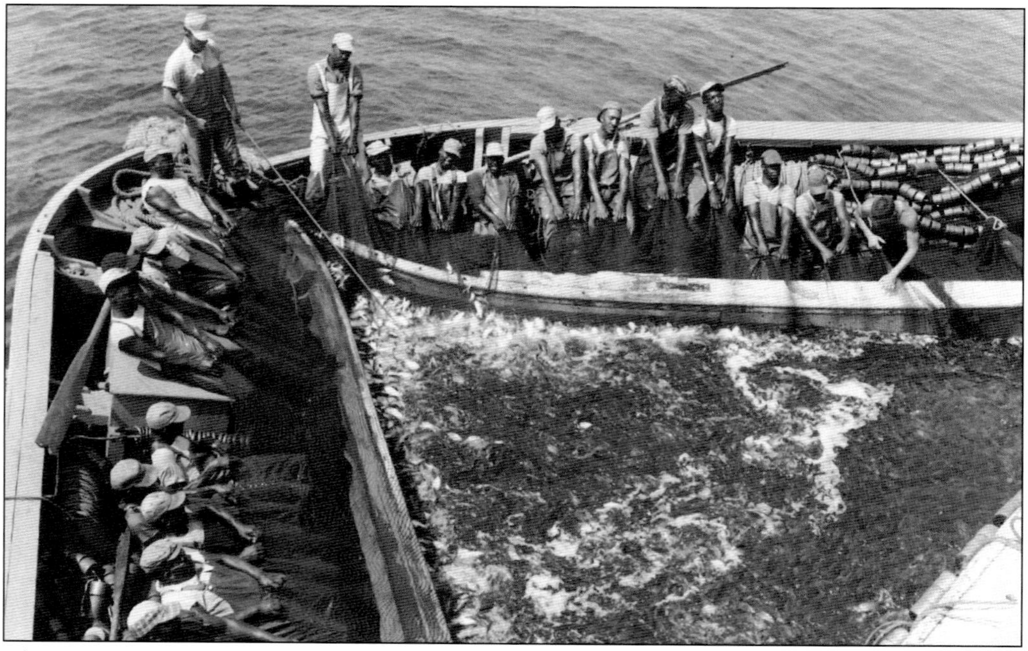

The stress and strain of pulling in the nets before the arrival of the power block is obvious here. Most men suffered from back troubles and hands that would not straighten due to the stress on the hands while pulling in the thin net lines. It was a long and arduous process to slowly compress the net, especially since it got tougher with each pull.

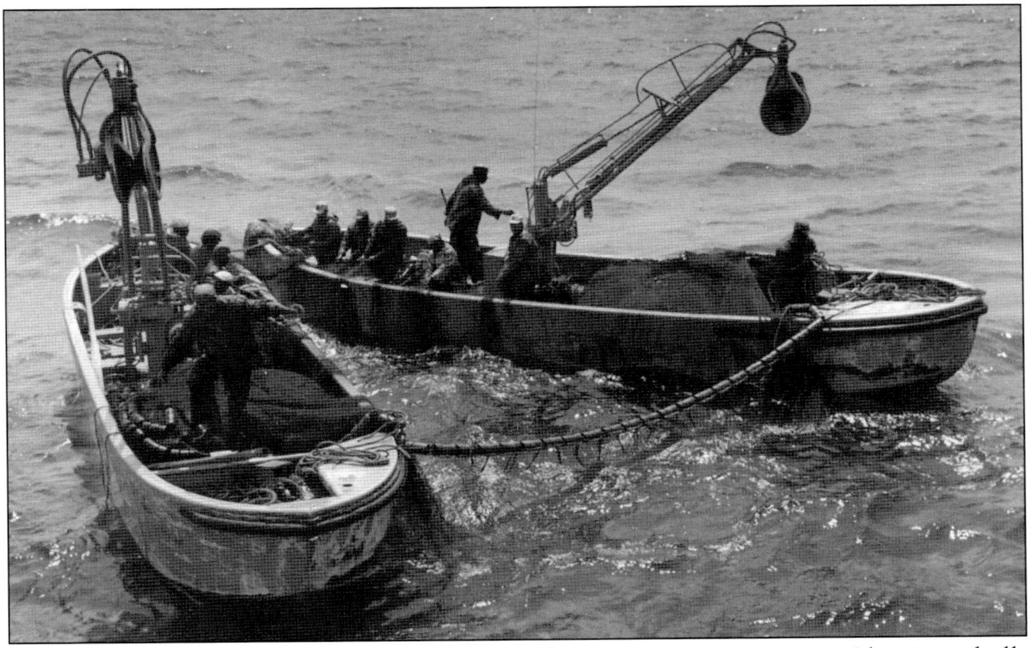

During the 1960s and 1970s, the purse boats underwent a new innovation. Aluminum hulls became the norm due to their durability and lighter weight. The difference in the size of the crew needed is clear here. However, the boats were much more efficient, and the time saved meant higher production.

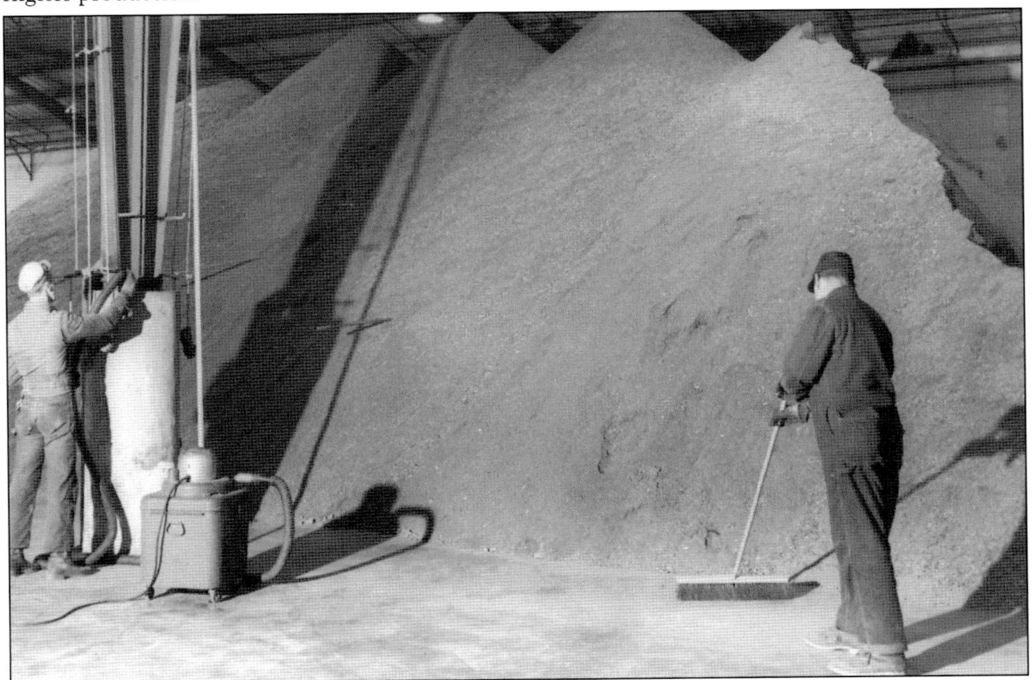

In the fish factories, once all of the oil has been removed for use in supplements, fish meal is left over. Menhaden was first used as fertilizer by the Native Americans, and its by-products are still used for this purpose. It is also used for commercial products such as paints, soaps, lubricants, and pet foods.

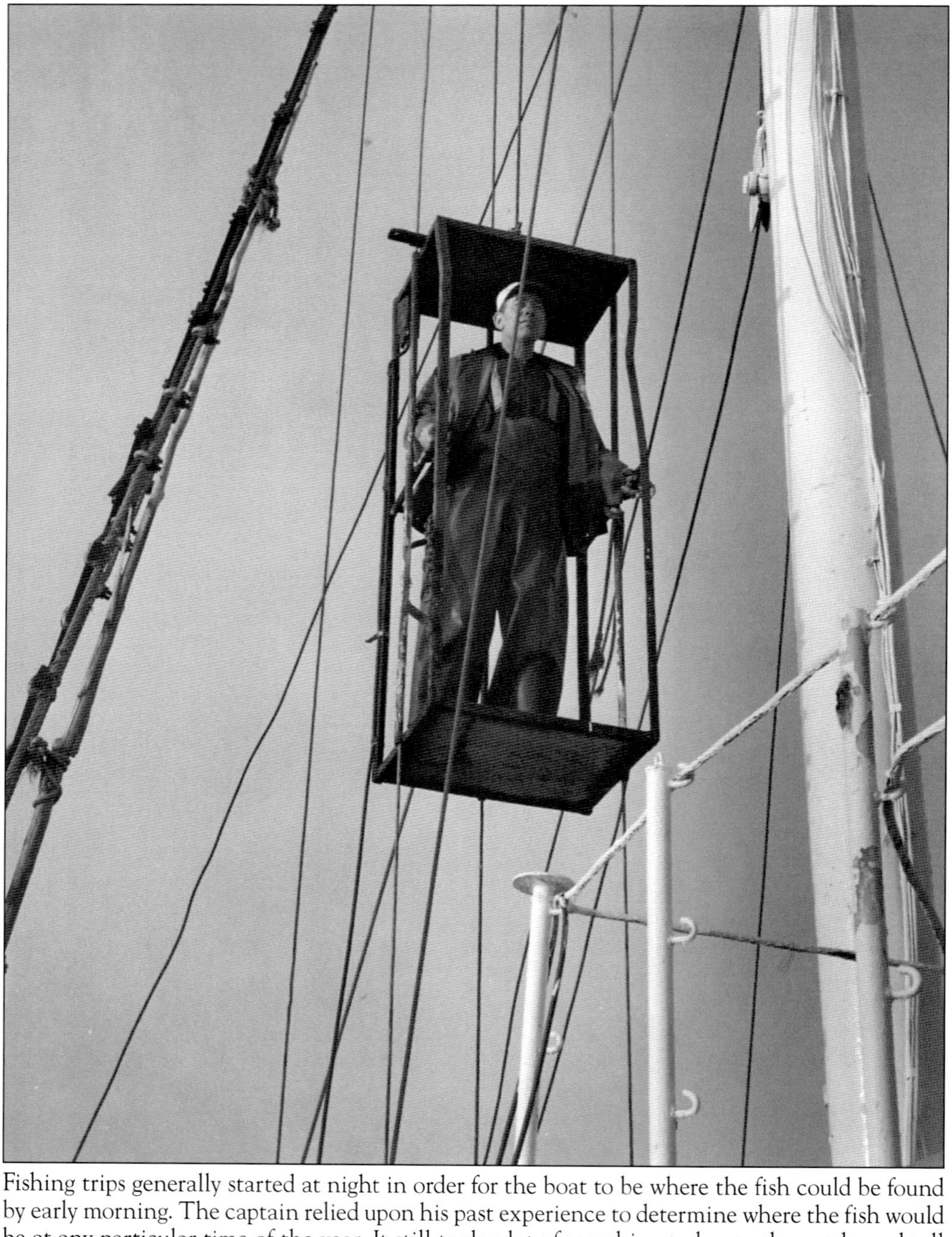

Fishing trips generally started at night in order for the boat to be where the fish could be found by early morning. The captain relied upon his past experience to determine where the fish would be at any particular time of the year. It still took a lot of searching to locate the catch, and tall crows' nests were needed. The more-expensive boats were able to afford elevators to take one up to the crows' nest.

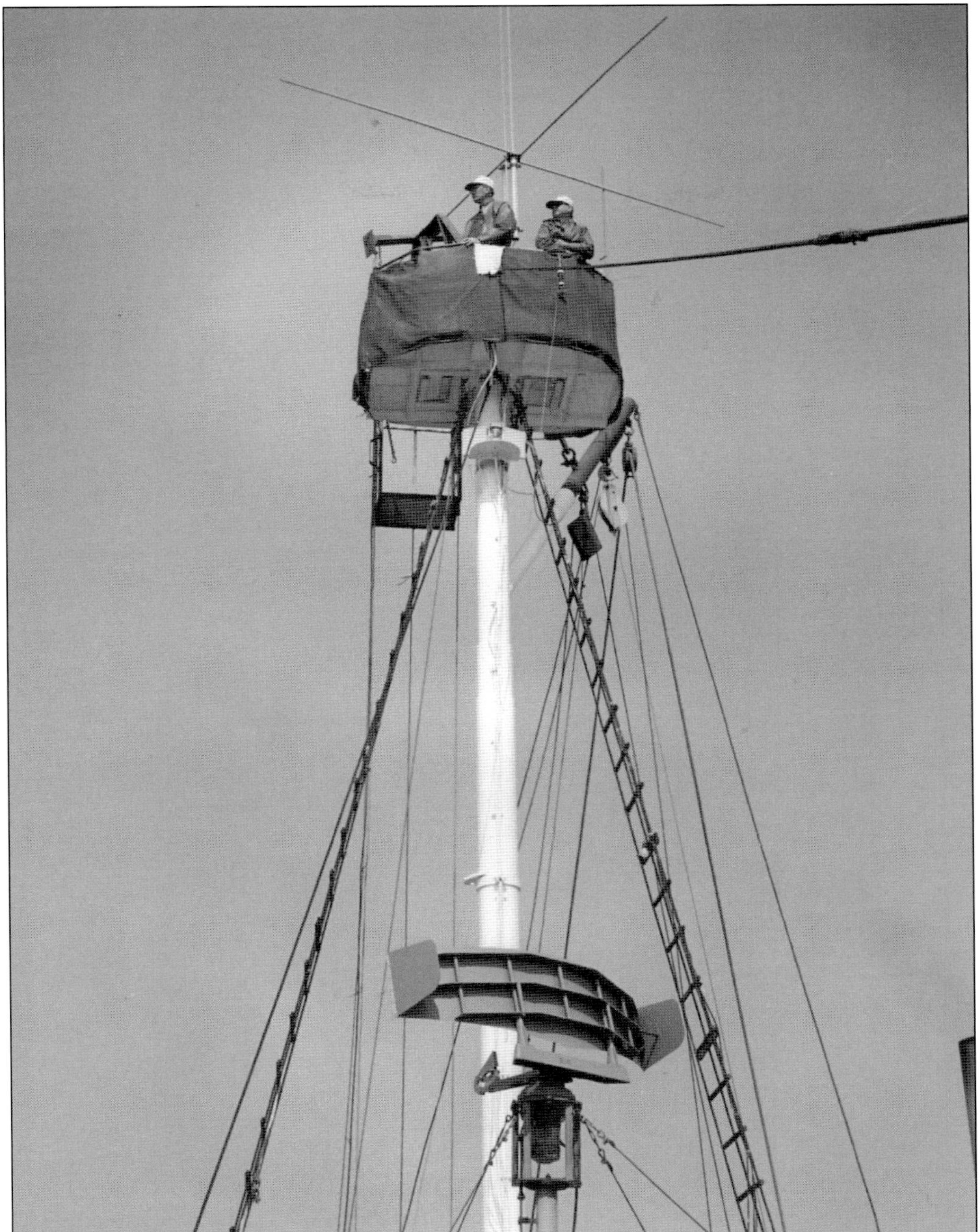

The captain, drive boatsman, and mate spent many hours in all kinds of weather up in the crow's nest searching for the telltale color and flapping of menhaden fish. However, once the innovation of spotter pilots was developed, for the larger companies that could afford it, the need for a crow's nest was gone.

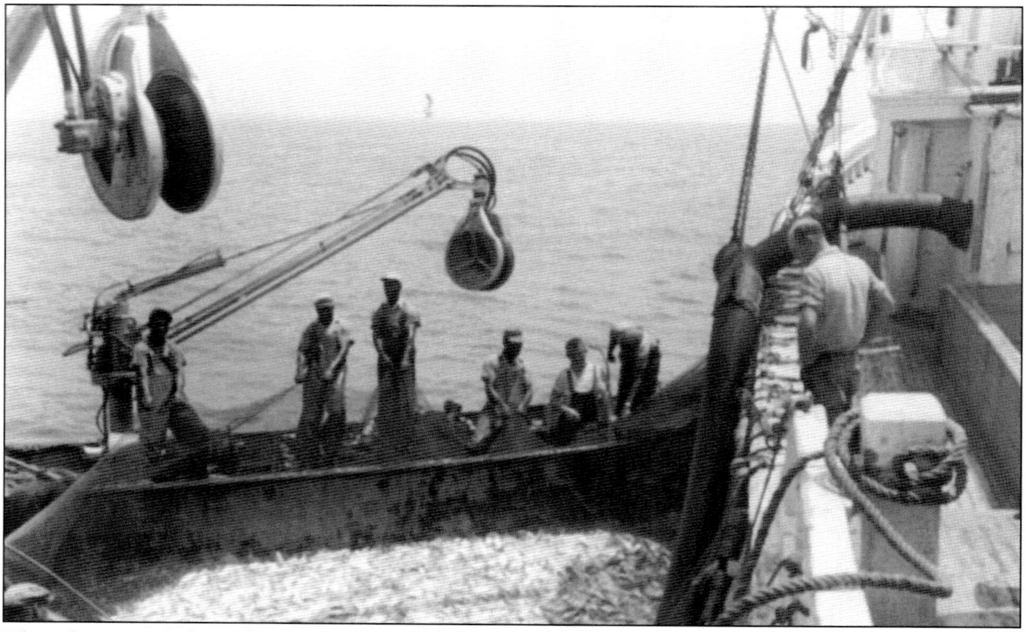

This photograph from the 1960s shows two inventions that revolutionized the menhaden industry: the power block and the fish vacuum. By vastly shortening the time required to catch and load the fish, production skyrocketed and made menhaden fishing more profitable in the long run.

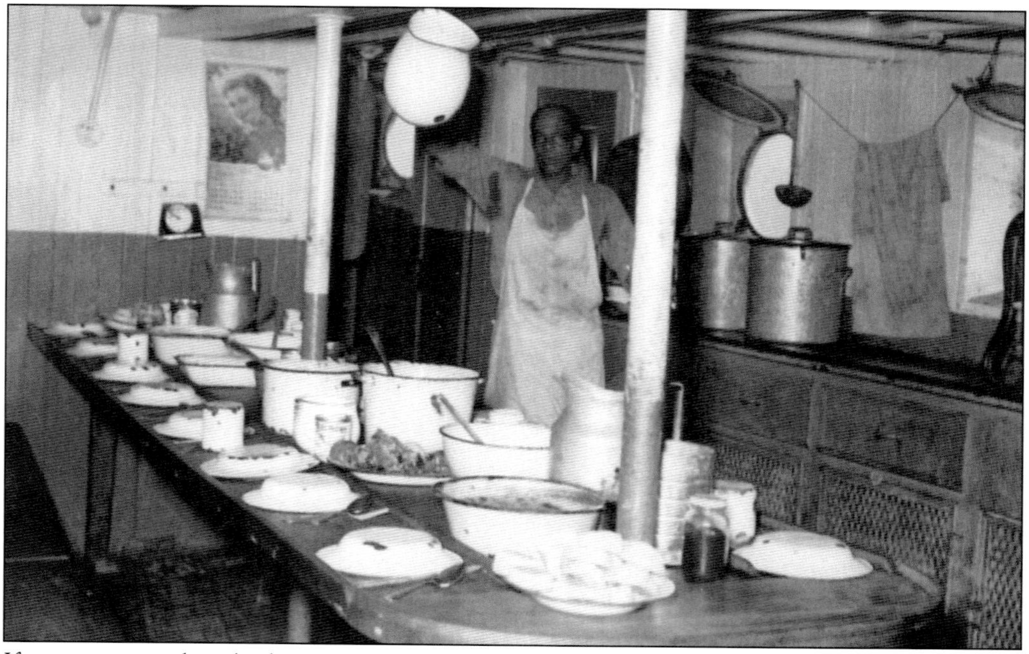

If one was a good cook, there were always a lot of friends on board. Typically, meals were served three times a day: breakfast from 4:00 to 5:00 a.m., dinner at 10:00 a.m., and supper at 3:00 to 3:30 p.m. After 3:30 p.m., the assistant cook would set the table, and the crew could serve themselves as they wished.

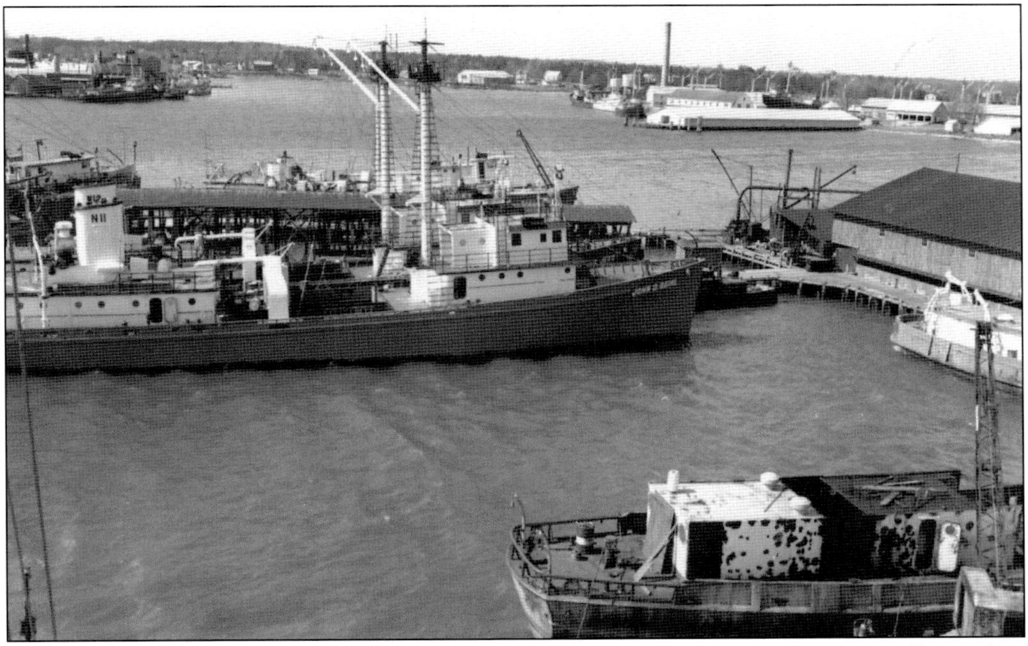

With modernization, a number of companies like Zapata Haynie Corporation (formed in 1972), Reedville Oil and Guano Company, Haynie Products Company, and Standard Products Company survived and continued to keep Reedville at the forefront of fish production for the United States.

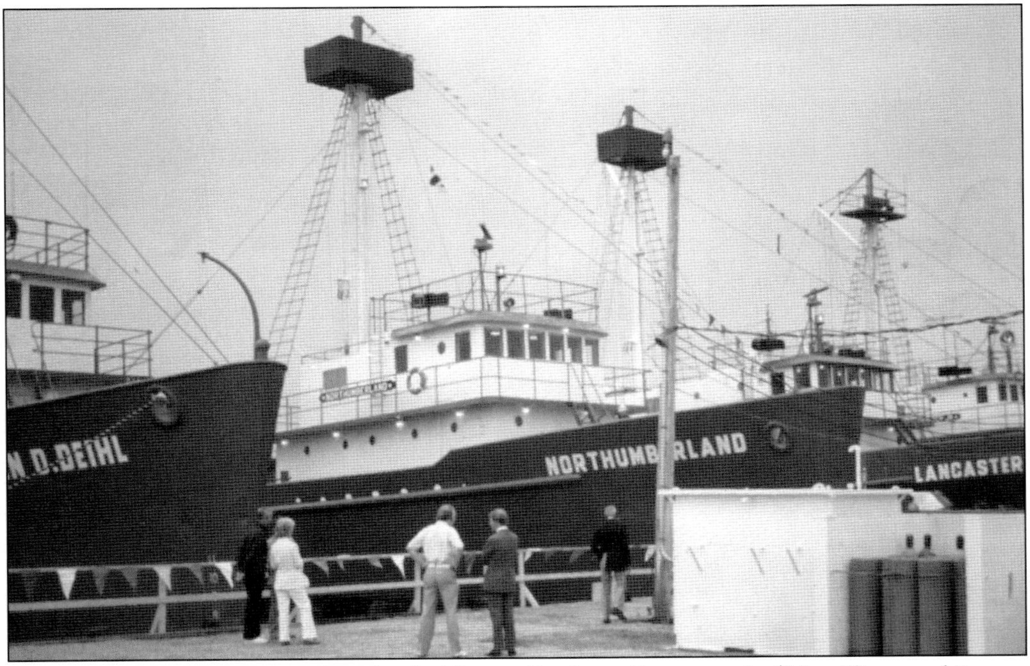

In 1972, Zapata Corporation bought the Haynie Products Company for $11 million, and Zapata Haynie became one of the largest fishing companies in the United States, with operations in the Gulf of Mexico in addition to Reedville. Over the following years, a fleet of new and much-larger steel vessels were built to increase production.

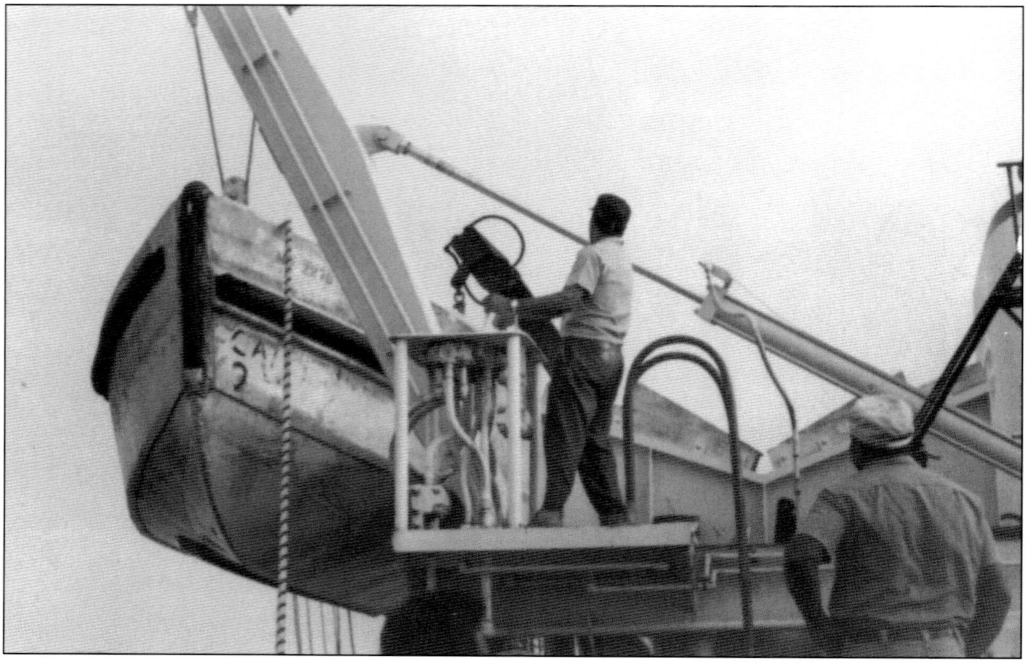

The heavy-duty hydraulics on the modern fishing boats did not have any problem lifting the purse boats on board. In 2015, Omega Protein Corporation generously donated a completely restored aluminum purse boat to the Reedville Fishermen's Museum to join their functional collection of historical boats at the museum dock.

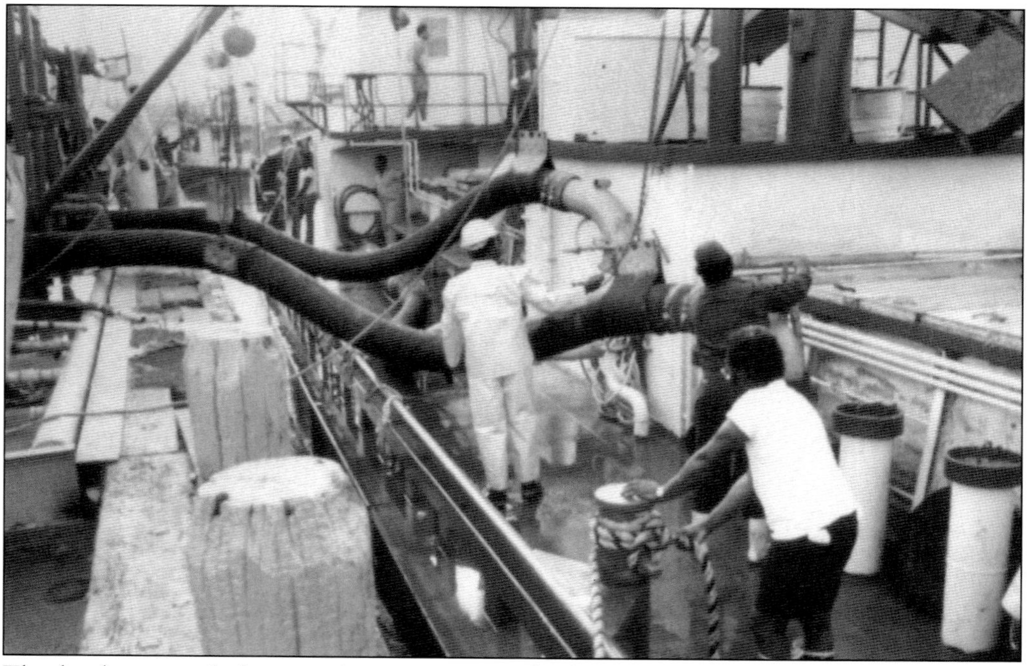

The development of a functional pumping system for the menhaden fish greatly cut down loading and unloading times, allowing for higher production. One of the most time-consuming parts of a fishing trip was getting the menhaden from the nets onto the boat. Another was the hours spent docked while unloading at the factory, one full net at a time.

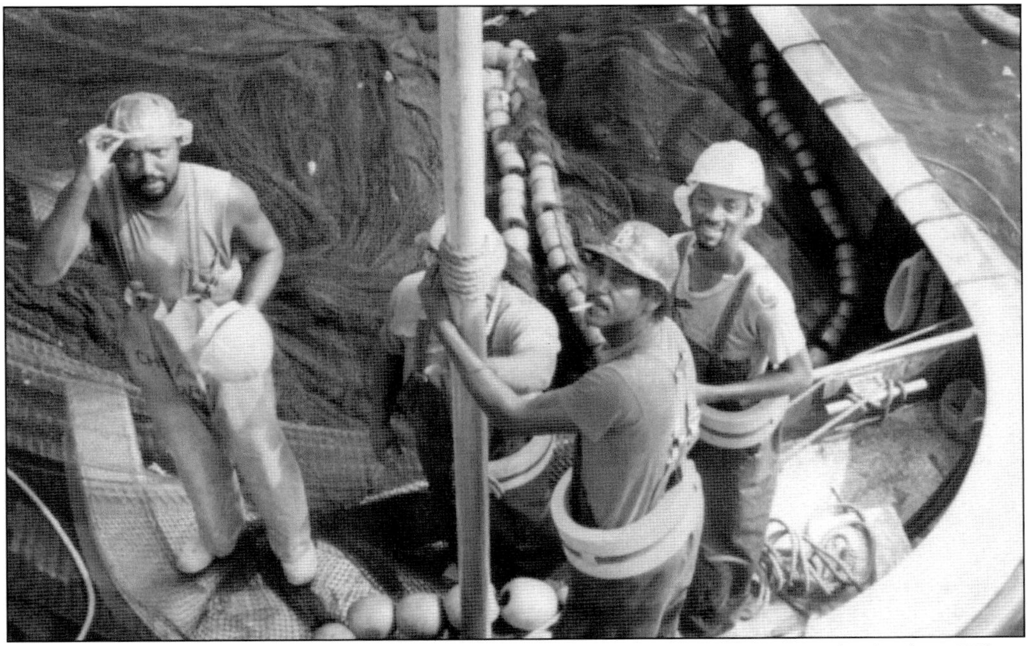

When the fish boat was where menhaden would be spotted, the crew was on high alert. When the crew was not fishing, they spent much of their time caring for the nets. They were constantly picking them over to mend holes. In the days when nets were made of cotton, the crew had to wet the nets down twice daily with brine to keep them from rotting too quickly.

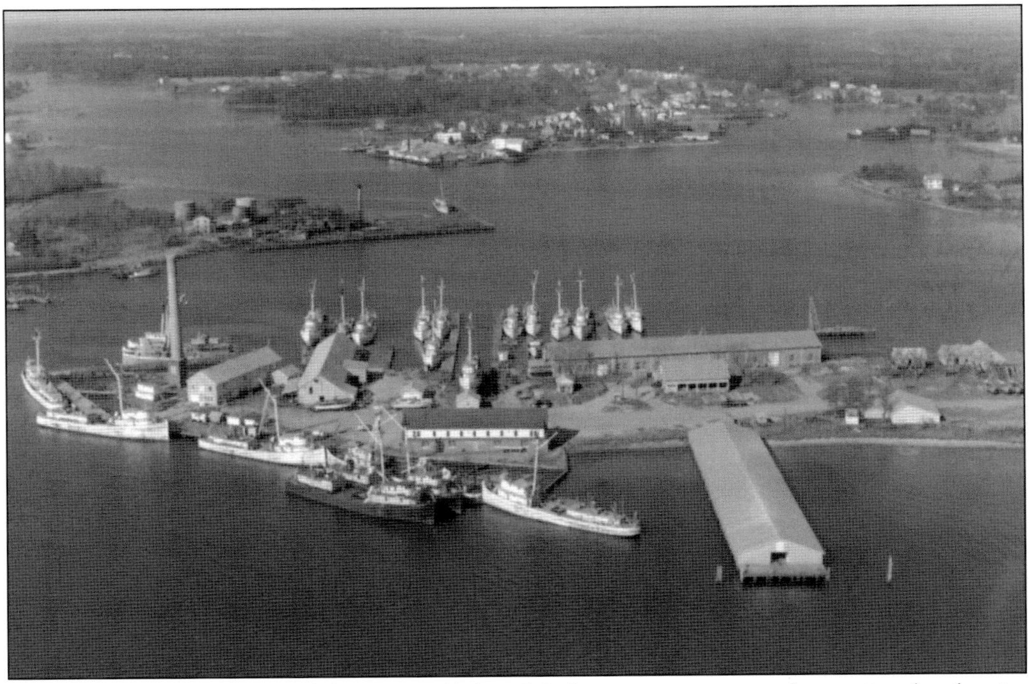

While only the old stack of the Morris-Fisher fish factory remains on the peninsula, the site served as a huge boat repair and maintenance yard for the Zapata Haynie group. On the narrow peninsula in the background is the town of Reedville. All of the buildings around the stack are now gone except for the white two-story one in the foreground.

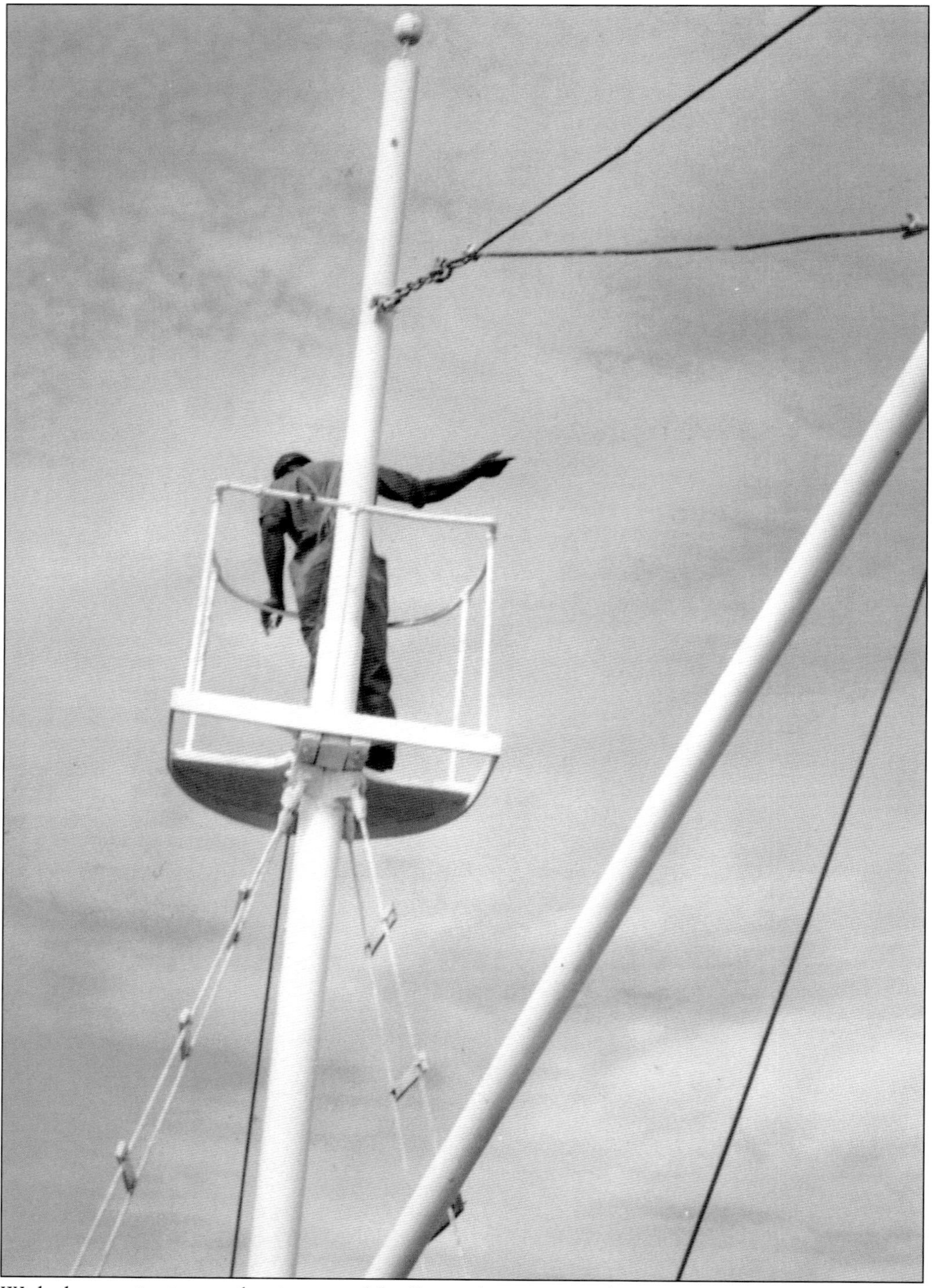

With the continuing modernization of the fleets, the once-popular and iconic crow's nest became obsolete. Now, Omega Protein Corporation employs a squadron of spotter planes. The airborne spotter pilot can direct the captain by radio to the most desired position for launching the purse boats and tell the captain where and how to set his net.

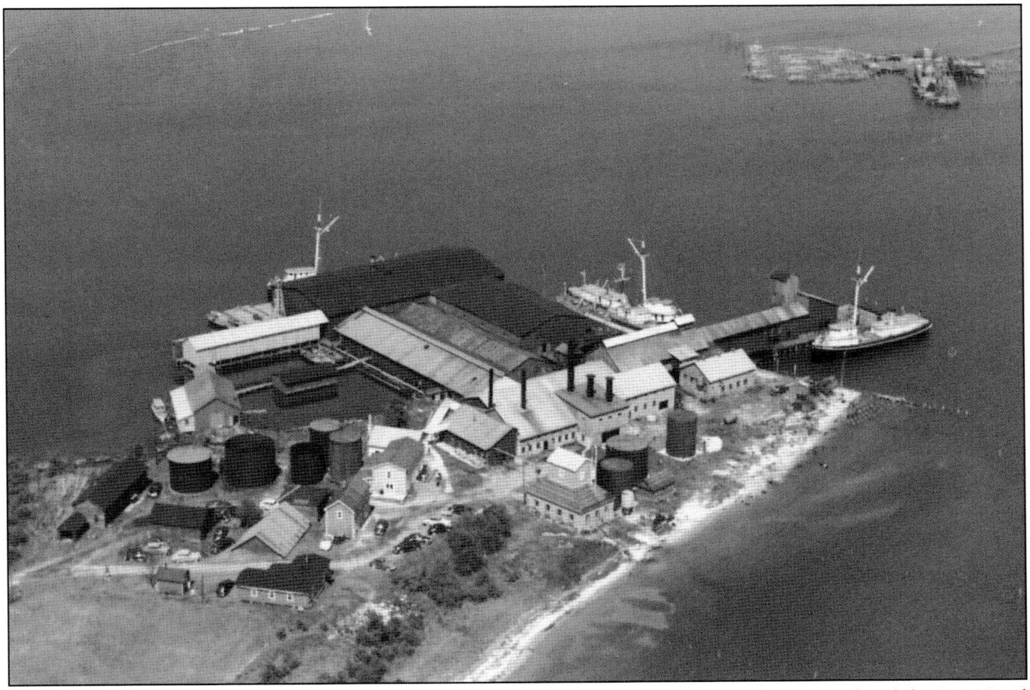

Nearby Fairport also had an active menhaden industry. This is a 1950 photograph of the McNeal Company. The ruins of the Douglas Company are at the top. The McNeal factory burned in 1953. The boats docked at the company are, from left to right, *George H. McNeal III*, *Henry W. Conant*, and *E. Warren Edwards*.

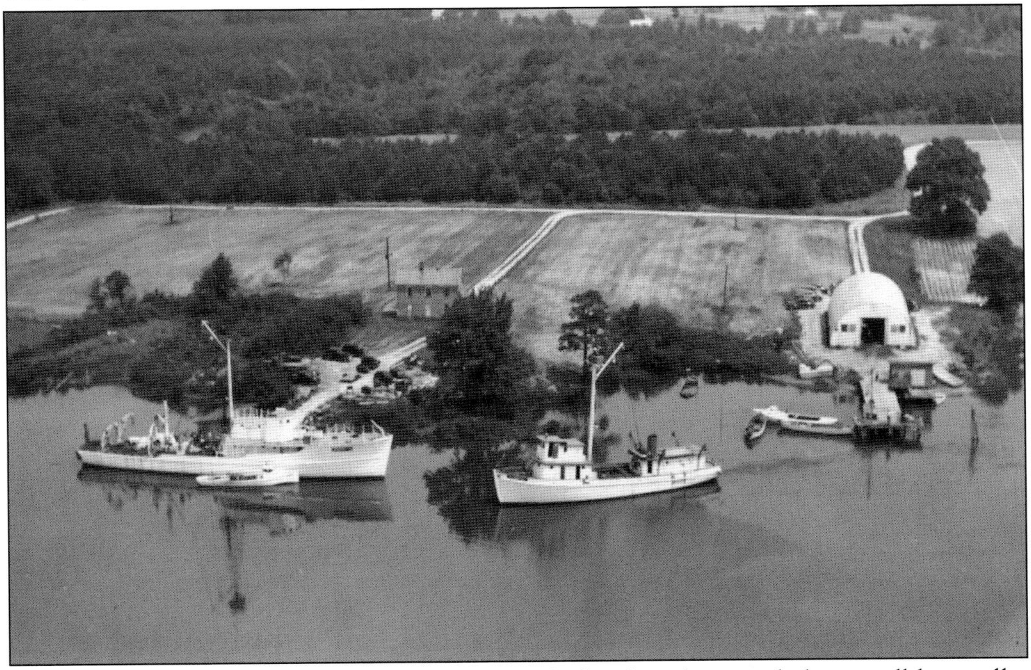

While the big factory companies dominated Reedville, there have and always will be smaller operators working hard to make a living on the bay. To the left is the Haylow fish house with the *John-O* at the dock. On the right is the Wallace Lewis plant with the *Hiawatha* berthed by it.

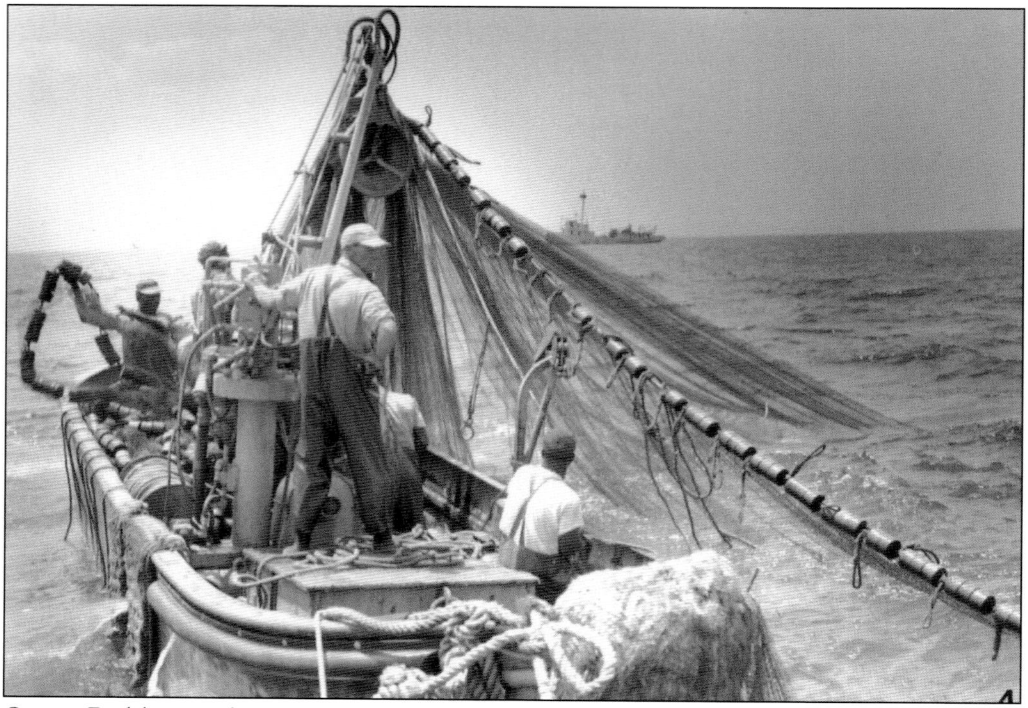

George Deihl, part of a multigenerational Reedville fishing family, takes charge of a purse boat. This illustrates the difference the power block made in retrieving nets. Invented by Mario Puretic, a steelworker, the innovation was introduced to the menhaden industry in 1955.

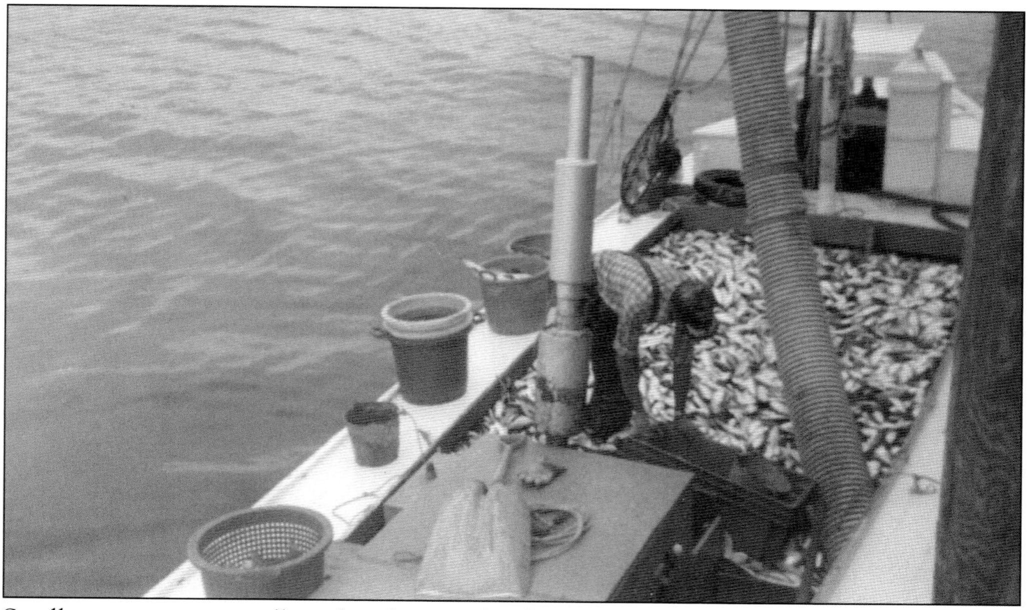

Smaller operators, normally with only a couple of watermen, have continued to this day, fishing for menhaden and other seafood in the waters around Reedville. A favorite boat is the flat-bottom deadrise boat, which was developed in Virginia. Its low draft made shallower waters accessible.

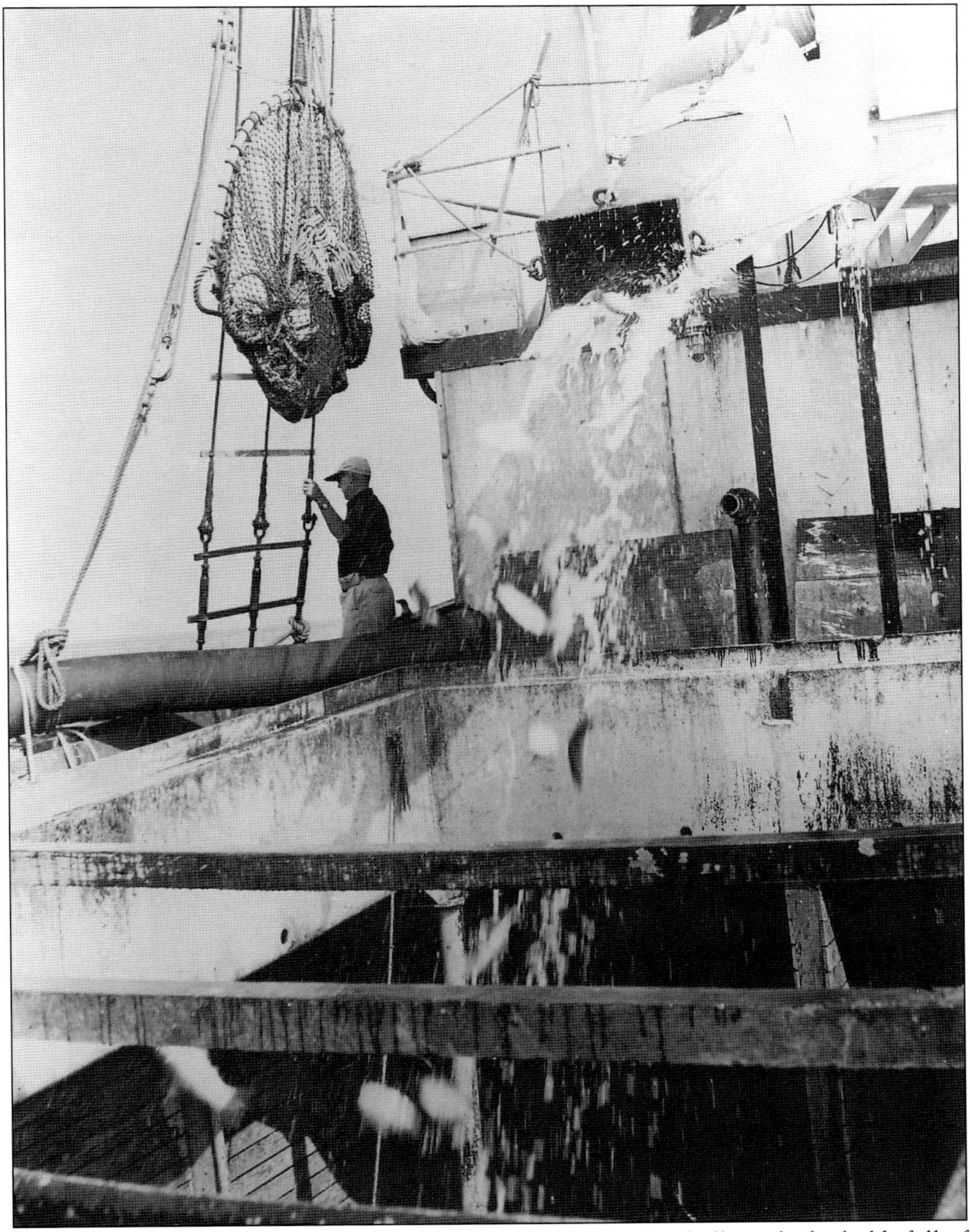

On the big fleet boats, the goal was always to head back to Reedville with the holds full of menhaden. The advent of the hydraulic power block, refrigeration, and a vacuum system to bring the fish into the boat greatly increased efficiency and raised production.

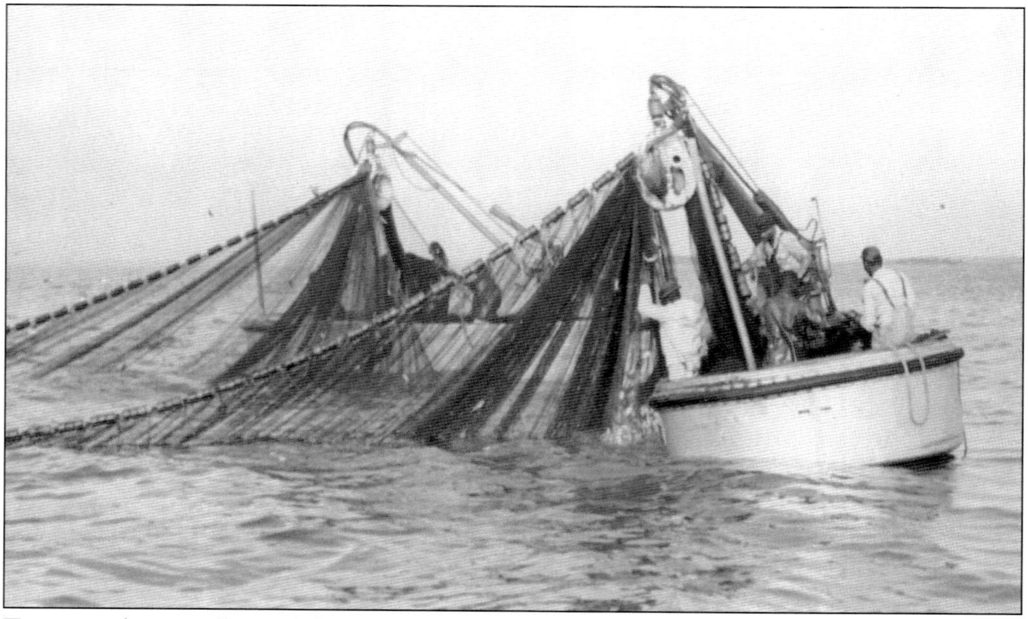

Two purse boats pull in a full net of menhaden. Note how fewer men are needed to man the modern purse boats compared to older ones before the power block came into use. The block was first used by Capt. Wallace Lewis on the *Joseph F. Bellows* while fishing for the Standard Products Company.

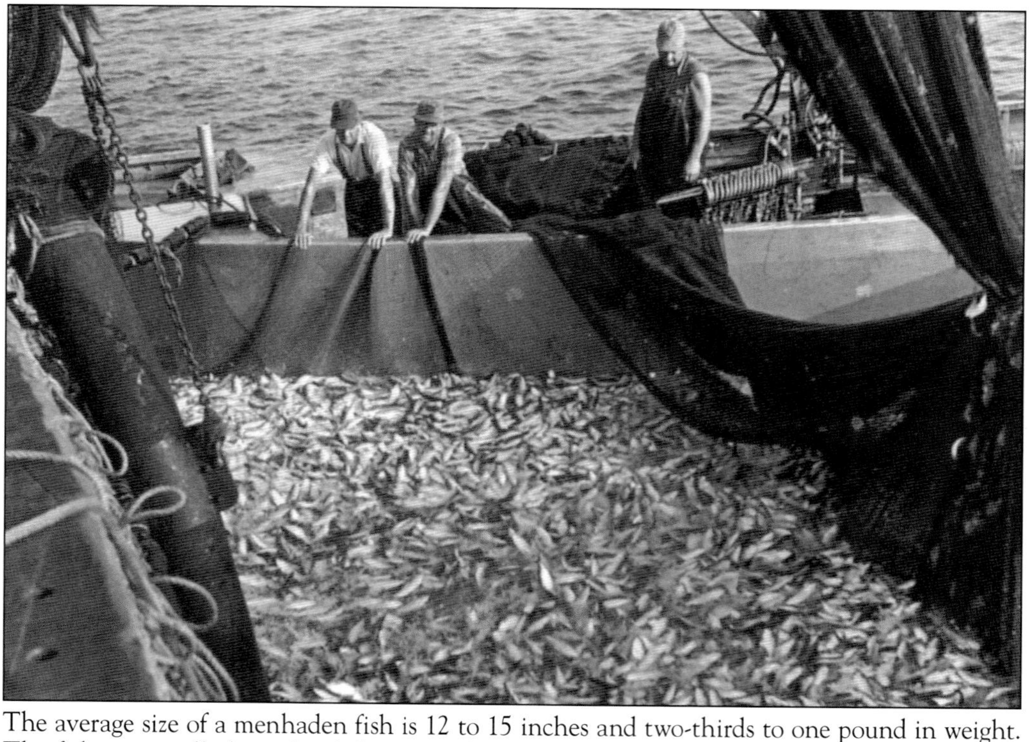

The average size of a menhaden fish is 12 to 15 inches and two-thirds to one pound in weight. The fish ranges all along the Atlantic Seaboard and into the Gulf of Mexico. Menhaden are thought to spawn in the ocean over the continental shelf in winter. One female can lay an estimated 22,000 eggs.

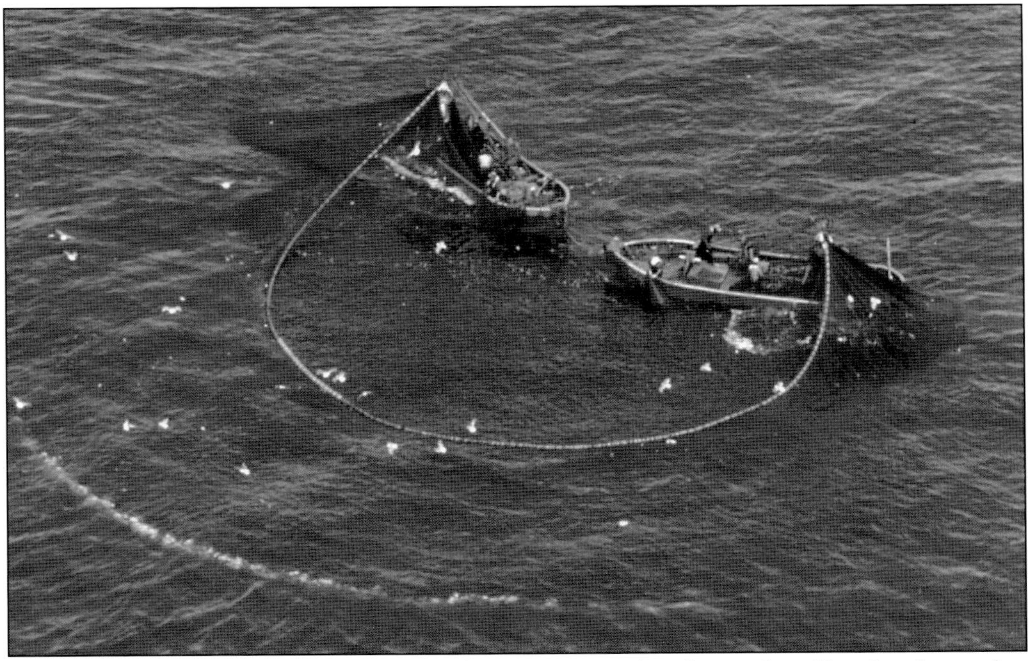

Two purse boats work on closing the net and preparing to gather the catch and head to the mother boat. The fishing season on the Chesapeake Bay and nearby waters extends from the last week of May to the first of November. Omega Protein Corporation also has a facility in Louisiana, and many of the crews rotate there to continue fishing.

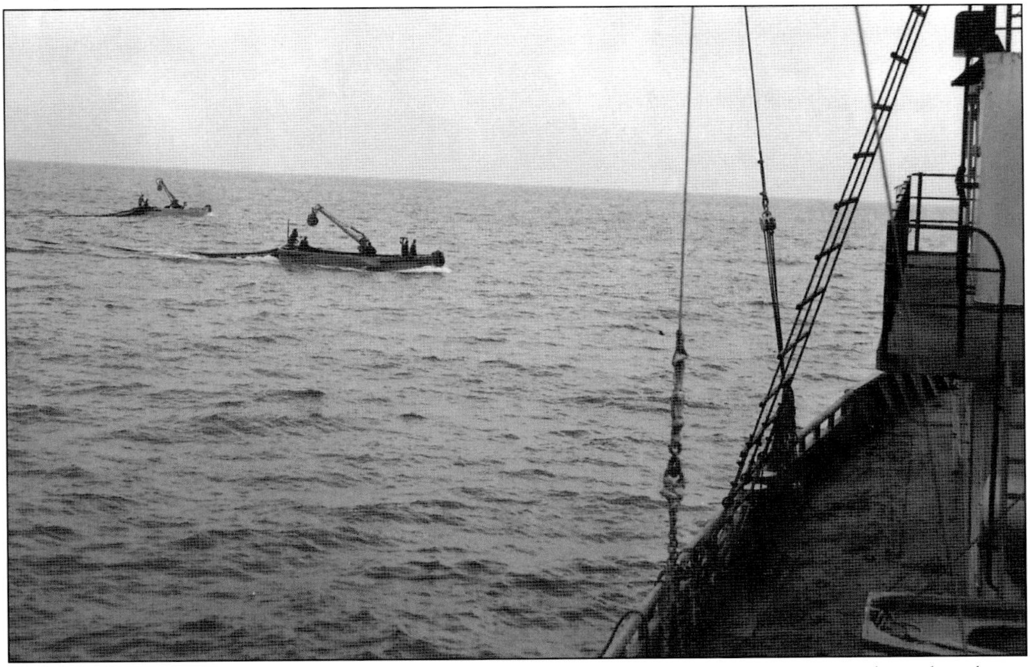

Two purse boats drag the net toward a school of menhaden. Over the years, there has been increasing regulations governing the menhaden industry and quotas set to assure the regeneration for the lost fish. However, the bay is rebounding, and in 2015, the limits were raised due to a dramatic increase in the menhaden.

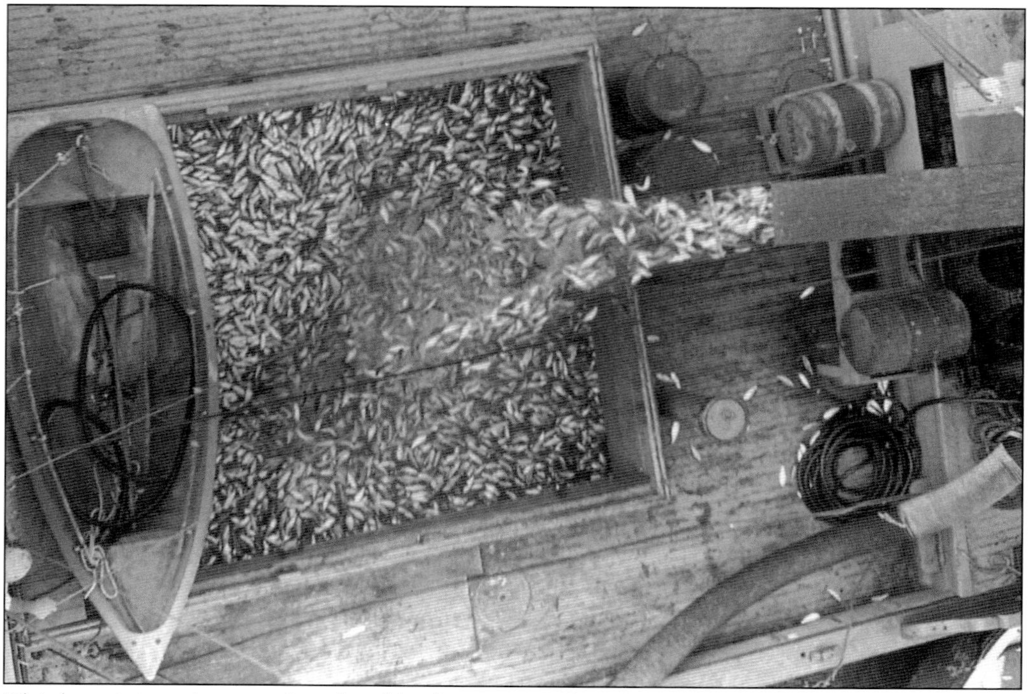

This boat is just about ready to head back to port with its hold full to the brim with menhaden. Menhaden perform a vital role in the bay's ecosystem as both a feed fish for striped bass, weakfish, bluefish, and predatory birds such as osprey and eagles, as well as serving as a filter feeder, as they feed on phytoplankton and zooplankton.

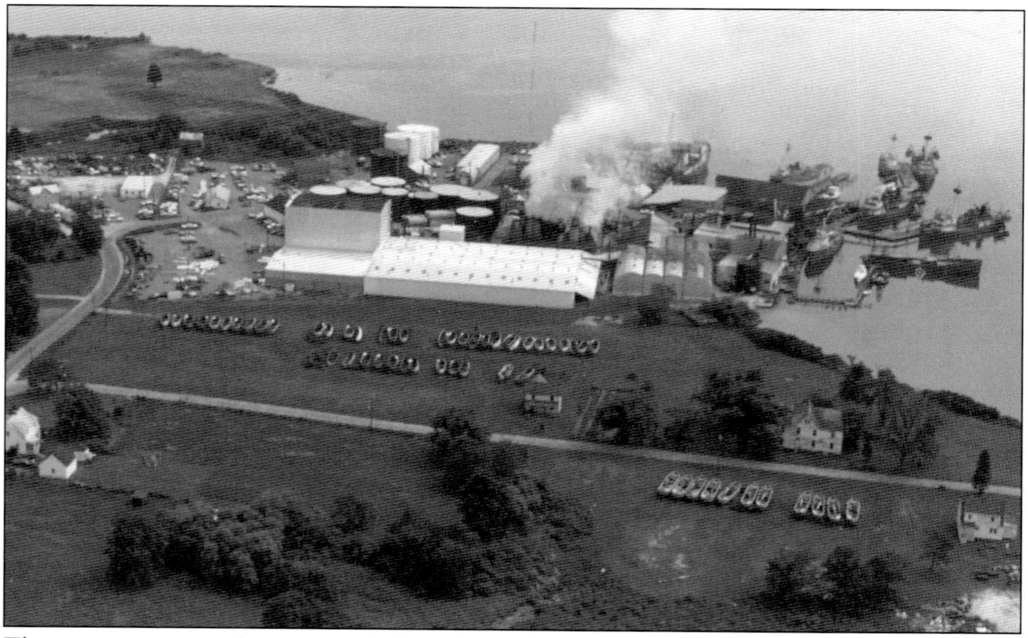

This is an overview of the Omega Protein Corporation plant in Reedville. Between its facilities in Reedville and Louisiana, the company produces about 80 percent of all menhaden processed. With the FDA certification in 1995 of fish oil as an additive and supplement, the company began to produce the popular Omega-3 fish oil supplements.

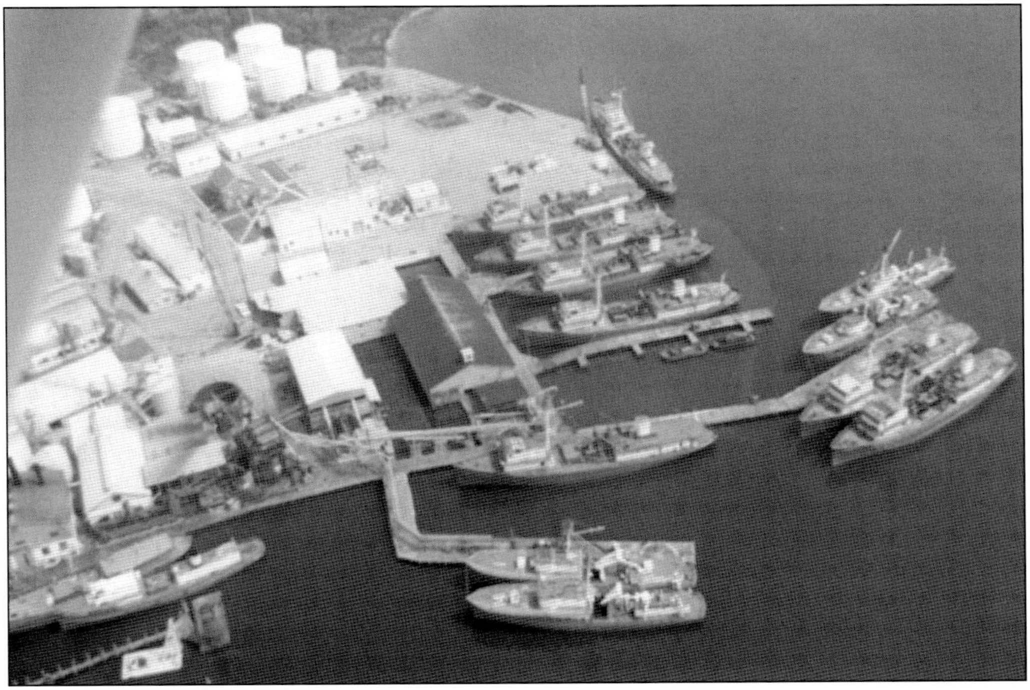

This is an aerial view of the menhaden fleet of ships that Omega Protein Corporation maintains. The amount of fish tonnage processed by Omega Protein each year ranks Reedville second to only Dutch Harbor, Alaska, in production. The company employs 250 to 350 workers and maintains a modern fishing fleet and a squadron of spotter aircraft.

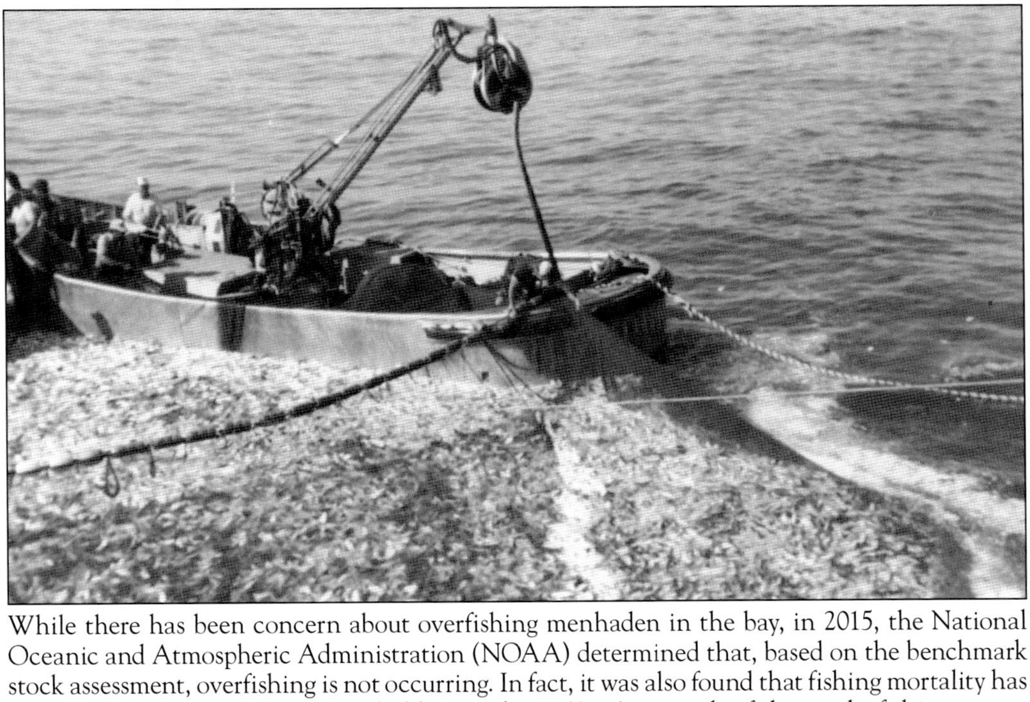

While there has been concern about overfishing menhaden in the bay, in 2015, the National Oceanic and Atmospheric Administration (NOAA) determined that, based on the benchmark stock assessment, overfishing is not occurring. In fact, it was also found that fishing mortality has stayed below the overfishing threshold since the 1960s. As a result of this study, fishing quotas were raised, but not to the original level before the cuts were made.

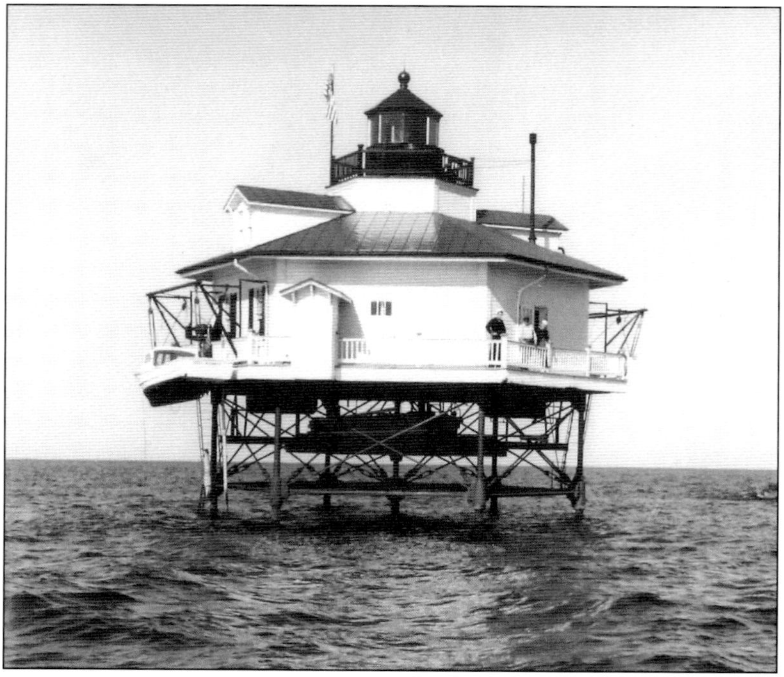

The Great Wicomico River lighthouse was built offshore from Fleeton, a few miles north of Reedville, in 1889. It was at the entrance to the river and also served as a signal for the nearby Potomac River. The hexagonal screw-pile lighthouse was dismantled in 1967 and replaced with a small automatic light on a steel tower.

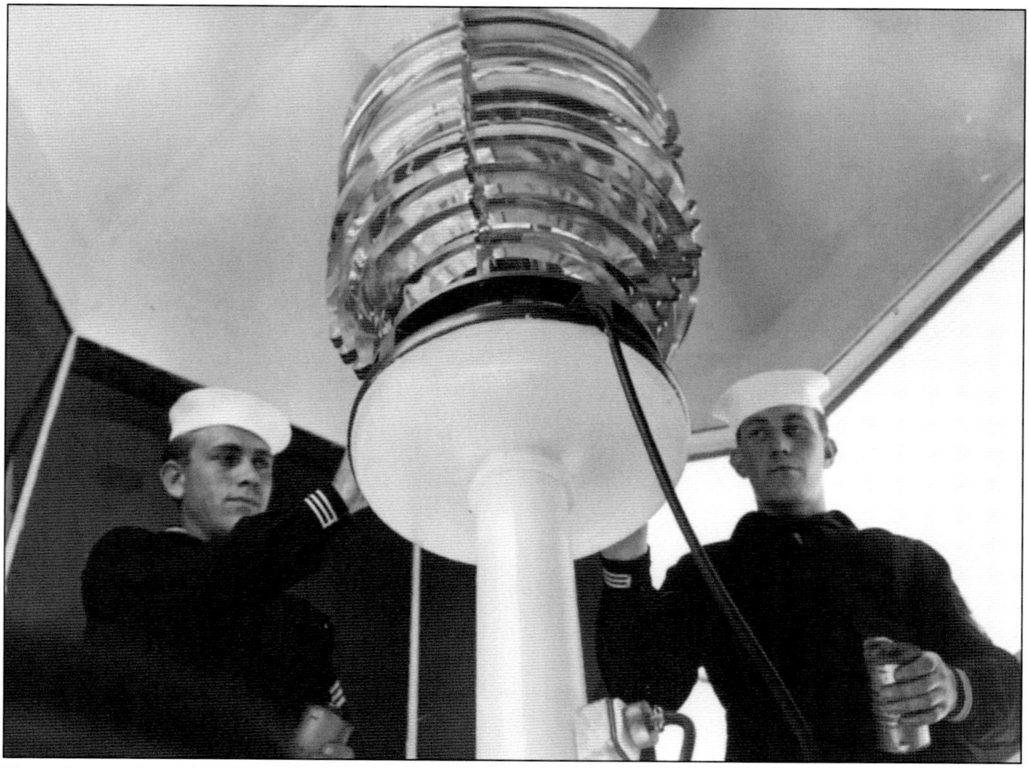

Two Coast Guard sailors clean the Fresnel lens in the Great Wicomico River lighthouse. For many years, most of the lighthouses on the bay were manned by sailors year round, but starting in the 1960s, all the lighthouses were made automatic and no longer needed the sailors. Many were dismantled and replaced with just an automatic light on a small steel tower. An era was over.

Three

Fishing Boats of the Chesapeake Bay

Many different styles of fishing boats have been used on the Chesapeake. The earliest was the log canoe used by the early watermen for fishing and harvesting shellfish. It was much larger than typical canoes. Up to five hollowed-out logs were fastened together to make the hull. They also featured one or two masts and were fairly easily to sail. At one time, they were quite prevalent throughout the bay, but motorized boats led to the downfall of popularity of the log canoes. Today, only about 20 of these original boats survive.

The skipjack was another popular bay boat and is still the official state boat of Maryland. The boat came into vogue in the late 19th century and, for a long time, was the preferred boat for oyster harvesting. Many were still in use during the 1960s, but today barely 30 of these sleek boats remain, mainly at museums, although a handful are still actively fishing the bay.

The Virginia deadrise was another of the line of unique boats developed to fish the bay. This was, and is, one of the classic workboats of the bay, featuring a sharply pointed bow with a flat-bottom hull. The cabin was at the very front, and the rest of the boat was open, with plenty of space for the catch. Because it only drafted two or three feet, it was able to fish areas that the larger boats could not. This boat is still heavily used by individual watermen on the bay today.

Buyboats, also known as deck boats, were popular on the bay during the early 20th century. In the days before large dredging operations became more prevalent, buyboats would travel out into the bay and load oysters from the tongers and dredgers. This allowed the watermen to harvest for longer periods each day by eliminating the need for multiple trips back to the docks when their small boats were full. Buyboats were also used for buying spat (seed oysters) destined to be planted in oyster beds. Many buyboat owners also used their vessels to haul freight during the off season. By the 1950s, the need for buyboats declined dramatically, and by the 1980s, very few still existed. Today, most of the surviving boats are parts of museum collections.

Schooners were another popular boat among watermen, who used these workboats to harvest oysters, blue crabs, and fish from the bay. Typically, the boats had two masts, although more were not uncommon. Today, schooner races are held around the bay and used to promote the history of the watermen and the heritage of the bay.

The bugeye was one of the early boats on the bay, having been developed during the 1860s as an alternative to the log canoe boats. As the dredging of oysters became more popular, the larger size of the bugeye allowed it to have more dredging power and production. However, beginning in the 1880s, the development of the even larger skipjack led to the downfall of the bugeye. The only bugeye left on the bay that is still used for fishing is the *Edna Lockwood*.

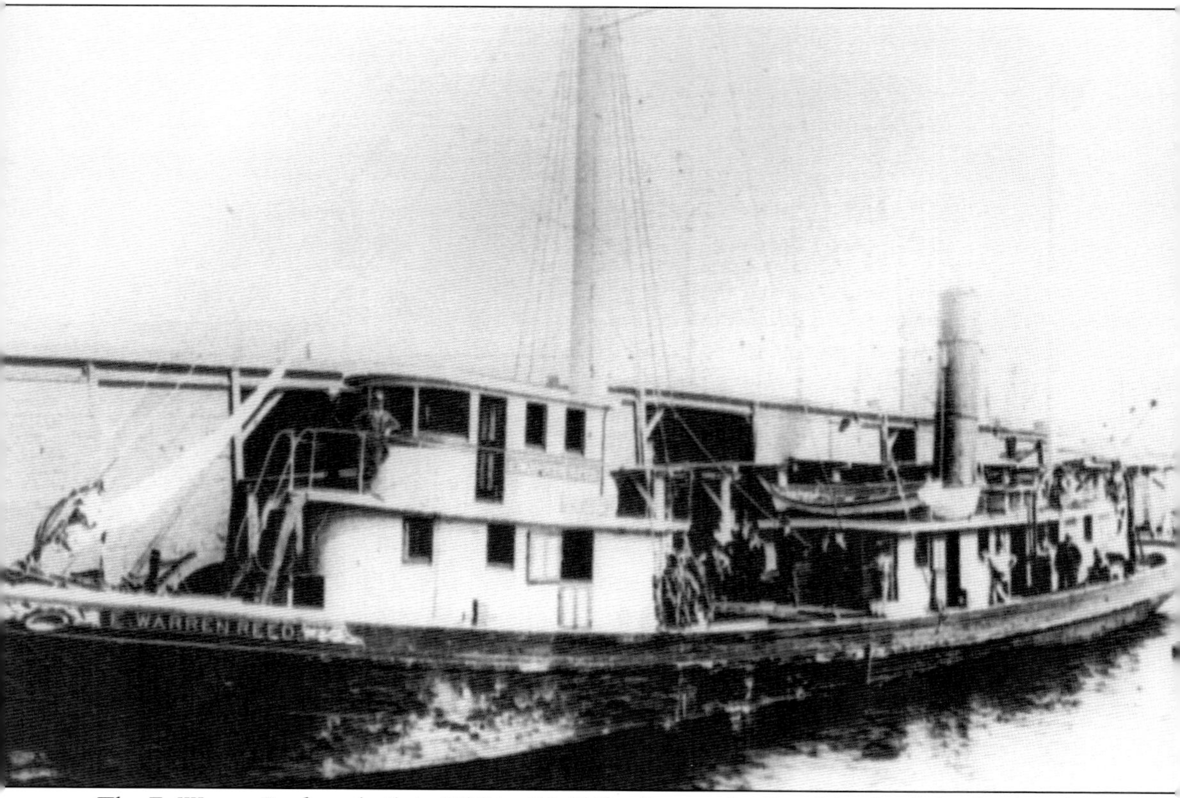

The *E. Warren Reed* was built in 1899 by E.J. Tull at Pocomoke City, Maryland, for the founder of Reedville, Elijah Warren Reed, who proudly named the boat for himself. Reed, a native of Maine, started the menhaden fishing industry in Reedville and the Chesapeake Bay. Originally steam-driven, it was converted to diesel in 1931. During World War II, the *E. Warren Reed* was leased by the US Navy and stationed at San Juan, Puerto Rico, before it was returned to the owners, the McNeal Company, in 1943. It later served the Standards Products Company and was sunk for use as a fishing reef near the Cape Charles light station.

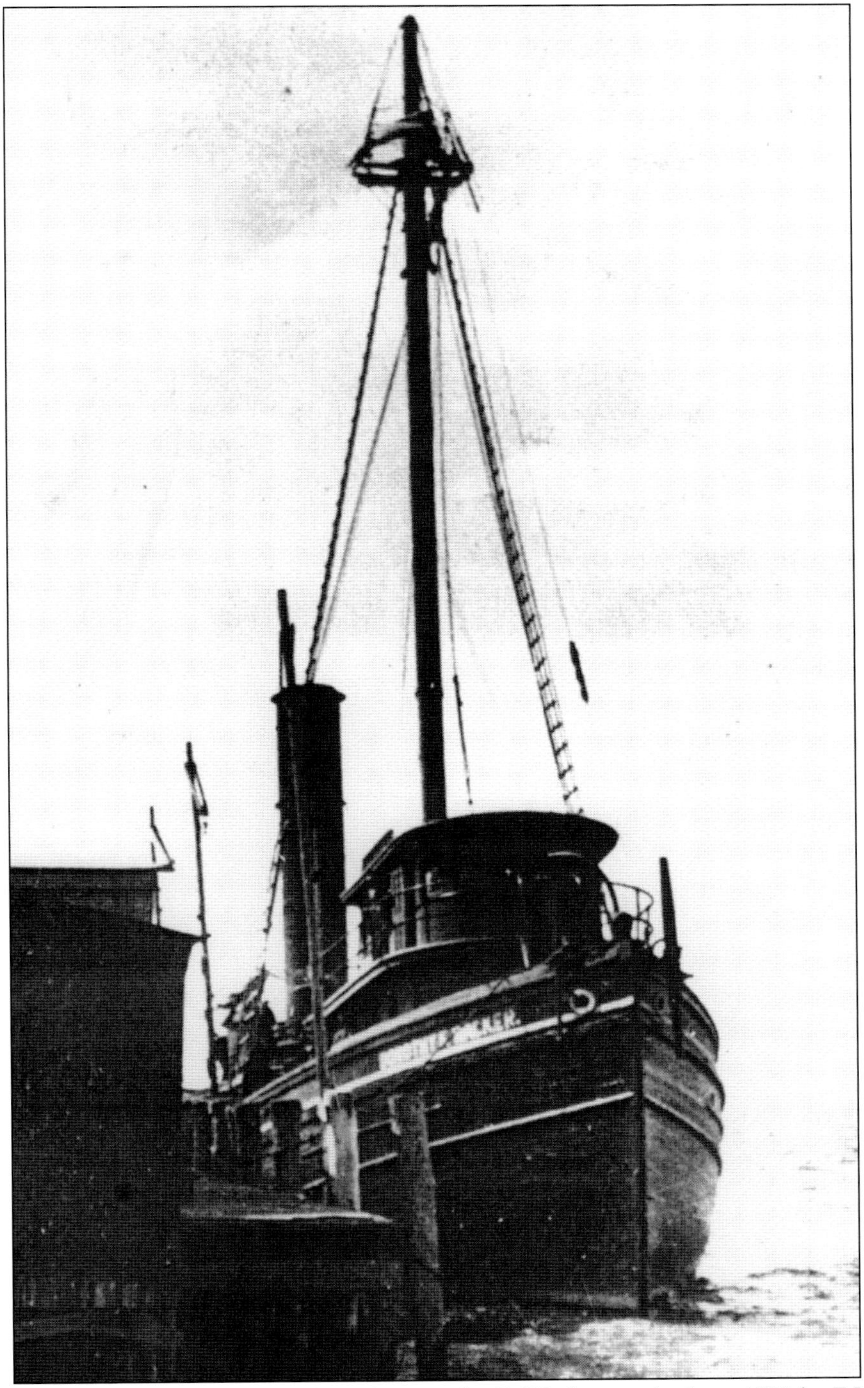

Named for the wife of Charles Wacker, the *Dorothy F. Wacker* was built in 1897 by E.J. Tull at Pocomoke City, Maryland. It was based out of Reedville and owned by the Struven & Wacker Company. Charles was a partner also in the Indian River Fertilizer Company and one of the developers of the steam fish cooker. Here, the *Wacker* is docked in Reedville around 1910. It appeared on active ship lists in 1916 but had disappeared from those lists by 1931. No one seems to know what ever happened to it.

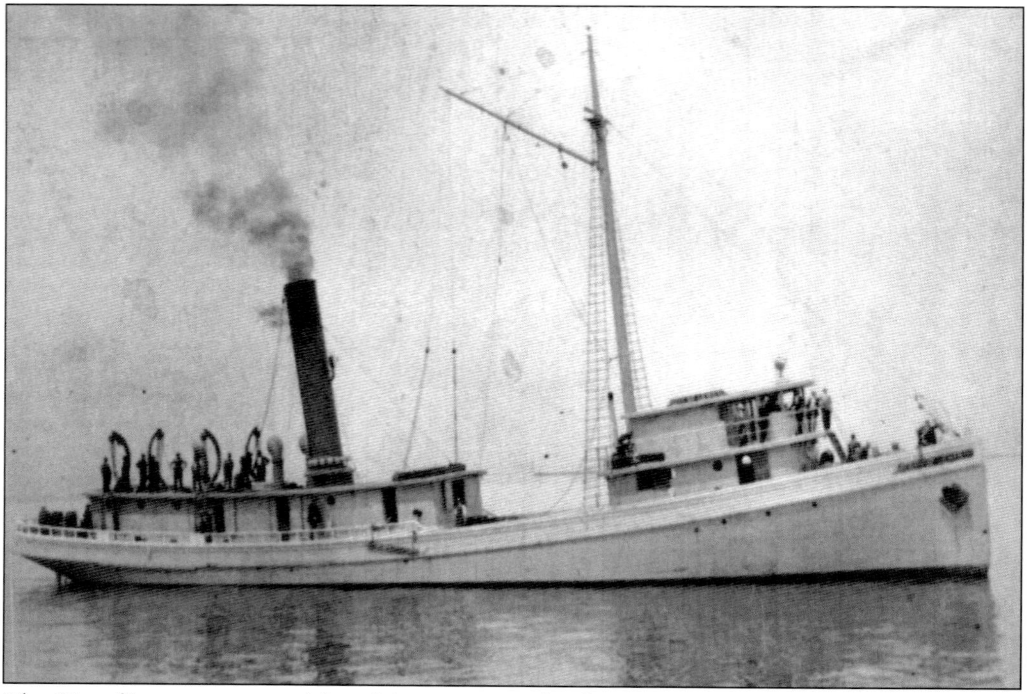

The *City of Lewes* was named for a fishing port inside of Cape Henlopen in Delaware. It was built by W.G. Abbot in 1912 and fished the coastal areas of Virginia and inside Chesapeake Bay. In 1917, the *Lewes* became part of a large group of menhaden fishing vessels that were converted by the Navy into minesweepers and sailed across the Atlantic Ocean to patrol and do escort duty. It was decommissioned at Brest, France, in 1919 and sold there, since the cost of bringing the boat home to the United States was prohibitive. After that, there is not any mention of the boat, and its fate is unknown.

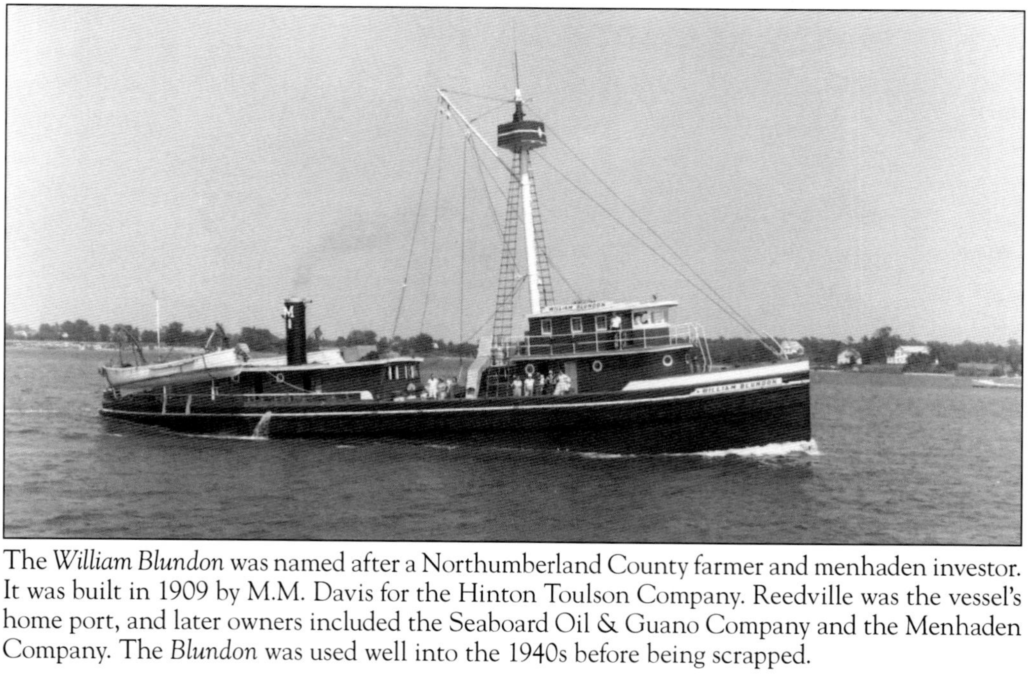

The *William Blundon* was named after a Northumberland County farmer and menhaden investor. It was built in 1909 by M.M. Davis for the Hinton Toulson Company. Reedville was the vessel's home port, and later owners included the Seaboard Oil & Guano Company and the Menhaden Company. The *Blundon* was used well into the 1940s before being scrapped.

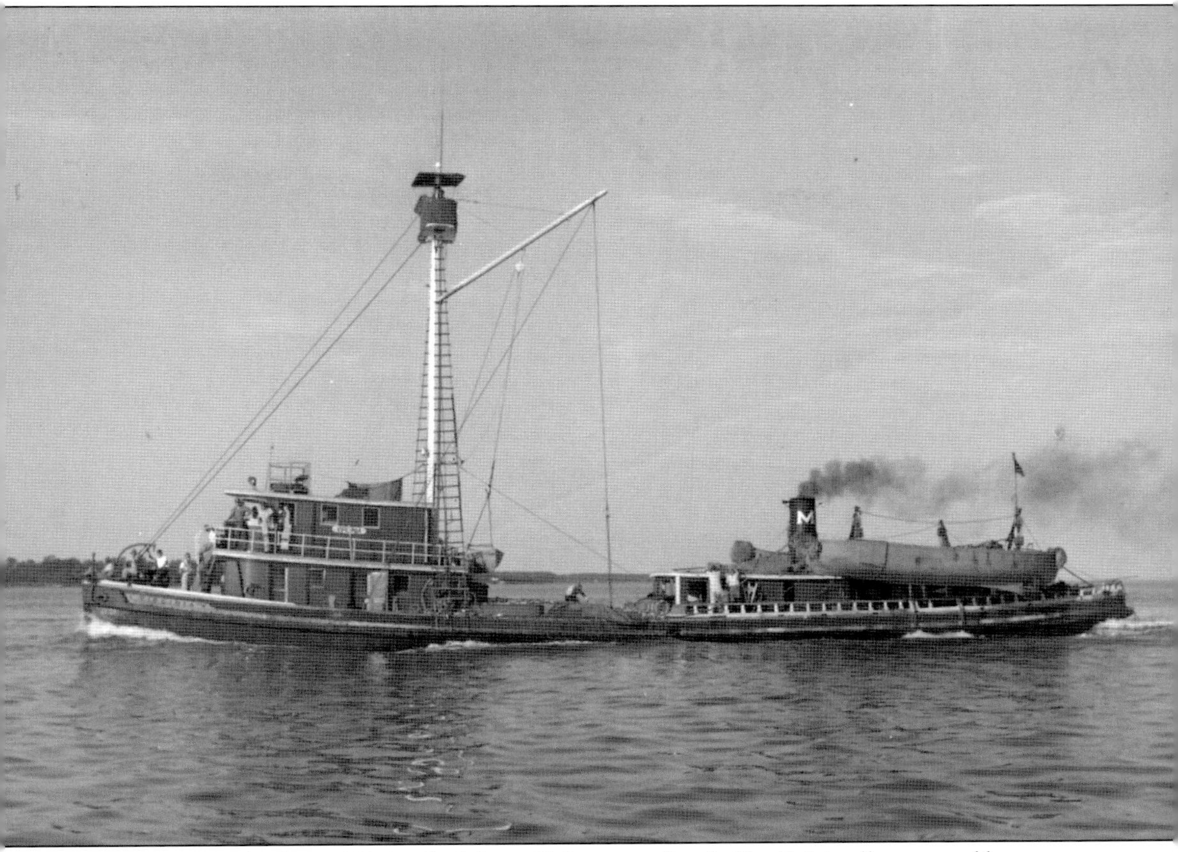

The *Virginia* was built in 1893 for the Morris Fisheries in Reedville. Originally powered by steam, it was converted to diesel in 1938. The *Virginia* also was later used by the Jett Menhaden Company and the Standard Products Company. Eventually, it was sold for scrap but wrecked near the Intracoastal Waterway while being towed.

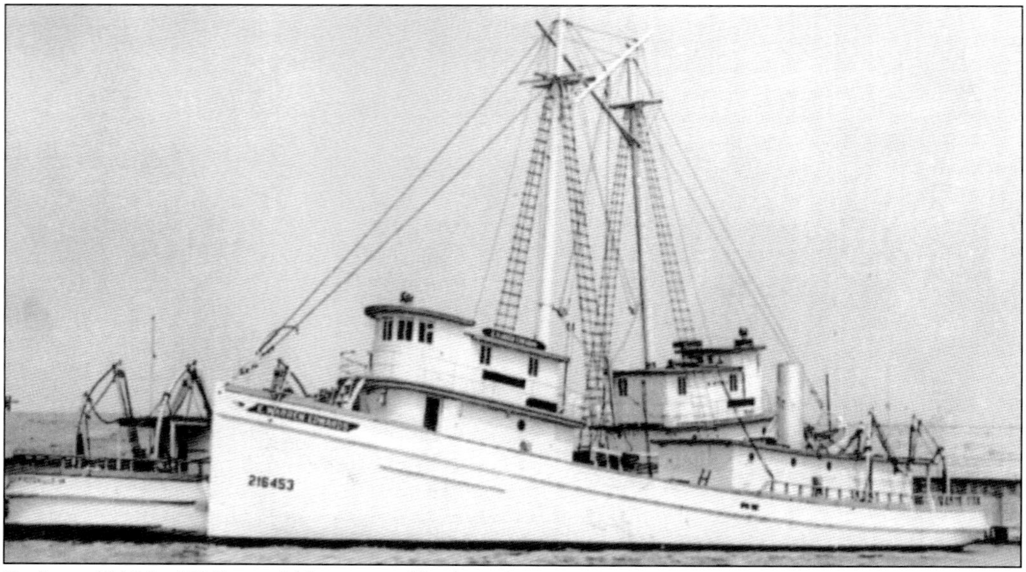

Built in 1918 by William Abbot at Milford, Delaware, the *E. Warren Edwards*, named for Elijah Warren Edwards, spent its entire existence in Reedville. Elijah and his brother Wilbur were owners of the Edwards and Reed Company. The *Edwards* was 125 feet long and had a draft of only 10 feet. It also featured one of the first diesel engines to run in Reedville-area waters. In 1943, the Coast Guard leased the boat, and it was stationed at Norfolk and San Juan, Puerto Rico. The boat was returned to its owners in 1953 and used for the next couple of decades before being sunk for a fishing reef near Ocean City, Maryland.

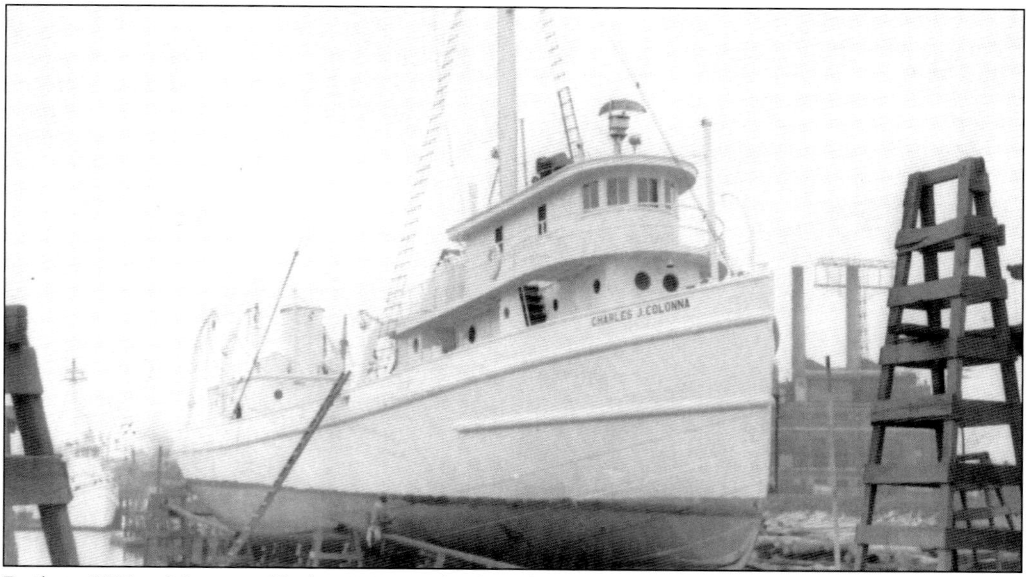

Built in 1920 at Mariners Harbor, New York, the *Charles J. Colona* became a menhaden boat in the Chesapeake Bay. While its homeport was Reedville, it was named for a part owner of the Colona Shipyard in Norfolk, Virginia. The family had numerous interests in many different menhaden fishing operations. The *Colona* was first owned by Ben and Will Colona and later the Atlantic Fishing Company of Reedville. It fished at Reedville and the Chesapeake Bay until the 1960s but was later sent to the Gulf of Mexico to fish for the Zapata Haynie Corporation. Nothing is known about the *Colona*'s ultimate fate.

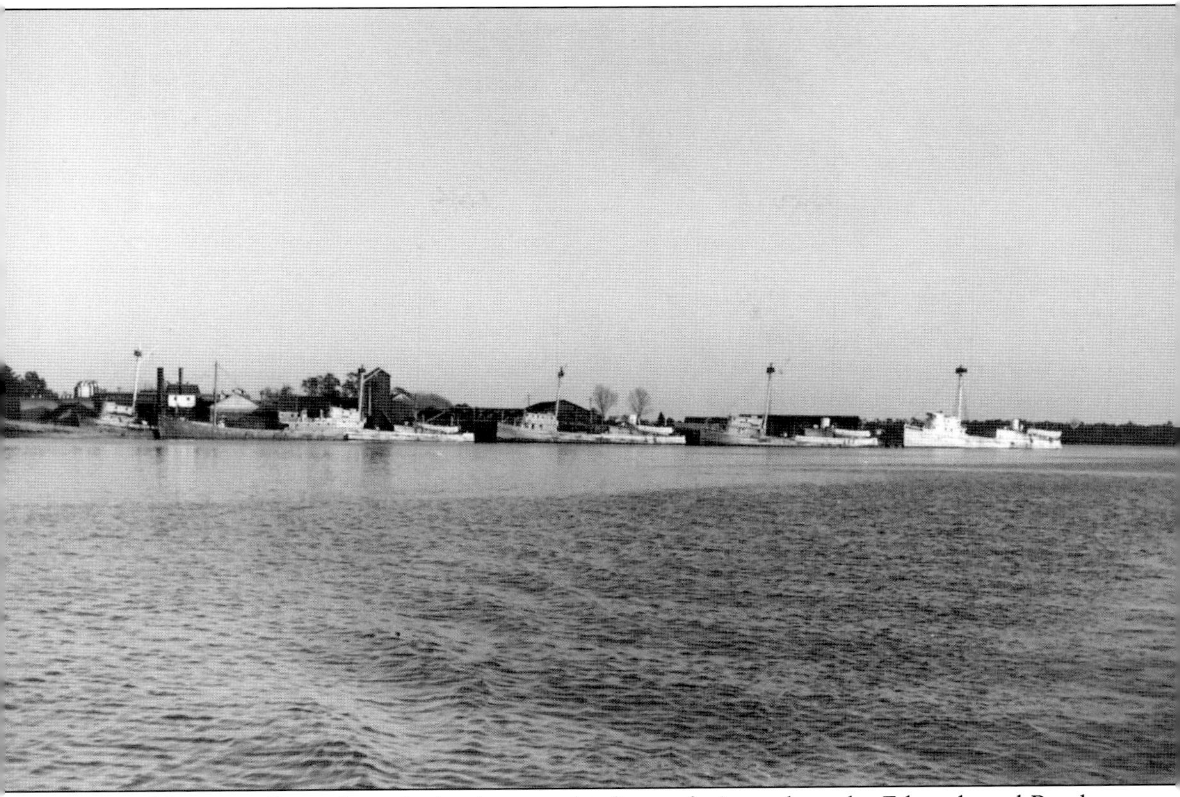

Pictured here is a fleet of menhaden boats unloading a day's catch at the Edwards and Reed fish factory, located at the end of the Reedville peninsula. The factory was spread out so that it could easily handle multiple boats unloading at the same time. The menhaden boats are easily recognizable from the purse boats hanging near the stern.

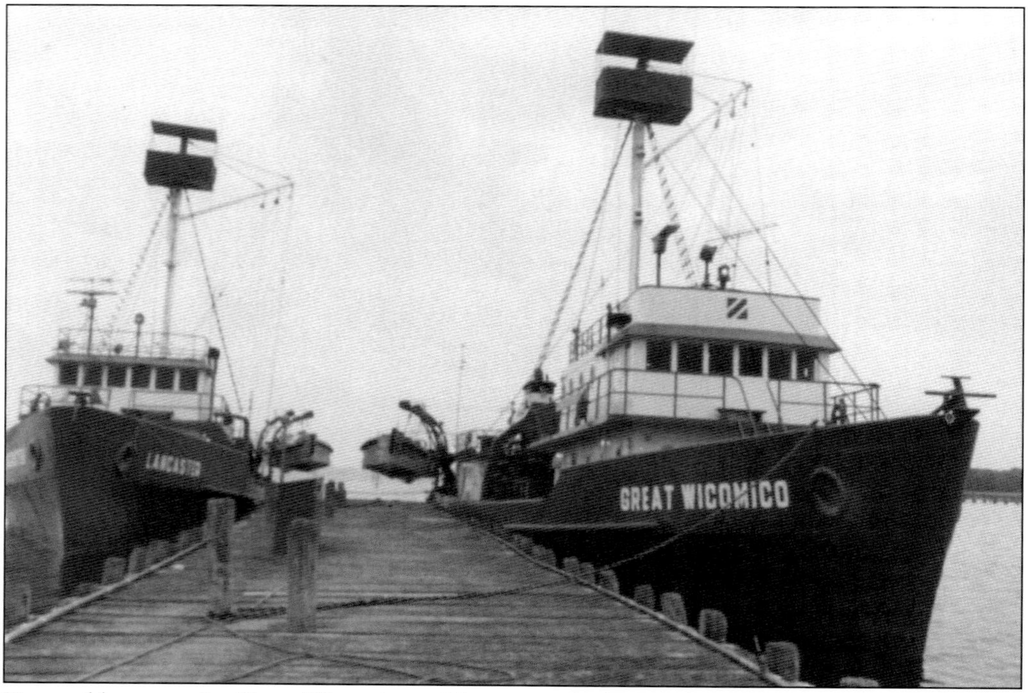

Pictured here are the *Great Wicomico* and *Lancaster* docked at the Zapata plant in Reedville in 1986. The Zapata Haynie Corporation would later evolve into the Omega Protein Corporation. During this time period, the *Lancaster* and *Great Wicomico* were state-of-the-art fishing vessels and were only recently retired from service.

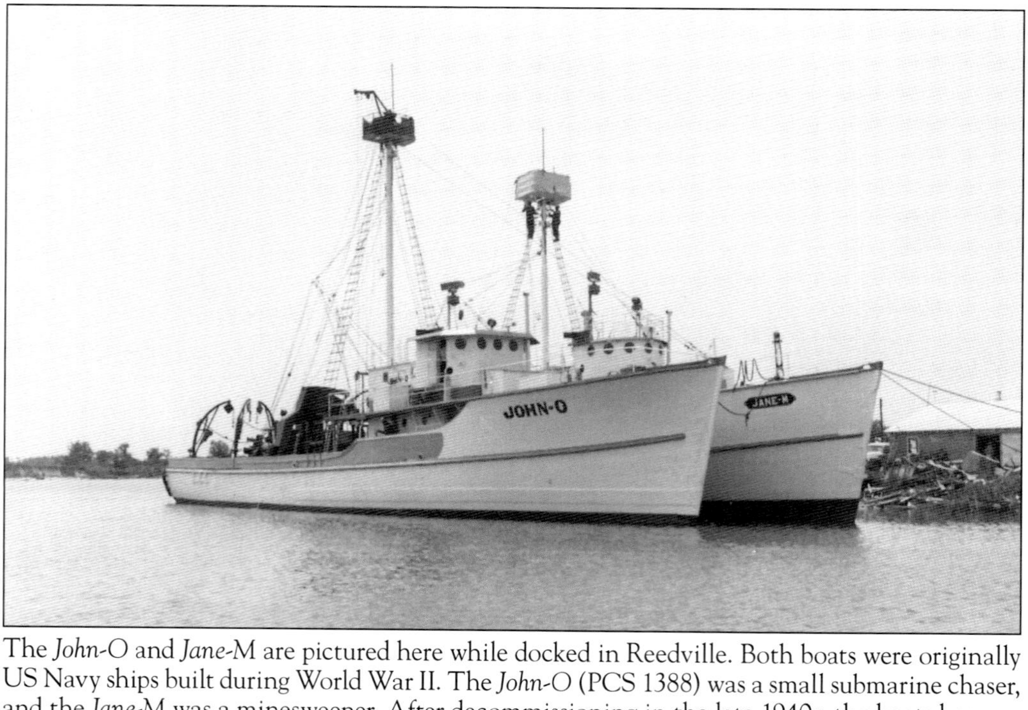

The *John-O* and *Jane-M* are pictured here while docked in Reedville. Both boats were originally US Navy ships built during World War II. The *John-O* (PCS 1388) was a small submarine chaser, and the *Jane-M* was a minesweeper. After decommissioning in the late 1940s, the boats became part of the Standard Products fishing fleet.

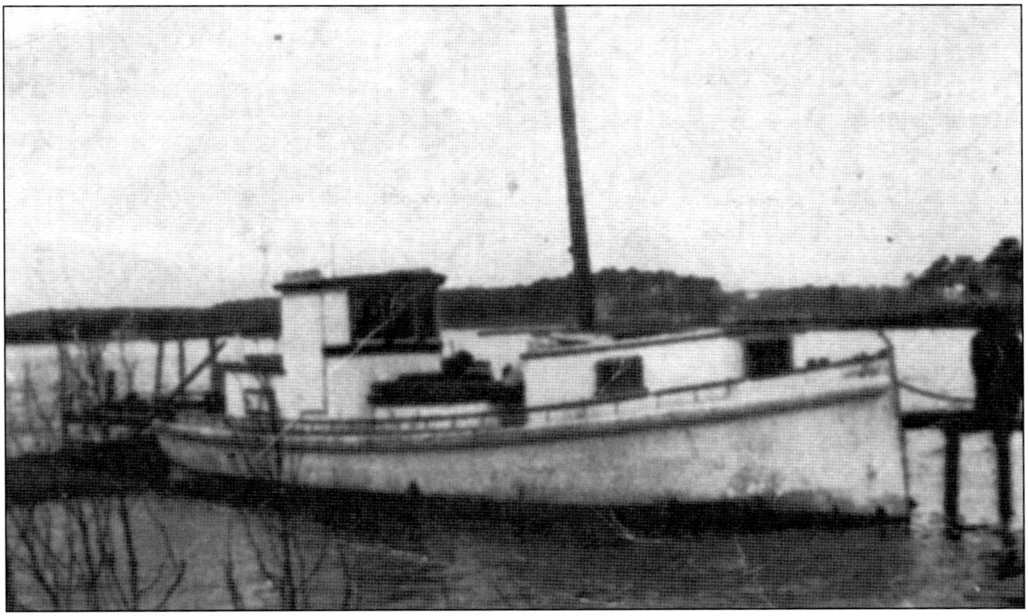

While the larger boats dominate, there are many smaller family fishing operations throughout the bay. The *Three Sisters* is a 46-foot oyster boat owned by Gilbert White of Foxwells, Virginia. He built the boat himself in 1931, and it had a capacity of 350 bushels, which did not leave too much room for more than one person.

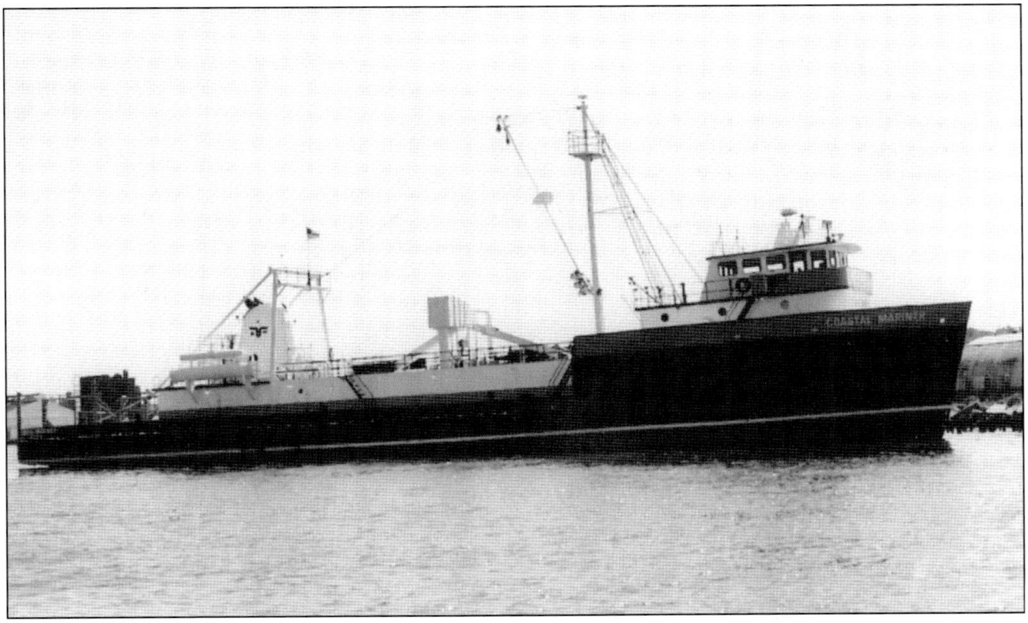

The *Coastal Mariner* was an impressive state-of-the-art boat when she was built in 1970. The *Mariner*, constructed in Port Arthur, Texas, was originally an oil-service boat but was later converted in the 1980s for menhaden fishing. It was more than 166 feet long and 38 feet in breadth. Ampro Fisheries owned the *Mariner* and stationed it at Reedville for a number of years. The vessel was later purchased by Beaufort Fisheries and spent the remainder of its days fishing the coastal areas of North Carolina and inland on the Chesapeake Bay. In 2006, having outlived its usefulness, the *Mariner* was taken to Norfolk and later sunk to become an artificial reef.

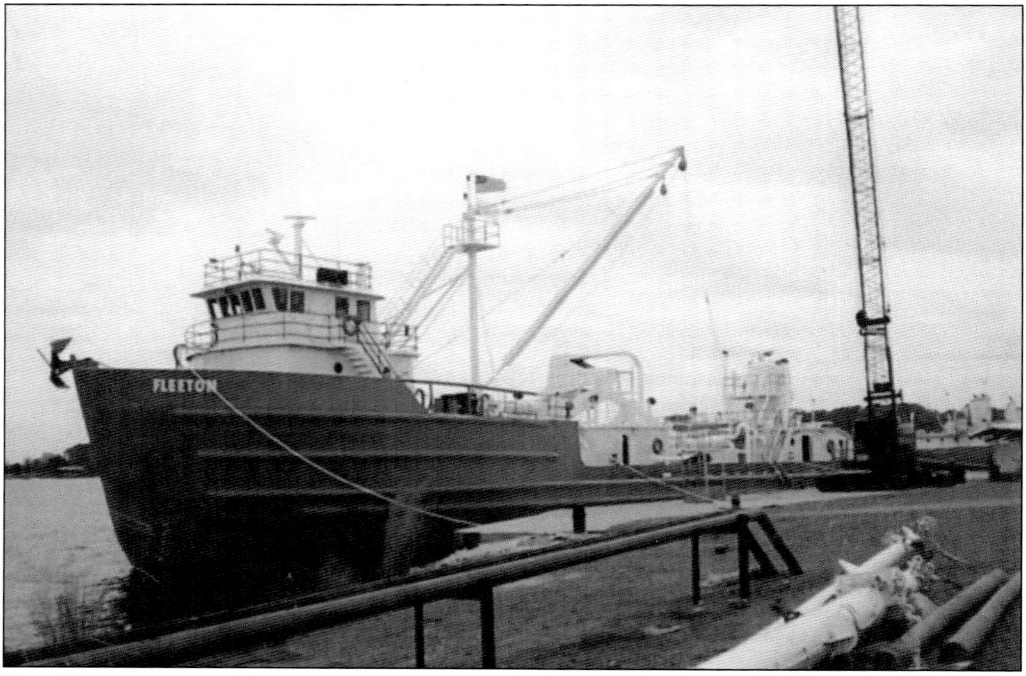

The *Fleeton* is part of the current menhaden fleet of Omega Protein Corporation in Reedville. Between its operations in Reedville and Louisiana, the company is the largest producer of menhaden products in the United States. The *Fleeton* was named for a small community located just a couple miles north of Reedville.

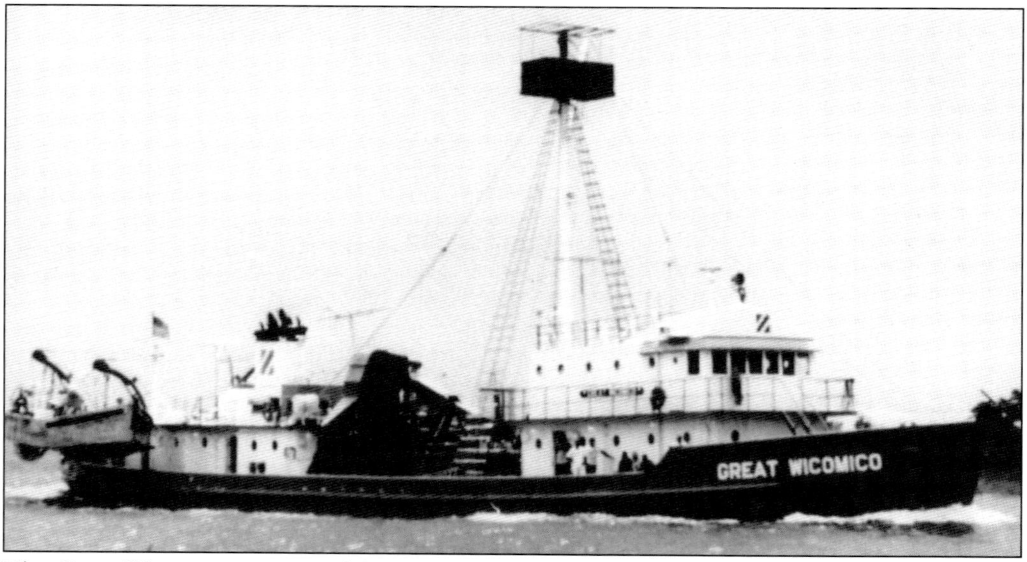

The *Great Wicomico* was named for a river that flows through Reedville. The ship was built in 1945 by the US Army and originally called the *Alaminos*. It was used as a Coast Guard ship, FS227, until its decommissioning. It was then converted to a menhaden fishing vessel with a home port of Reedville. The powerful twin diesel engines generated 1,800 horsepower. The *Great Wicomico* was used for many years by the Zapata Haynie Corporation of Reedville and, more recently, by its successor, Omega Protein Corporation. During the early 2010s, it was abandoned and later scrapped.

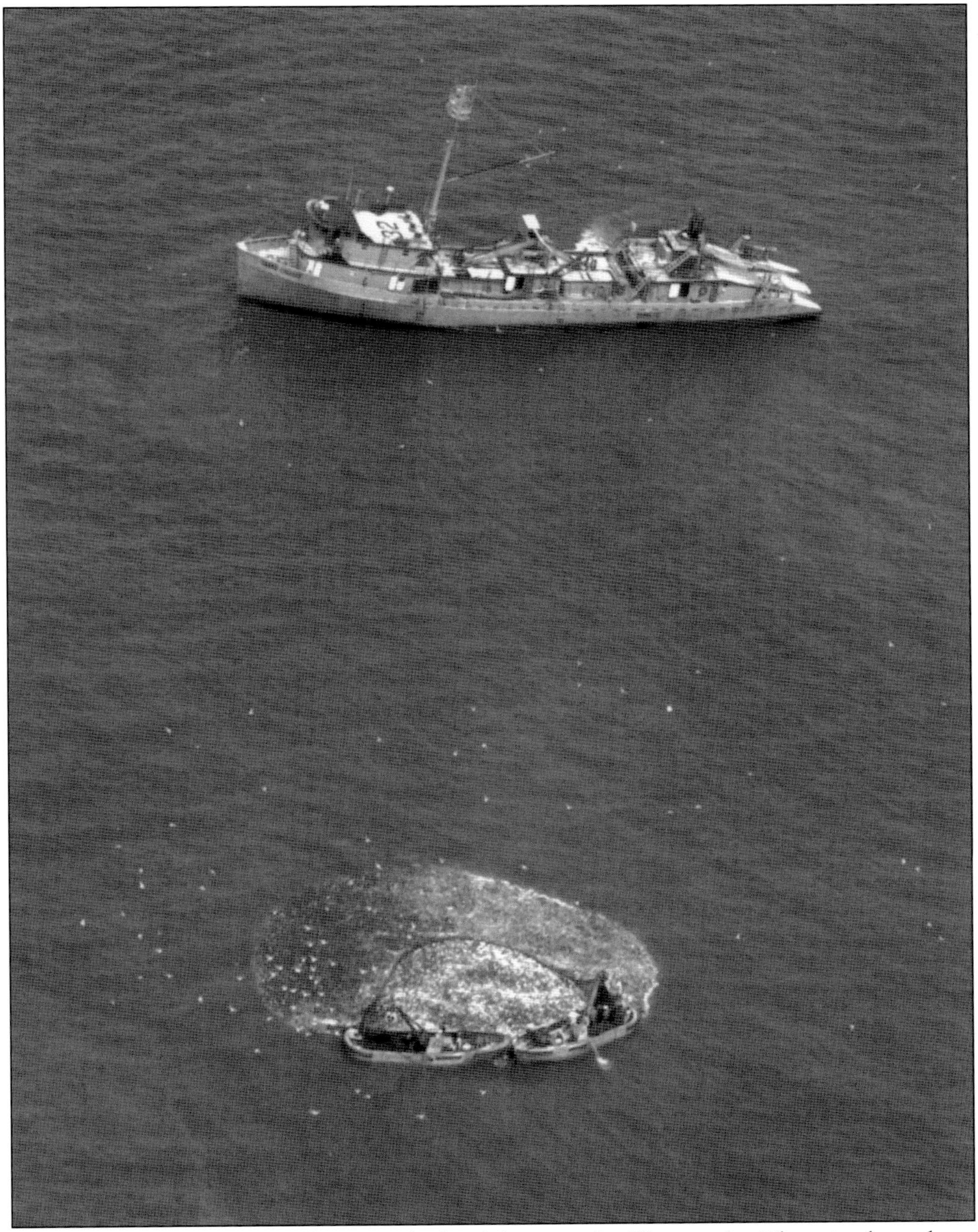

The *Grand Caliou* is pictured here menhaden fishing on the Chesapeake. The seine boats have already tightly closed up the net, which is full of fish. The *Caliou* is preparing to approach and hoist up the net and empty it into the hold. The boat was built in 1967 and specifically designed as a steel menhaden fishing boat for the Reedville-based Zapata Haynie Corporation. The *Caliou* measured 162 feet in length and had a minimal draft of 12 feet. It split its duties between the Chesapeake Bay area and the Gulf of Mexico, off of the Louisiana coast. The boat is still fishing, now under the Omega Protein Corporation flag.

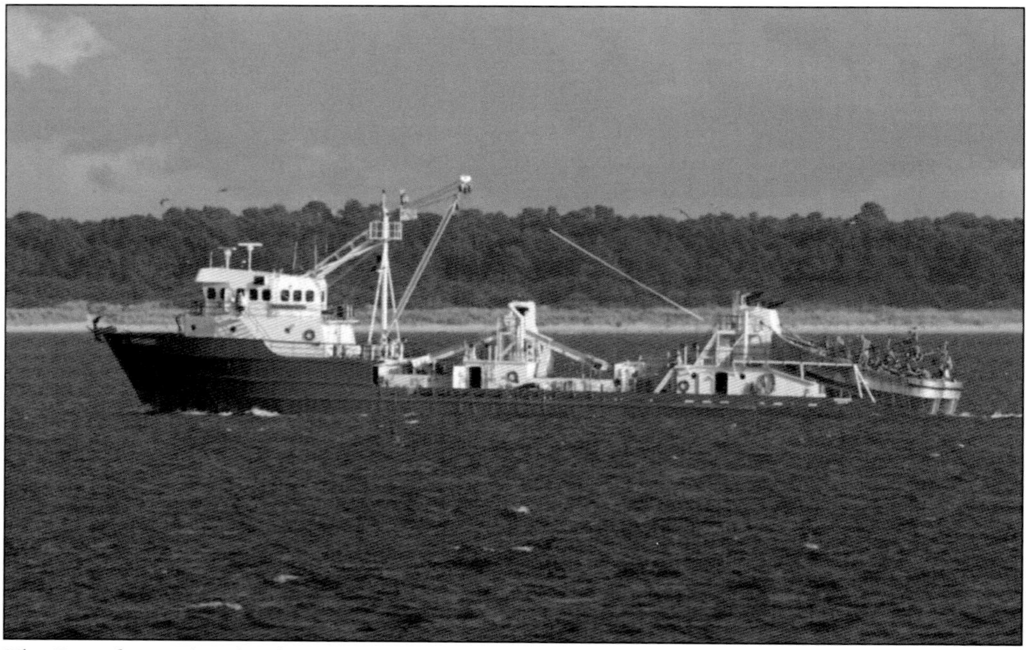

The *Rappahannock* is the showpiece of the current fleet of large menhaden boats owned by Omega Protein. Its new style greatly improves the efficiency of fishing. The purse boats no longer hang on davits on the sides but are pulled up the slanted end of the boat. The fleet not only fishes in Chesapeake Bay but also off the coasts of the Carolinas and the Maryland shore.

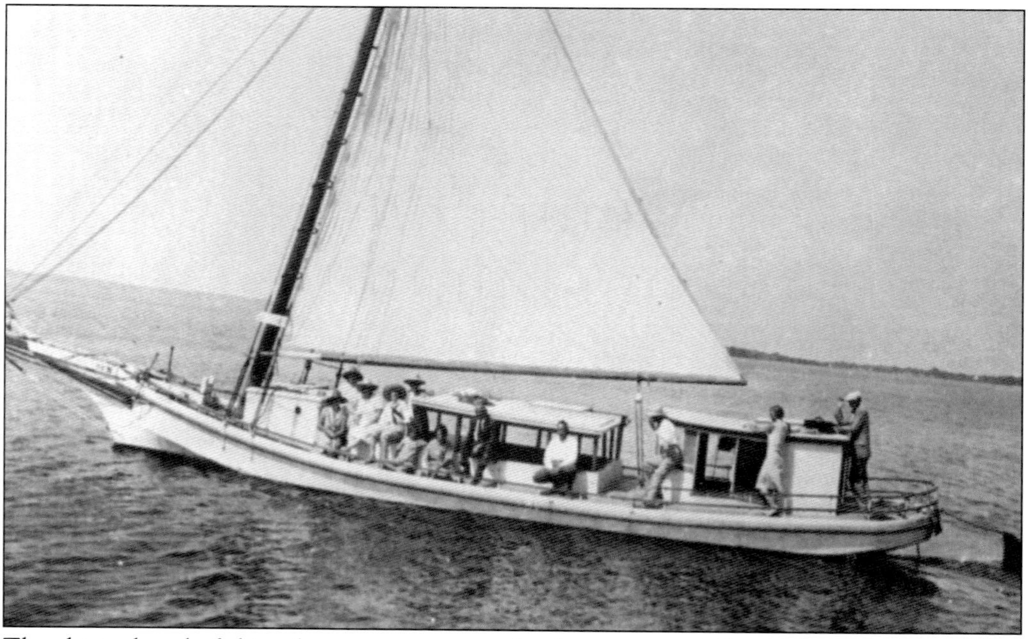

The skipjack-style fishing boat was very popular for oystering. This style was prominent in Maryland, although a number of them were built in Reedville. As more modern vessels took over, the skipjacks were sometimes purchased for use as tourist excursion boats. There are still a very few skipjacks actively being used for fishing boats.

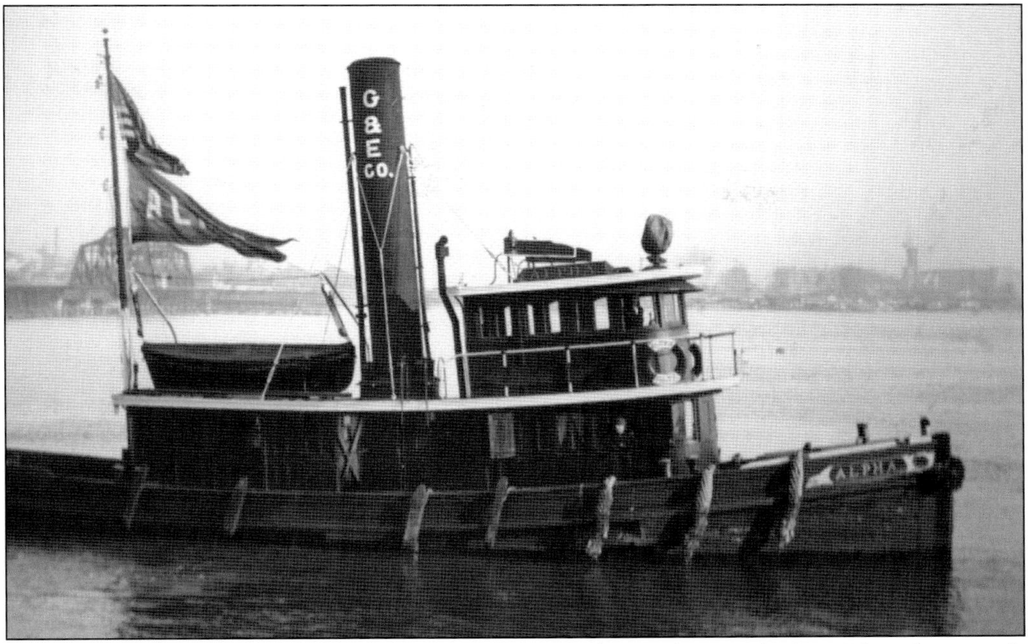

The *Alpha* was one of the earlier tugs to work the northern Chesapeake Bay. This photograph of the tug was taken before it was sold in 1927. It was owned by the Baltimore Gas and Electric Company and used to haul coal for its electric plants. The tug was sold to the New York City soon after this photograph was taken.

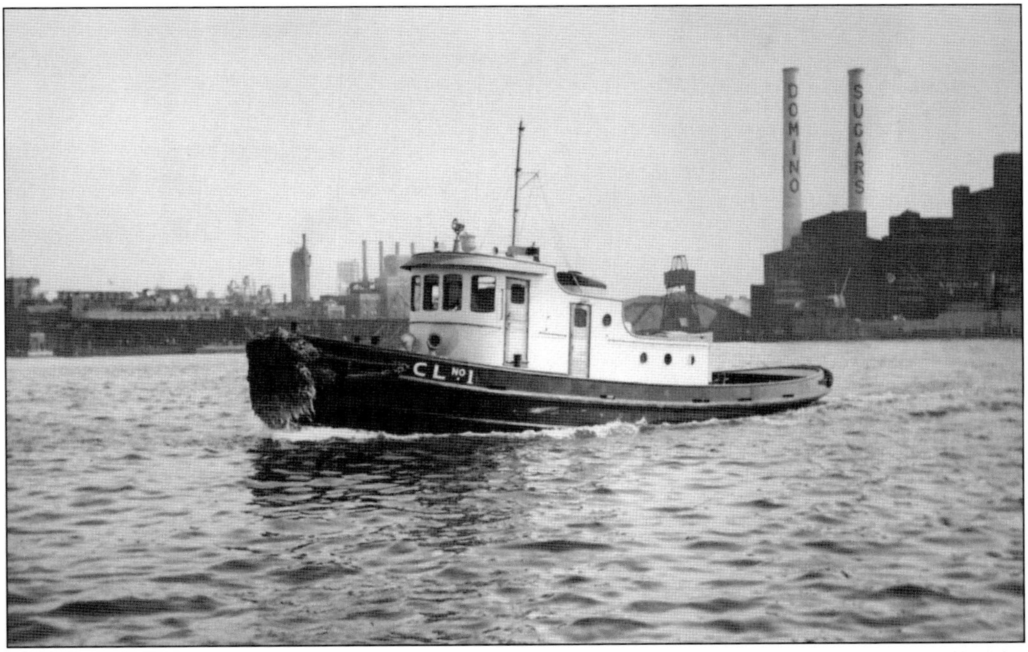

The tug *C.L. No. 1* was used primarily in the northern end of the Chesapeake Bay but called for duty to other areas outside of greater Baltimore. This 1940 photograph was taken in front of the Domino Sugar plant on the north branch of the Patapsco River, near the inner harbor. In the background is the American Electric Welding Company.

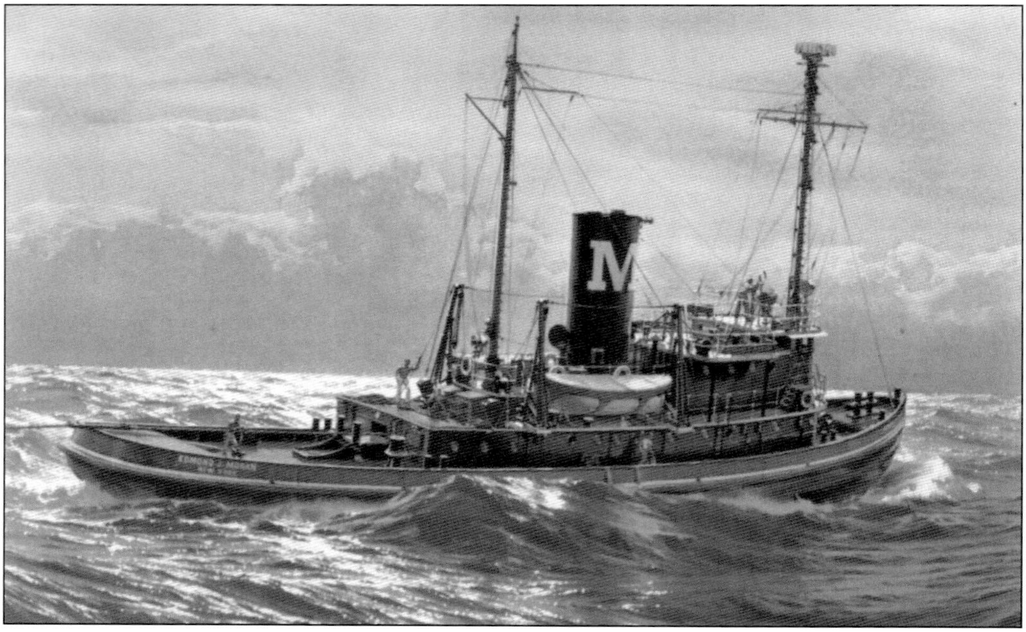

The *Edmond J. Moran* served throughout the Chesapeake Bay for many years. The powerful ocean tug was captained by Ira S. George of Fairport, Virginia. He made his longest tow from Port Arthur, Texas, to Thule, Greenland, towing two floating docks for the early warning station.

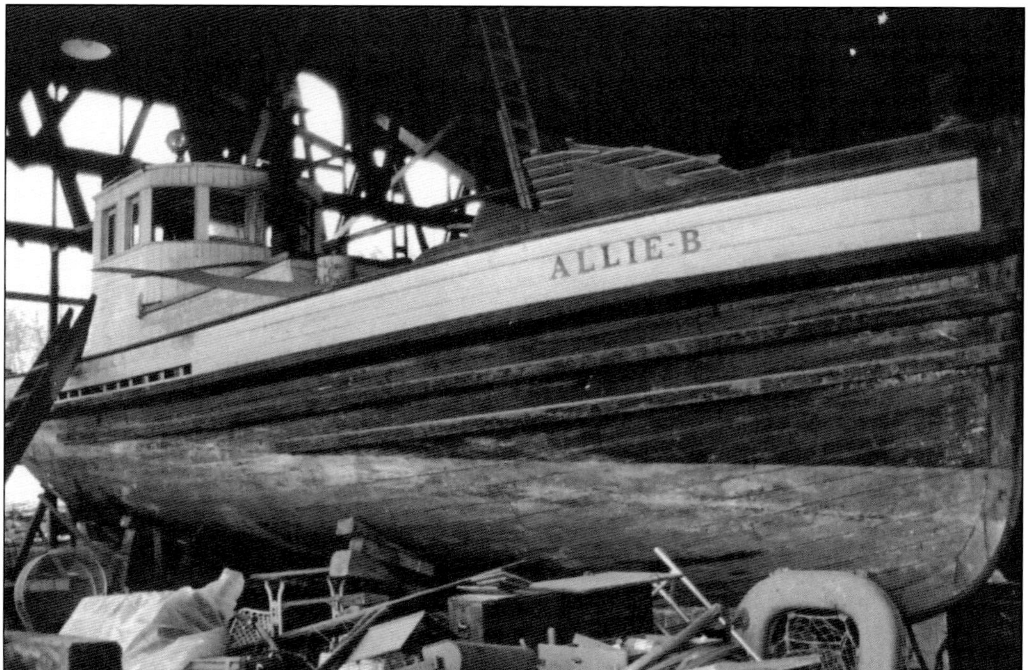

The tug *Allie B.* was built in West Bay City, Michigan, in 1902 but ended up spending most of its service life plying the waters of the Chesapeake Bay. It was used in toward on the Chesapeake and Delaware Canal for many years by Dann Marine Transportation. Tom Howell, head of the Chesapeake Bay Maritime Museum Boat Shop, bought the *Allie B.* in 1991 and then moved it to Cambridge, Maryland, for restoration. It remains a part of the museum's collection.

The *Brian McAllister* is still an active tug working the Chesapeake Bay, owned by McAllister Towing. This venerable and large tug operator is based in New York City with tug fleets in major East Coast locations, including Norfolk and Baltimore. The *Brian McAllister* is part of the Hampton Roads fleet, which docks at the Newport News Maritime Pier.

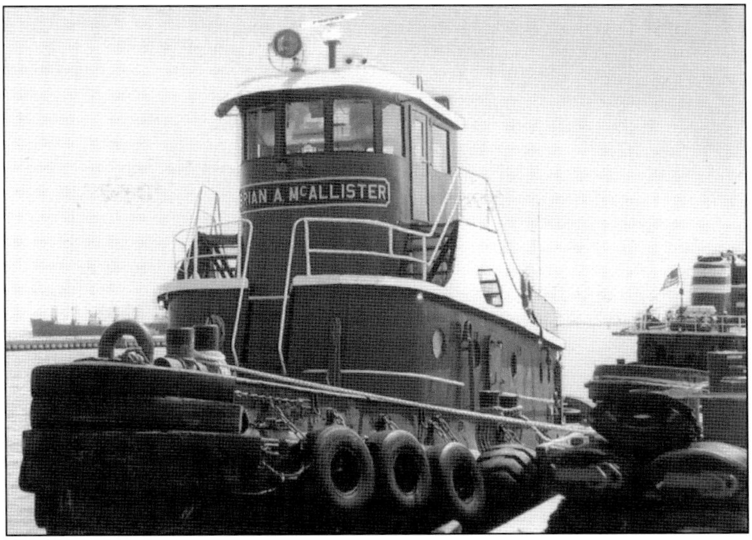

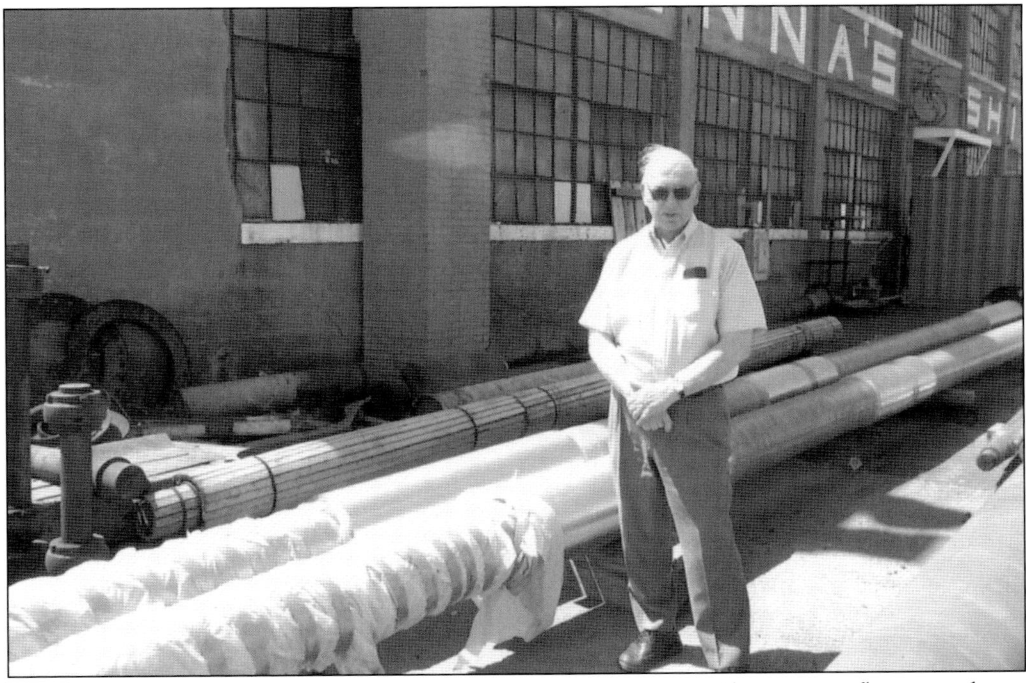

The Colonna Shipyard has worked on tugs for more than 100 years. This image reflects a tradition of special relationships and care with many different types of maintenance and construction projects. Bill Colonna is seen here in front of the shaft shop. Two large steel tug shafts are in the scene. The Colonna family also operated its own tug company in the 1920s and 1930s, Norfolk Towing and Lighterage Company.

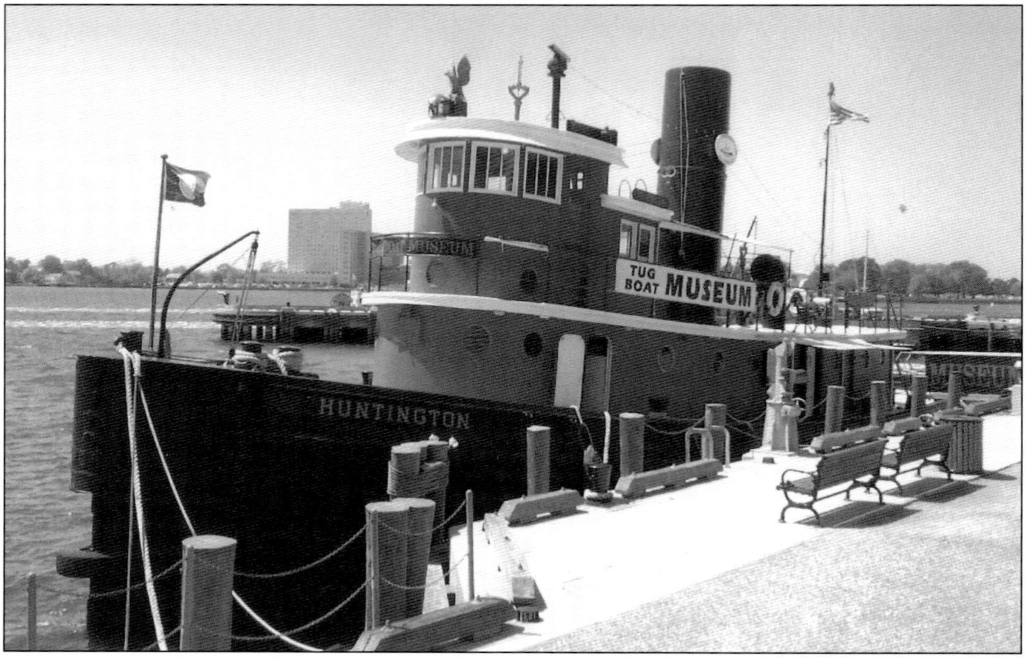

The tug *Huntington* was built in 1933 by Newport News Shipyard Apprentices. It worked as a docking tug in Hampton Roads for more than 50 years and is now retired and serving as a tug museum at the Nauticus Maritime Museum in Norfolk.

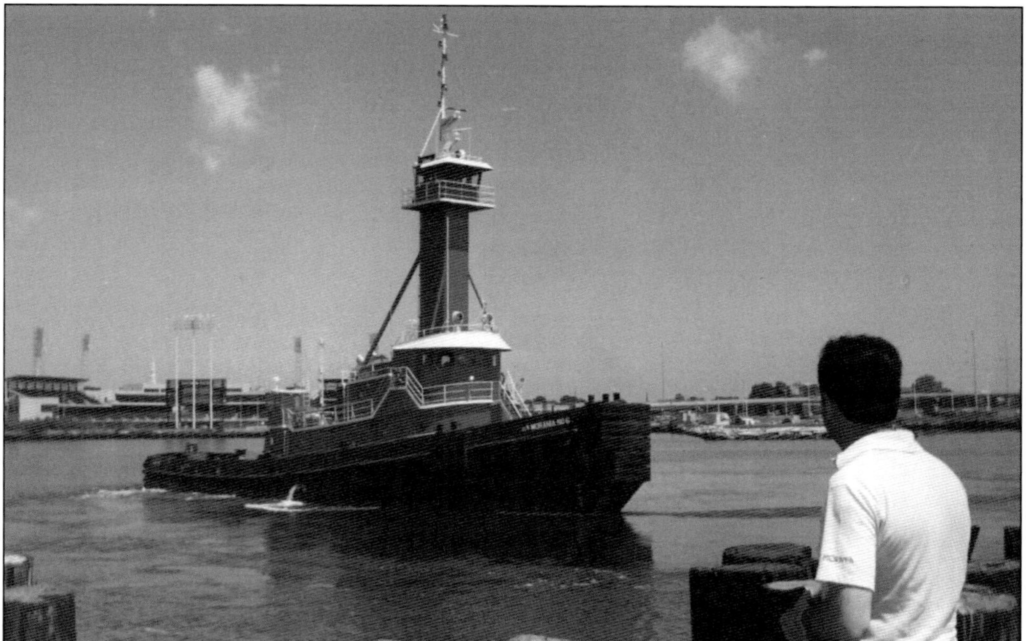

The *Morania No.* 6 is pictured here leaving Colonna Shipyard in Norfolk after a major refit, which included construction of a new extended pilothouse. As push barges became larger, the tug pilothouses had to be elevated to provide adequate visibility. The extension also contained an elevator. *Morania* port engineer Argie Barrieo inspects the tug after the refit was completed in June 1993.

Four

Chesapeake Boats in World War I

During both World War I and World War II, many menhaden fishing vessels from Reedville and the Chesapeake Bay were pressed into service as minesweepers, supply ships, and patrol boats. After both wars, vessels built for the Army and Navy were rebuilt for use as fishing vessels. These reconfigured ships performed cost effectively for many years.

During World War I, the US Navy crewmen on the converted menhaden steamers came from all walks of life and all parts of the country. The officers were a mixture of senior chief petty officers, average regular officers, and young newly commissioned ensigns and junior reserve officers, most of whom lacked maritime experience. Recruiting fishing crews from the Chesapeake Bay area proved beneficial to these inexperienced officers.

A flotilla of local fishing boats from the Chesapeake Bay area was sent across the Atlantic Ocean to patrol the French shoreline. While local fishermen served on boats elsewhere, only three known locals served on the Chesapeake boats in France. Robert Loder of Fairport was commissioned as an ensign at the ripe age of 58, and he served with distinction as the engineering officer on the USS *McNeal*. Lieutenant Loder was eventually made the assistant engineering officer for the whole squadron. W.W. Messick of Reedville was made a chief machinist's mate and served aboard the USS *Hinton*. Calvin Wootteon of Fairport served as a machinist's mate on the USS *Courtney*.

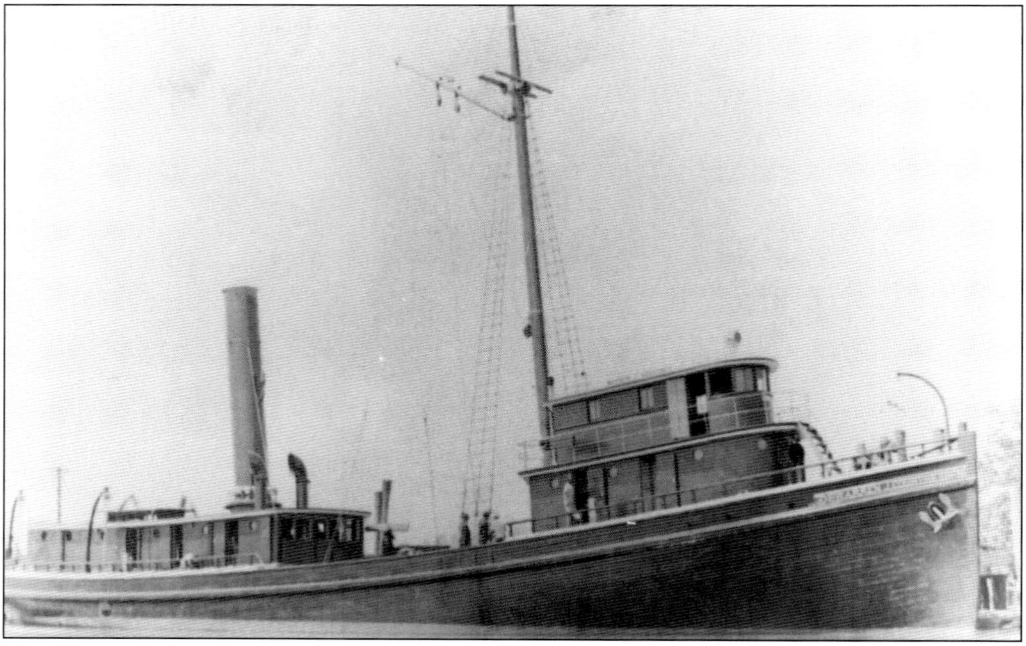

The *Warren J. Courtney* was built in 1912 for the C.E. Packing Company of Reedville. The US Navy took it in 1917 to be converted to a minesweeper, and *Courtney* was sent to France and served until the end of the war. The *Courtney*, pictured here in 1916, sank during a storm on the trip back to Virginia on April 27, 1919.

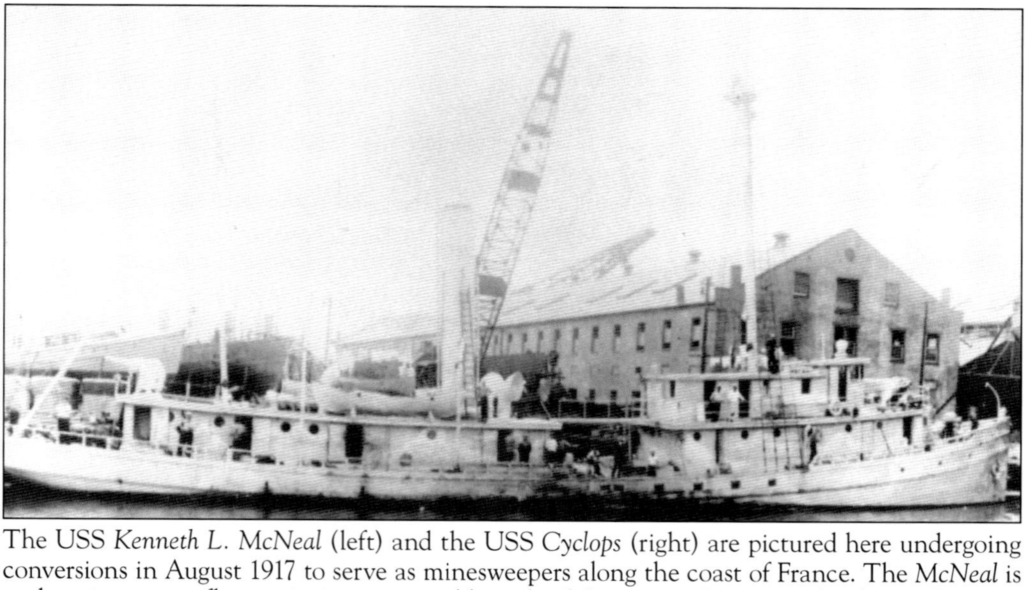

The USS *Kenneth L. McNeal* (left) and the USS *Cyclops* (right) are pictured here undergoing conversions in August 1917 to serve as minesweepers along the coast of France. The *McNeal* is undergoing camouflage painting to resemble a cloud formation. Interestingly, this is the same *Cyclops* that later disappeared into the Bermuda Triangle in March 1918, with a loss of 306 people. The remains of the ship have never been located.

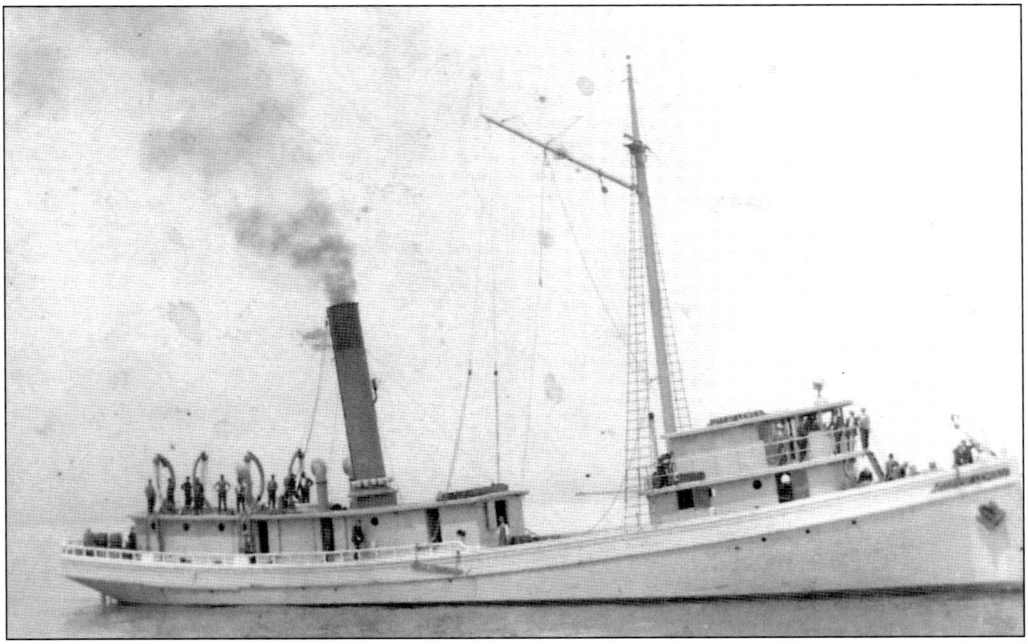

The *City of Lewes* was a commercial fishing boat built in 1912 by W.G. Abbott. It was purchased by the US Navy in May 1917 and immediately converted for minesweeping and patrol duties. The *Lewes* was part of the fishing vessel flotilla that sailed across the Atlantic to patrol the coast of France.

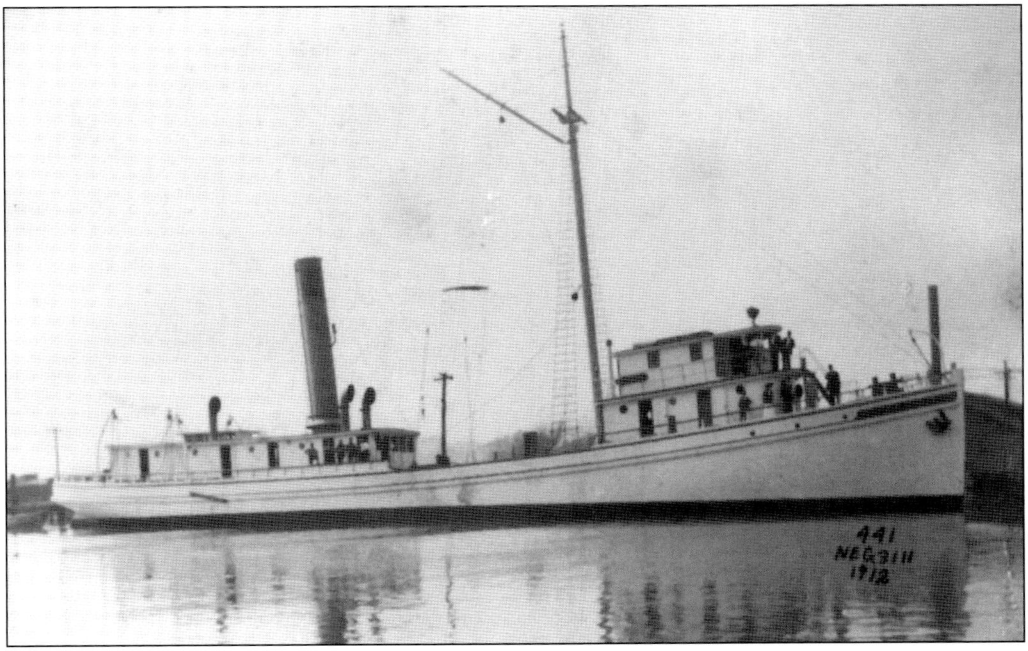

The *Otis W. Douglas* (later SP-313) was a freight boat built in 1912 for the Douglas Company of Reedville. In 1917, the vessel was commissioned into the US Navy and converted to a minesweeper. The *Douglas* was part of the flotilla of converted fishing boats that were sent to France. After departing for home in 1919, the boat encountered rough seas that sank it, along with the *Warren Courtney*.

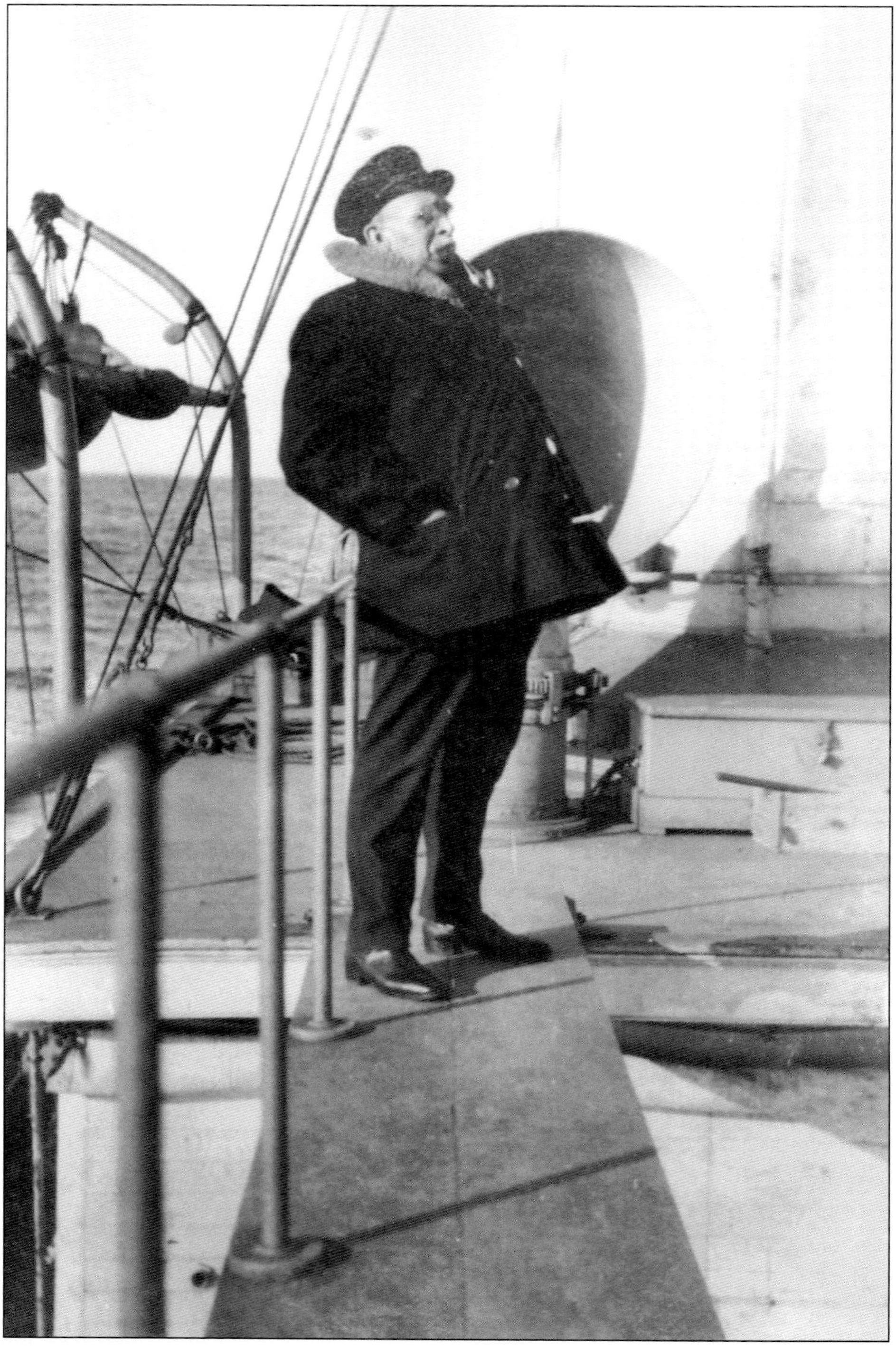

Lt. Robert Loder served as an officer on the USS *Kenneth McNeal* between 1917 and 1918. He hailed from Fairport, Virginia, and during his time on the minesweeper, Loder corresponded with his wife, Mildred, back home. These letters and photographs, like this one, provide a great insight to the role of the menhaden boats in France. His collection is housed at the Mariners' Museum in Newport News.

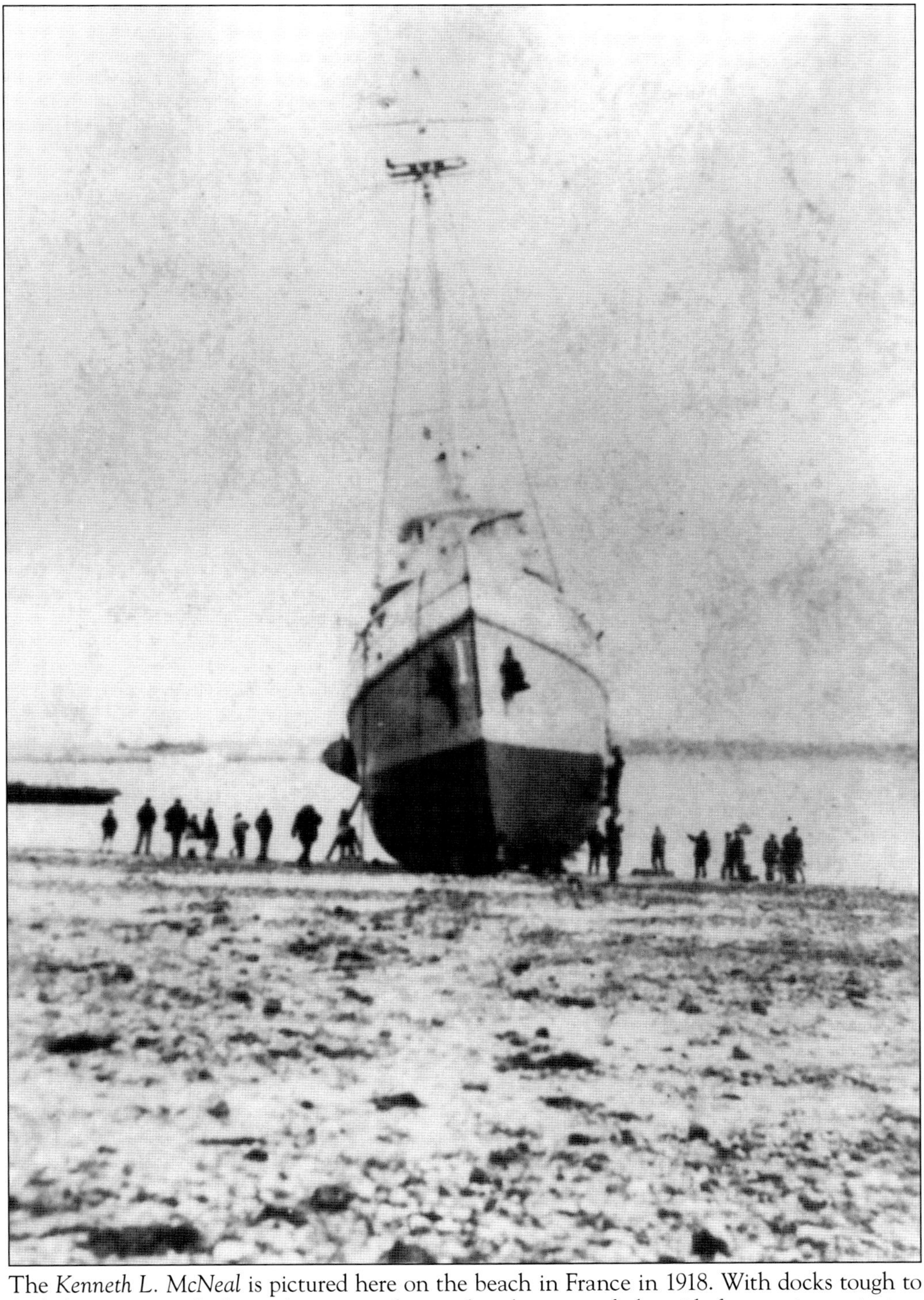

The *Kenneth L. McNeal* is pictured here on the beach in France in 1918. With docks tough to find, the crew uses the large change in tides to take advantage of a low tide for scraping, painting, and repairing the hull of the converted minesweeper. Later, the boat was damaged beyond repair and sold.

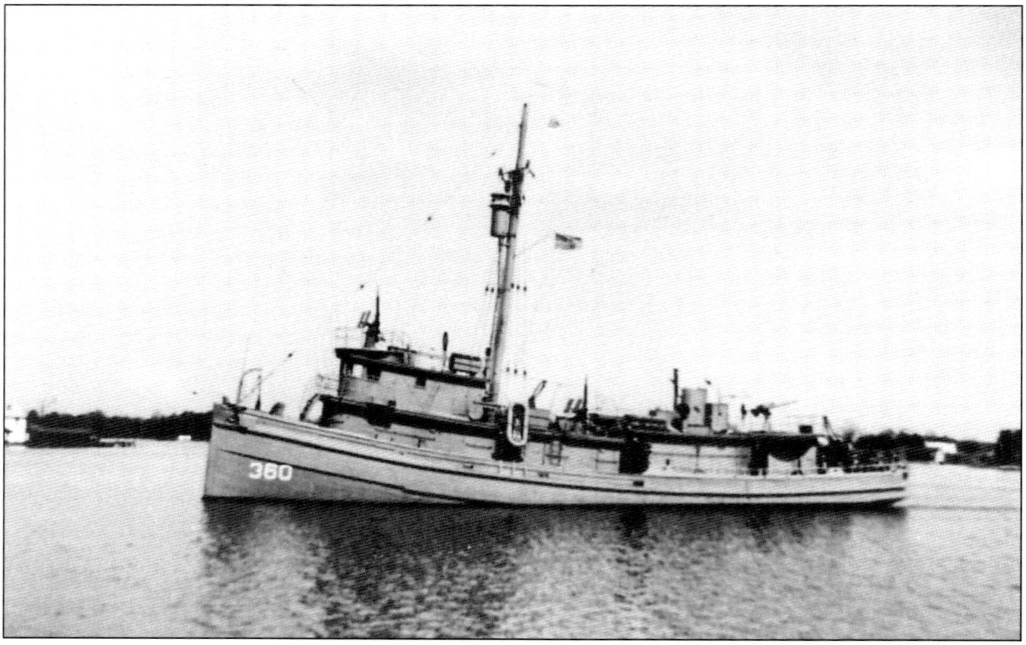

The *Elizabeth* M. *Froelich* (SP-380) was originally built as a fishing and freight boat. It was constructed in 1915, and in 1917, it was commissioned into the US Navy. It was outfitted as a minesweeper and served in the 5th Naval District, which was based at Norfolk, until 1919.

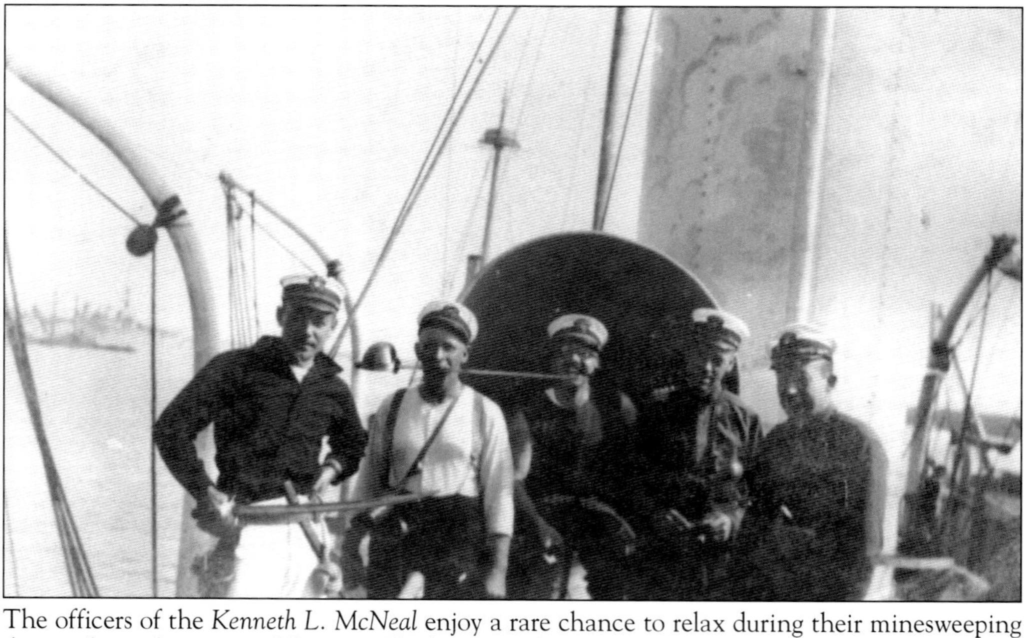

The officers of the *Kenneth L. McNeal* enjoy a rare chance to relax during their minesweeping duties along the coast of France. The boat was based in Brest along with a flotilla of other converted menhaden boats from the Chesapeake Bay area. Commanding officer Lt. C.B. Byrne is to the far left, and Lt. Robert Loder is next to him.

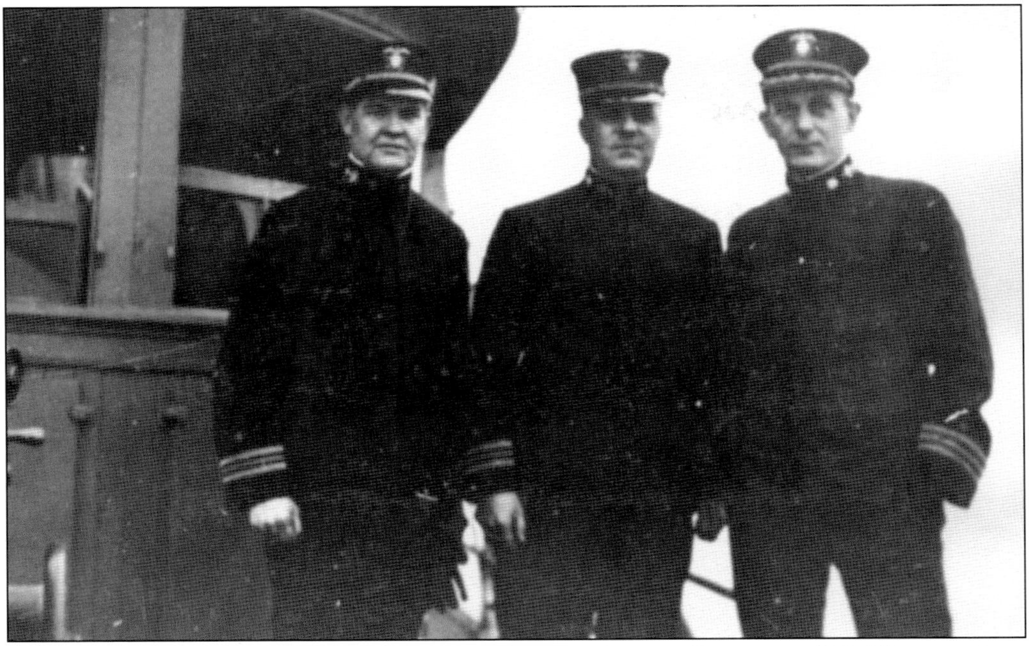

Pictured here are officers on board the *John B. Hinton* at Lorient, France, in 1918. They are, from left to right, Lt. Comdr. Fred L. Blaisdell, Lt. Comdr. Archibald McGlasson (commanding officer), and Comdr. Lemuel M. Stevens (senior aide to the Lorient District commander).

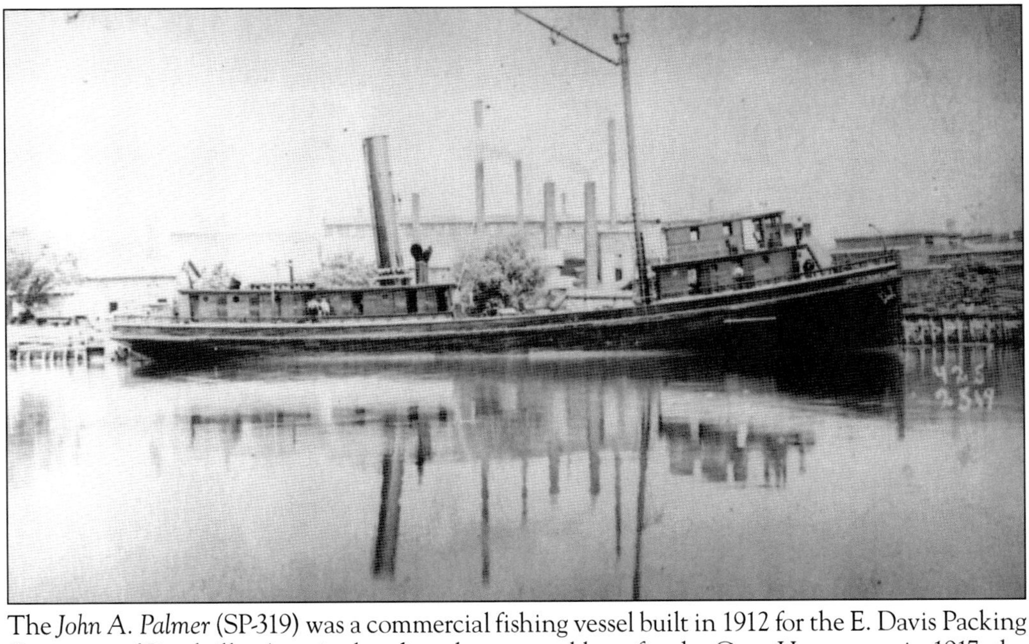

The *John A. Palmer* (SP-319) was a commercial fishing vessel built in 1912 for the E. Davis Packing Company of Reedville. Acquired and used as a patrol boat for the Cape Henry area in 1917, the *Palmer* was later converted into a cable boat for the Coast Guard in 1918. The boat was renamed the *Pequot* and used in that capacity until decommissioned in 1922.

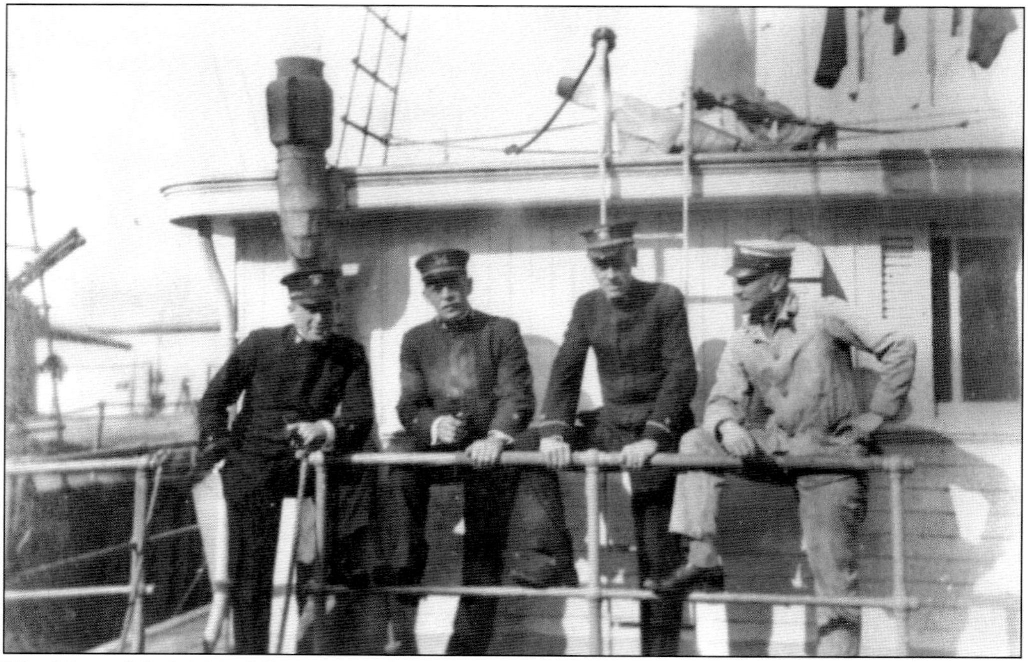

The *Kenneth L. McNeal* (later SP-333) was built in 1913 by M.M. Davis and used for fishing by the McNeal-Dodson Company of Reedville. It was commissioned into the US Navy for patrol duty as a minesweeper along the Virginia Capes area. Here are the *Douglas*'s officers, including Lt. Robert Loder of Fairport (second from left) and commanding officer Lt. C.B. Byrne (third from left).

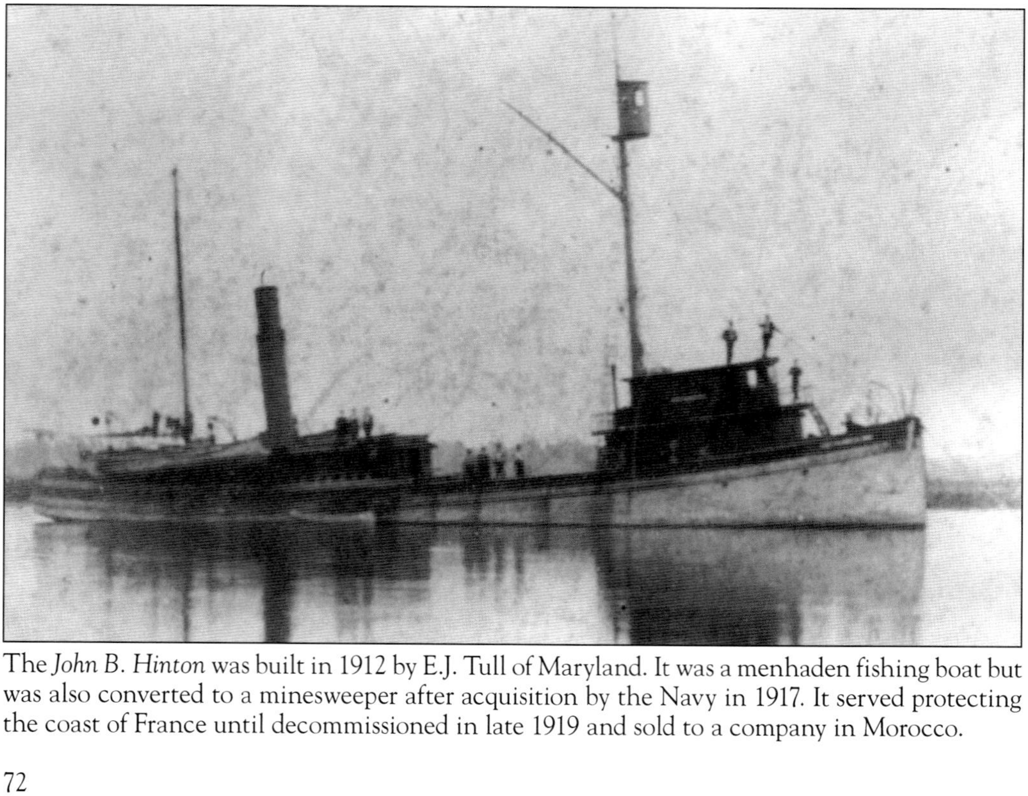

The *John B. Hinton* was built in 1912 by E.J. Tull of Maryland. It was a menhaden fishing boat but was also converted to a minesweeper after acquisition by the Navy in 1917. It served protecting the coast of France until decommissioned in late 1919 and sold to a company in Morocco.

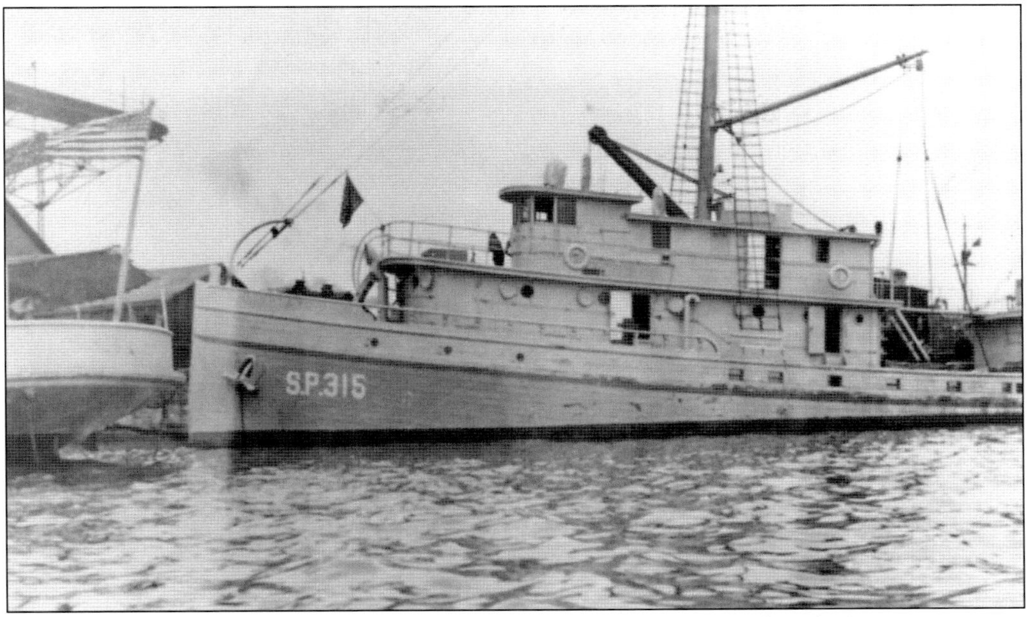

The *Wilbert Edwards*, later SP-315, was built in 1911 for the W.A. Edwards Corporation as a fishing boat. The Navy took it over, and the vessel was rechristened at the Norfolk Navy Yard in August 1917. Lt. D.C. Kindell commanded the *Edwards*, but after almost sinking on an attempted crossing to France, it remained stateside. The *Edwards* returned to commercial fishing and was active through the 1940s.

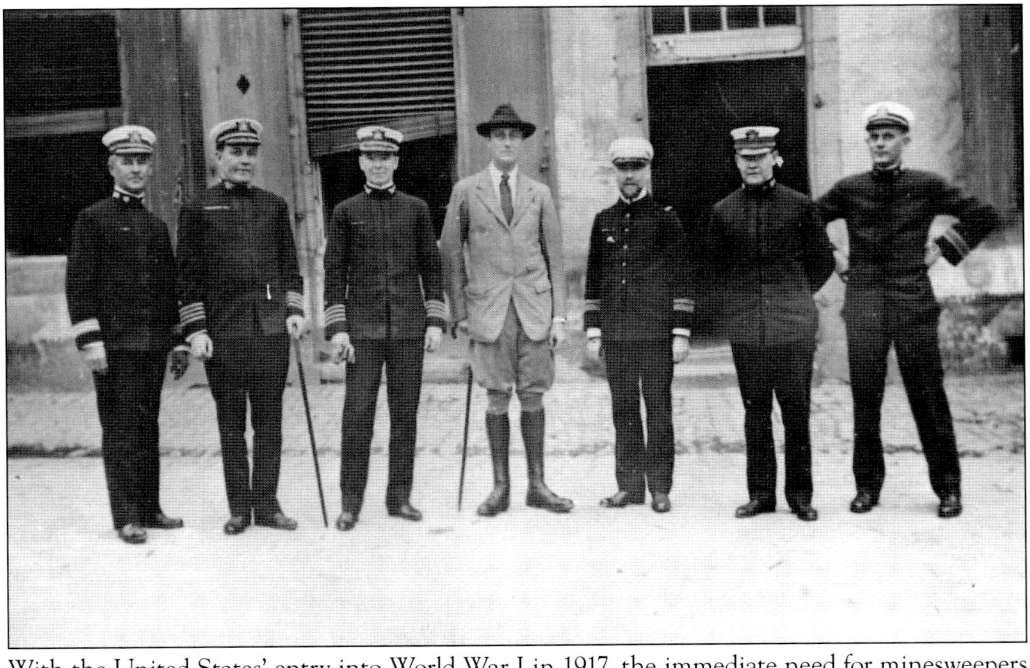

With the United States' entry into World War I in 1917, the immediate need for minesweepers and patrol boats led the government to acquire many of the menhaden fishing vessels. Due to their design, conversion to minesweepers was optimal. The then-Under Secretary of the Navy, Franklin Roosevelt, traveled to Norfolk to see the progress and meet some of the captains.

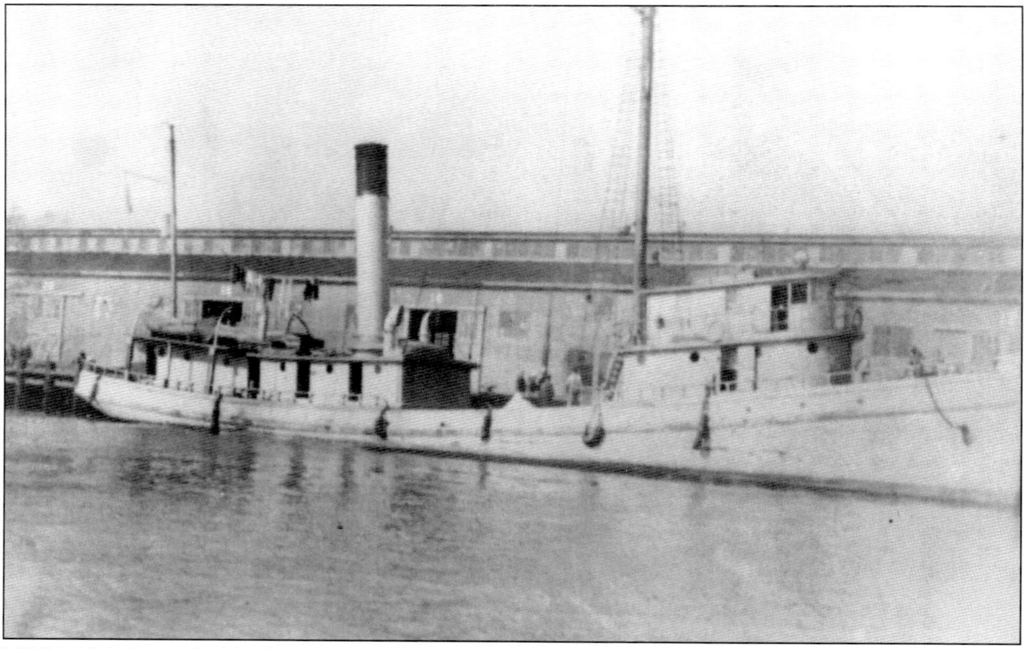

USS M.M. *Davis* (SP-314) was a menhaden vessel built in 1912. The Navy acquired the *Davis* in April 1917 and converted it into a minesweeper. The ship was decommissioned in May 1919 and sold in France rather than brought back across the ocean.

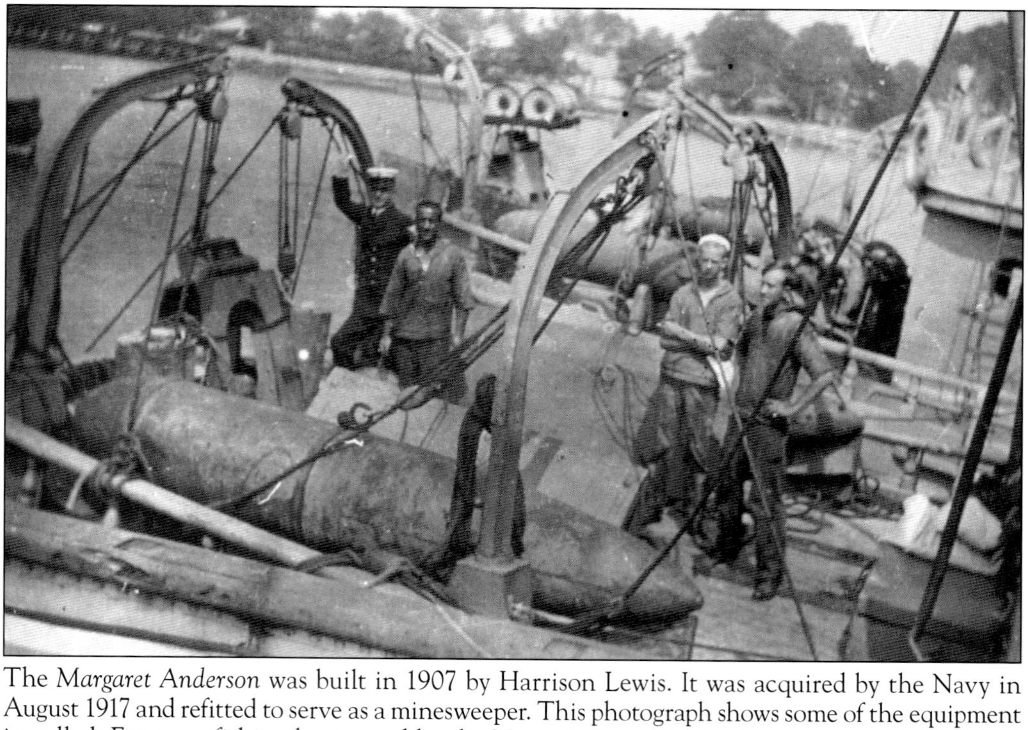

The *Margaret Anderson* was built in 1907 by Harrison Lewis. It was acquired by the Navy in August 1917 and refitted to serve as a minesweeper. This photograph shows some of the equipment installed. For most fishing boats used by the Navy, it was typical to keep most of the original fishing crew to run the minesweeper.

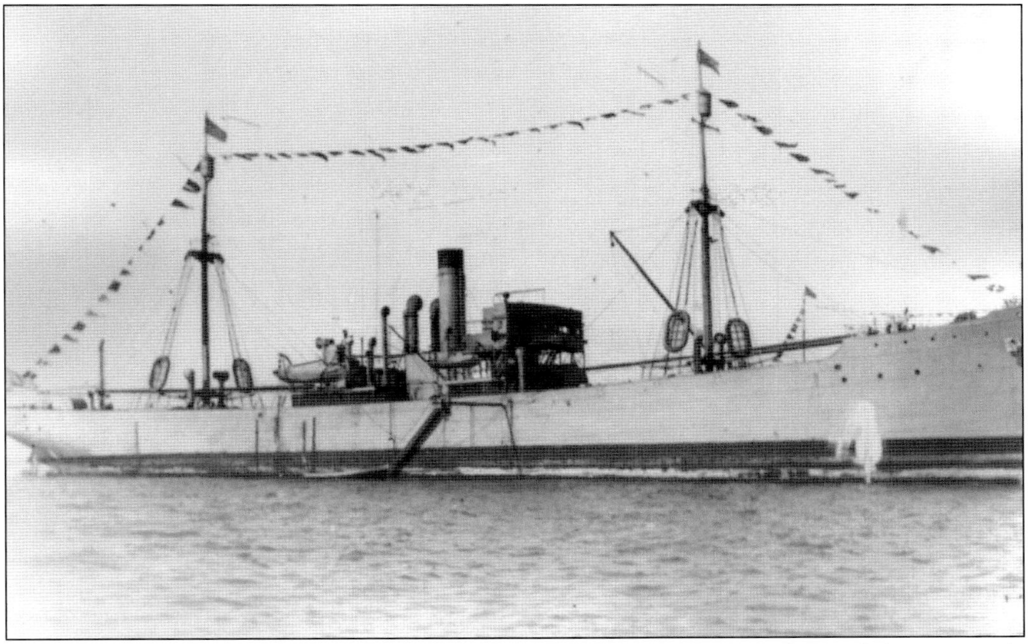

The USS *Bath* was a cargo ship built in 1913 by a German company, seized New Orleans in early 1917. The *Bath* then sailed to Norfolk, where it joined the flotilla of Chesapeake menhaden boats that had been converted to minesweepers. The *Bath* served as the lead for the boats heading to Brest, France. The group left Boston on August 2 and arrived in Brest on September 18.

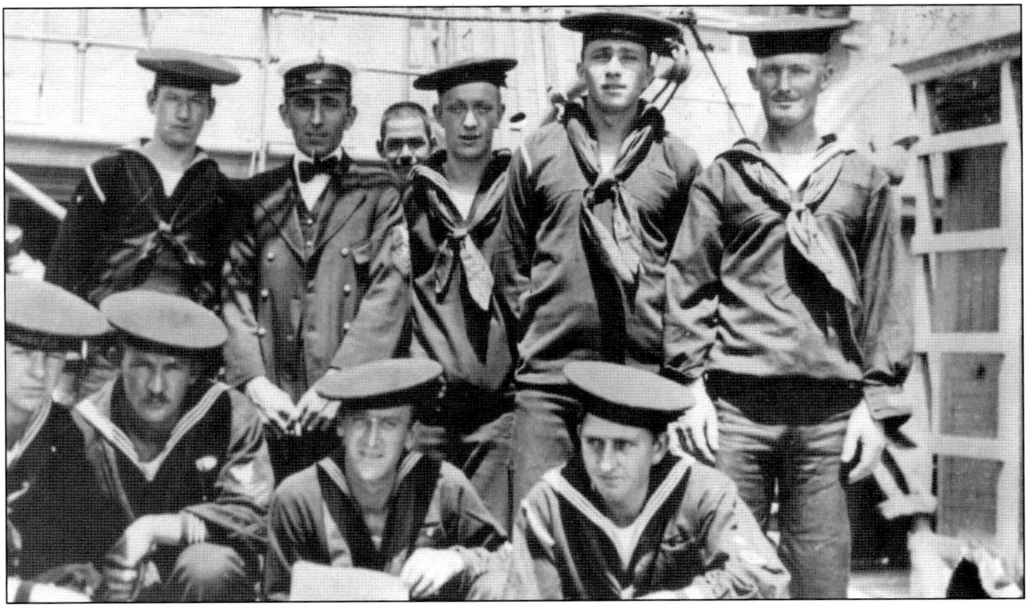

Pictured here are the captain and crew of the *Margaret Anderson* (SP-1203) around 1917. The boat was assigned to the 5th Naval District and based at Oyster, Virginia. After it was decommissioned in December 1917, the *Anderson* resumed serving as a menhaden boat with the Reedville Oil & Guano Company. The boat was taken by the Coast Guard during World War II and stationed at Cape May, New Jersey.

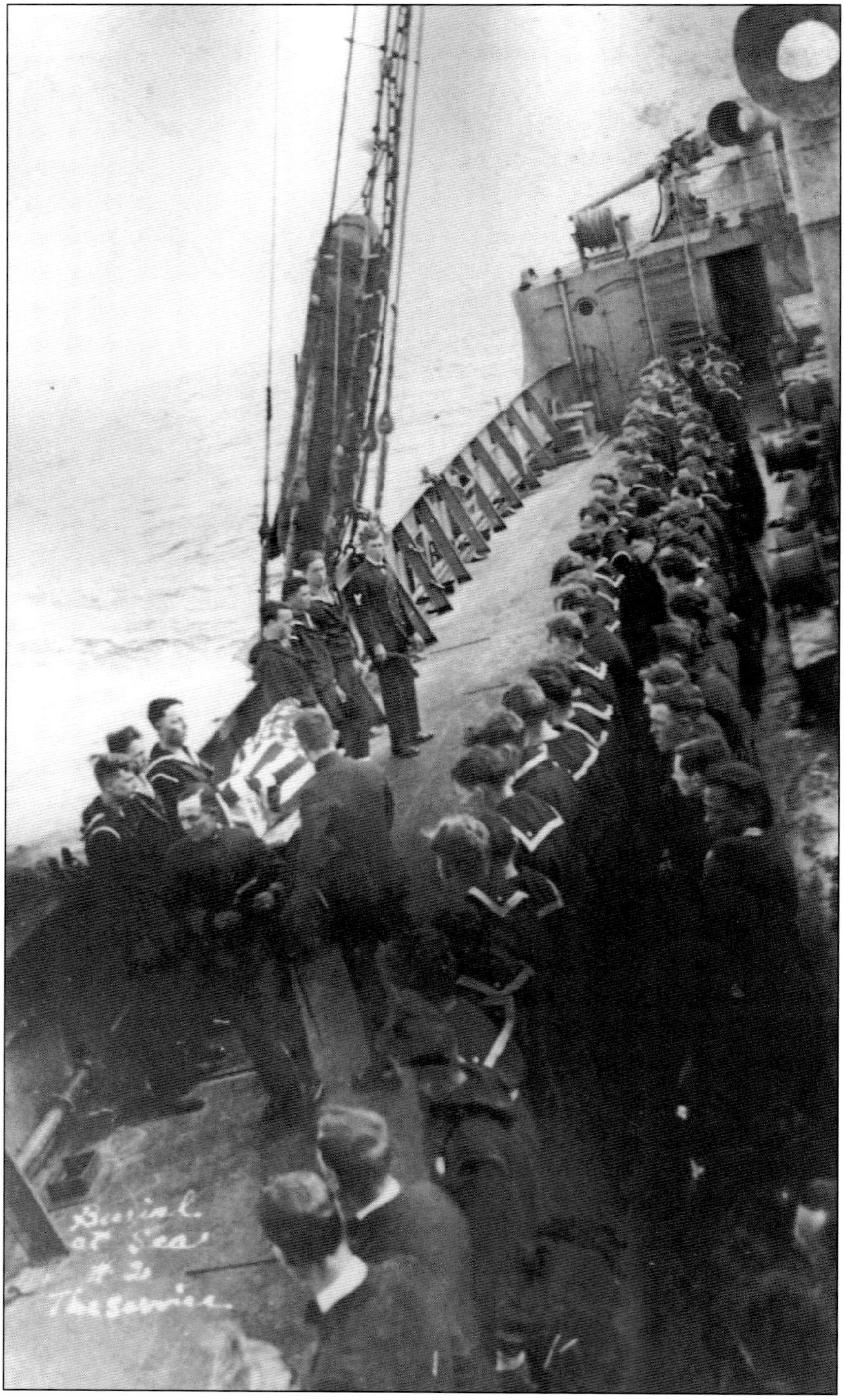

With so many local boats serving, protecting the coast of France during World War I, the risk of the loss of life was very real. Here, an unidentified sailor receives a burial at sea from the deck of one of the Reedville boats. A number of watermen from Chesapeake Bay perished during the war while serving on their ships.

Five

A Look at Reedville, Virginia

The story of Reedville, Virginia, is linked to the commercial fishing industry that developed here in the late 19th century. In 1874, Elijah Reed transferred his menhaden fishing operation from Brooklin, Maine, to the Chesapeake Bay. He purchased land on Cockrell's Creek that is now Reedville, and the industry flourished, especially in the early part of the 20th century. Today, Reedville is one of the major ports for the landing of commercial fish in the United States, second only to Kodiak, Alaska.

The town's Main Street, a National Historic District, is one mile long and flanked by water. The larger homes along Main Street reflect the prosperity of the early menhaden captains and plant owners. Most of the houses in the historic district have been carefully restored. Today, operating from Reedville, is a large, modern menhaden fishing fleet with 13 oceangoing vessels. There are smaller menhaden boats and numerous other boats used in pound net fishing, crab potting and dredging, soft crab processing, clamming, and oystering.

Reedville, during its heyday, had one of the highest per capita incomes in the United States. The long line of Victorian homes was nicknamed "Millionaires Row." While few businesses are left, it remains a cozy small town with a high density of retired residents.

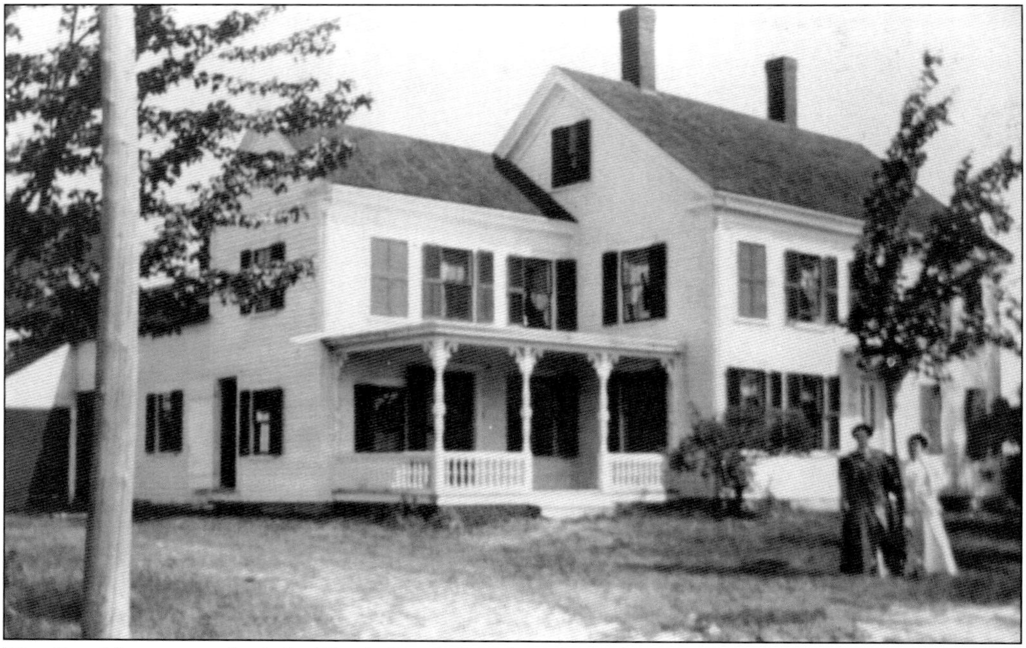

The Reed home was built by Elijah Reed, founder of Reedville. He was a sea captain from New England who came south to fish menhaden during the winter months. Reed established the industry in Chesapeake Bay, and his success allowed him to build one of the largest homes in town.

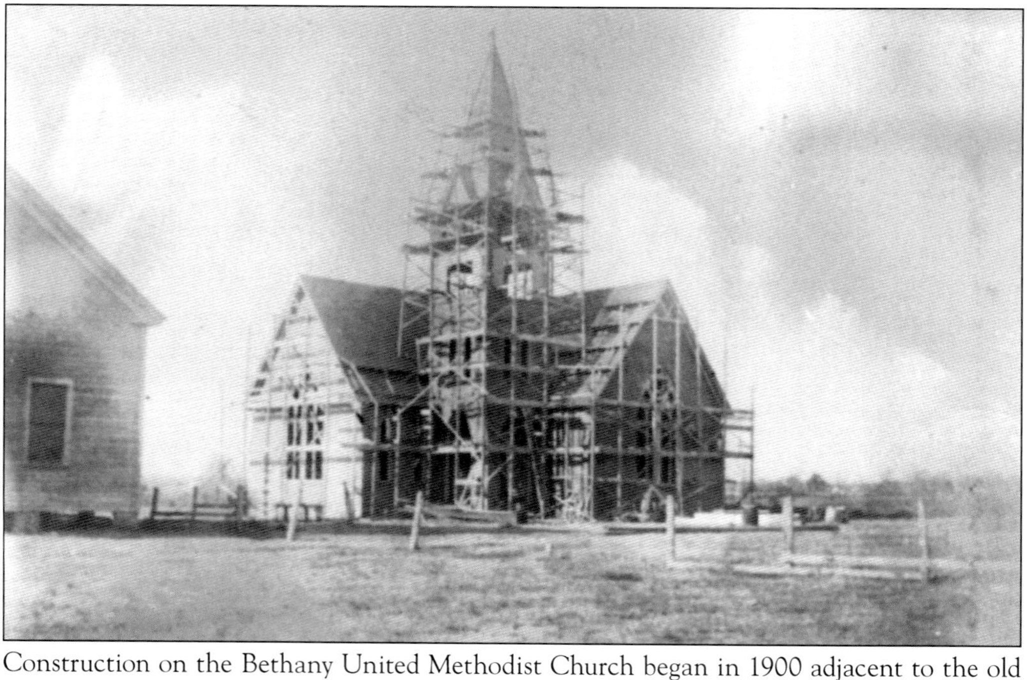

Construction on the Bethany United Methodist Church began in 1900 adjacent to the old Reedville Town Hall, visible to the left. It was built with brick and features a slate roof. The church was dedicated on June 30, 1901. While there were many churches in the Reedville area, this was the only one located in the main settlement on the peninsula.

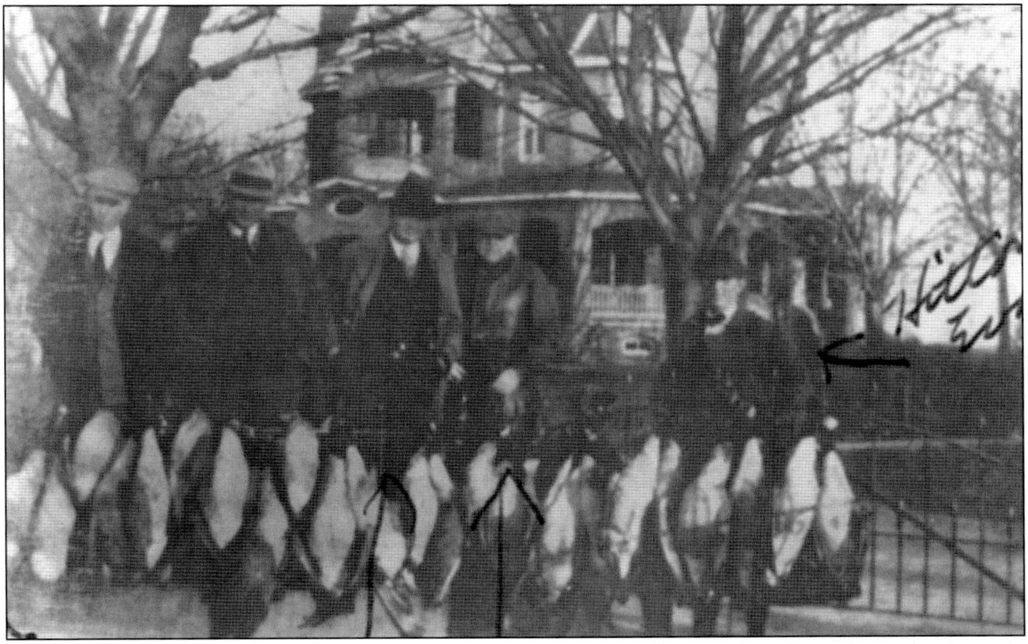

During the 1920s, local gentlemen from Reedville show off their prizes after a hunt for Canada geese. The prominent Reedville home, the Gables, is in the background. From left to right are Ira Lewis, T.C. Slaughter, Robert Moore, Capt. James Fisher, and Hilton Evans. Captain Fisher was a very important man in Reedville history. He was cofounder of the Morris-Fisher fish factory, one of the largest in the area.

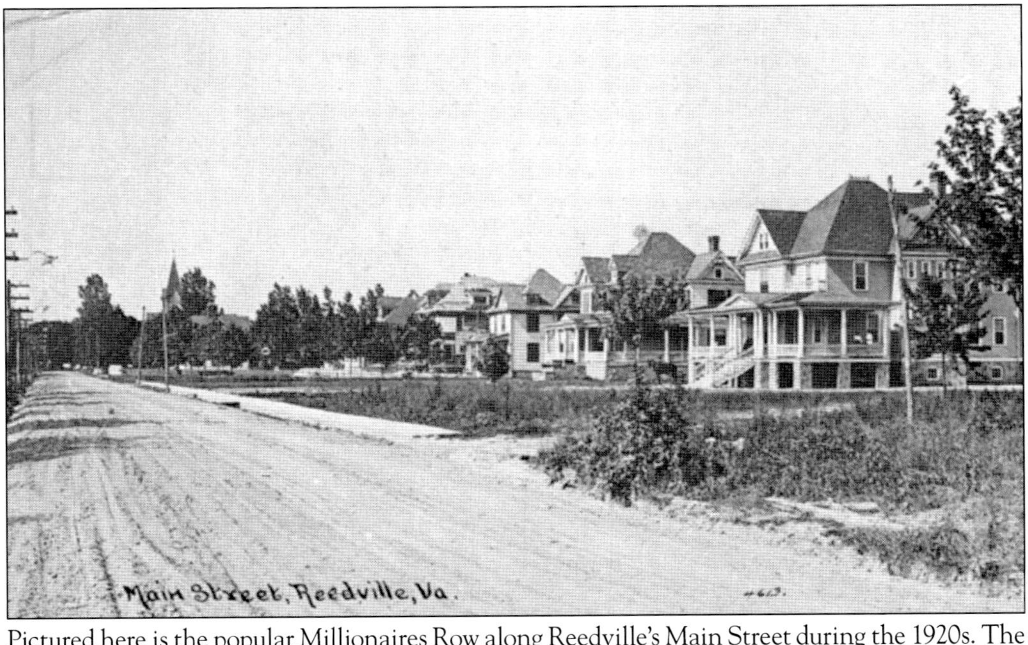

Pictured here is the popular Millionaires Row along Reedville's Main Street during the 1920s. The owners of the factories and other businesses accumulated great wealth from the fishing industry during the heyday of the town. Reedville, on a per capita basis, had one of the highest incomes of any town on the East Coast. Of course, the land area of the town was small, consisting of just the peninsula area, which had all the big homes.

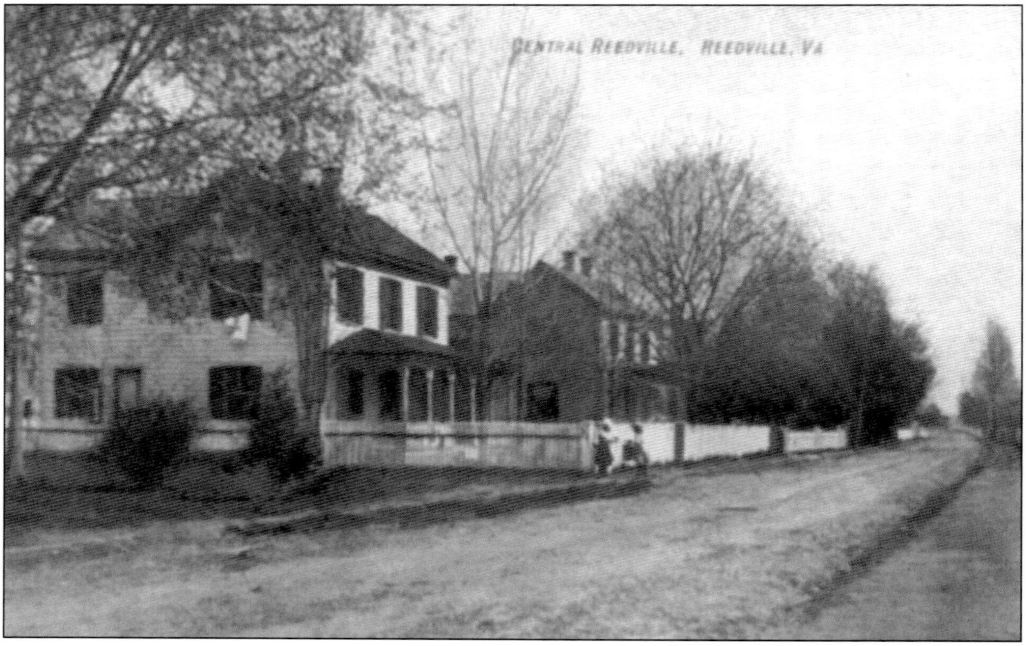

This is the lower part of Reedville's Main Street during the early 1900s. This area contains the original homes constructed after Reedville began growing in the 1880s. At the time, these were considered elegant homes and the original Millionaires Row, since it predates the Victorian homes located a short distance behind from where this photograph was taken.

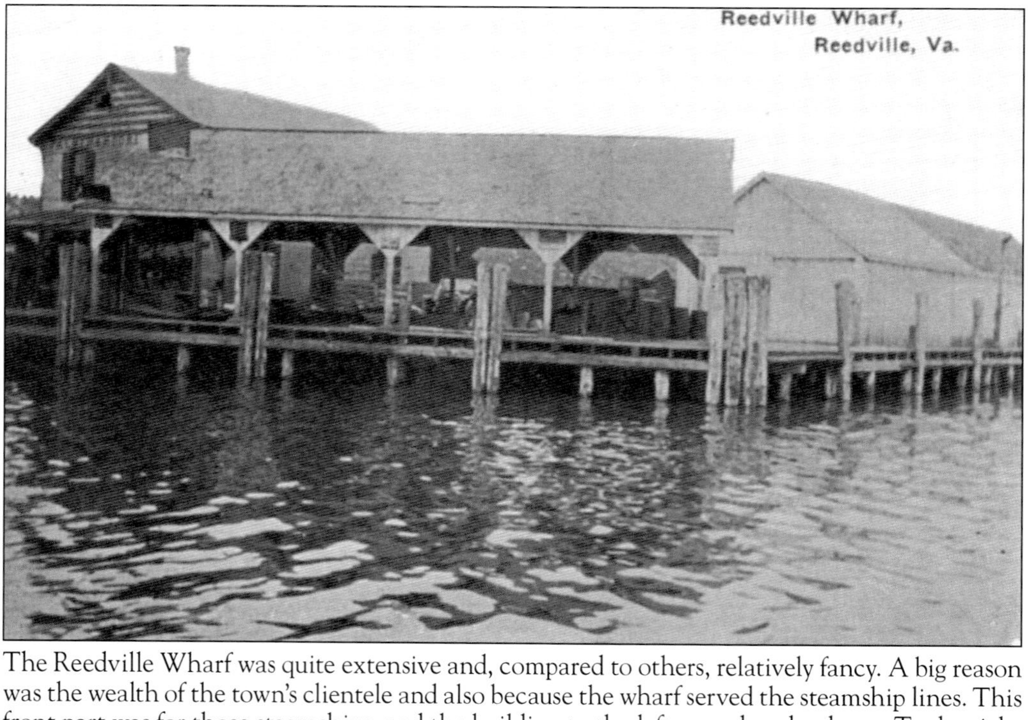

The Reedville Wharf was quite extensive and, compared to others, relatively fancy. A big reason was the wealth of the town's clientele and also because the wharf served the steamship lines. This front part was for those steamships, and the building to the left served as the depot. To the right are the freight buildings. Part of the wharf still remains, although in poor condition.

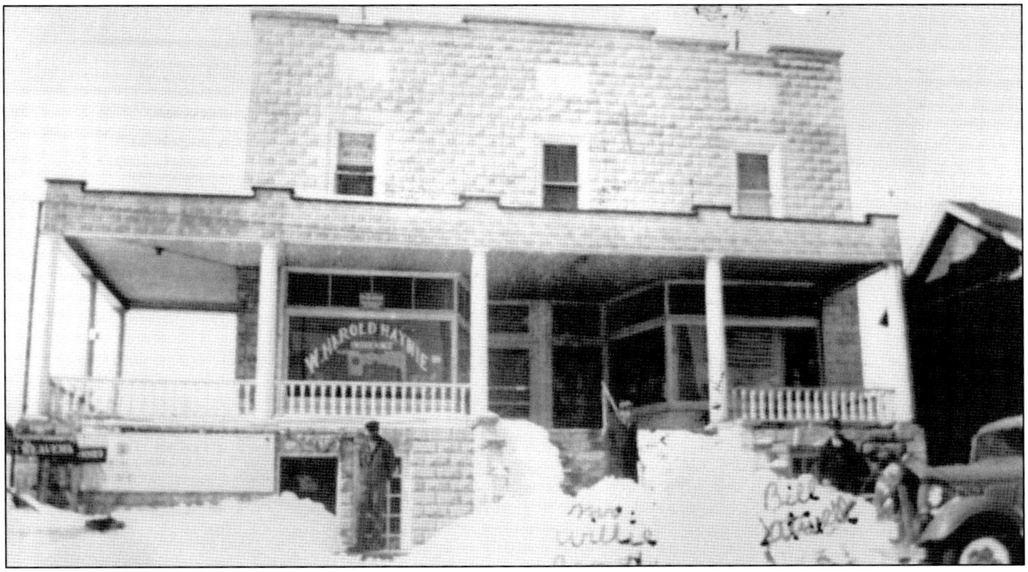

The Reed Company built the Dey Building in 1924, which was designed as an office and apartment house. Over the years, it hosted the post office, numerous food stores, clothing stores, and a dentist office, among other businesses. After years of being abandoned, the building was razed for a parking lot for the neighboring bank.

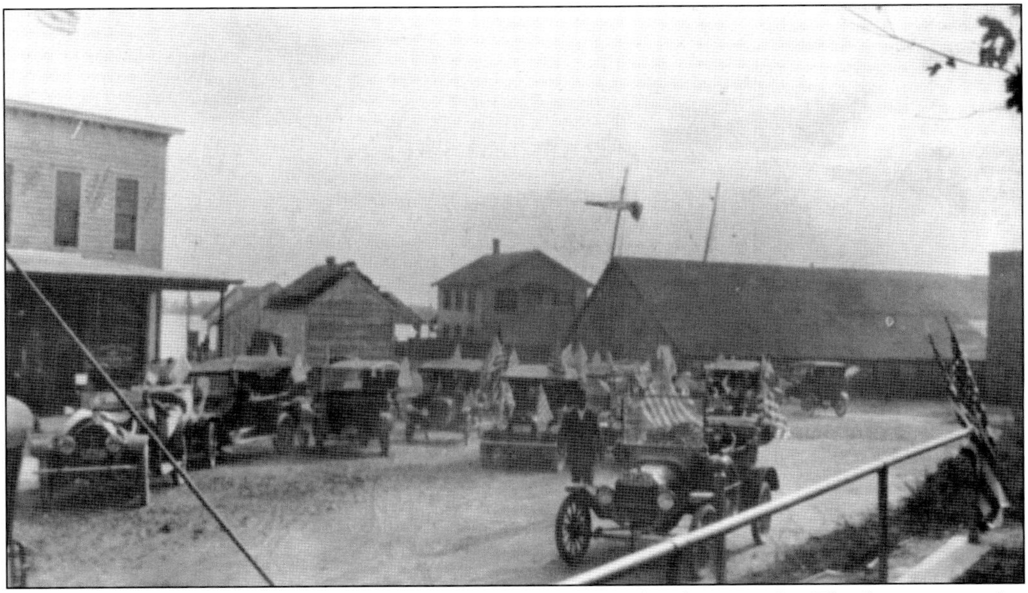

Reedville celebrated Armistice Day after World War I with a big parade. The location at the waterfront marks the end of Main Street. The Edwards and Reed Company factory is visible in the background. It burned to the ground in 1925. The Crazy Crab Restaurant is now located on the former site of the factory.

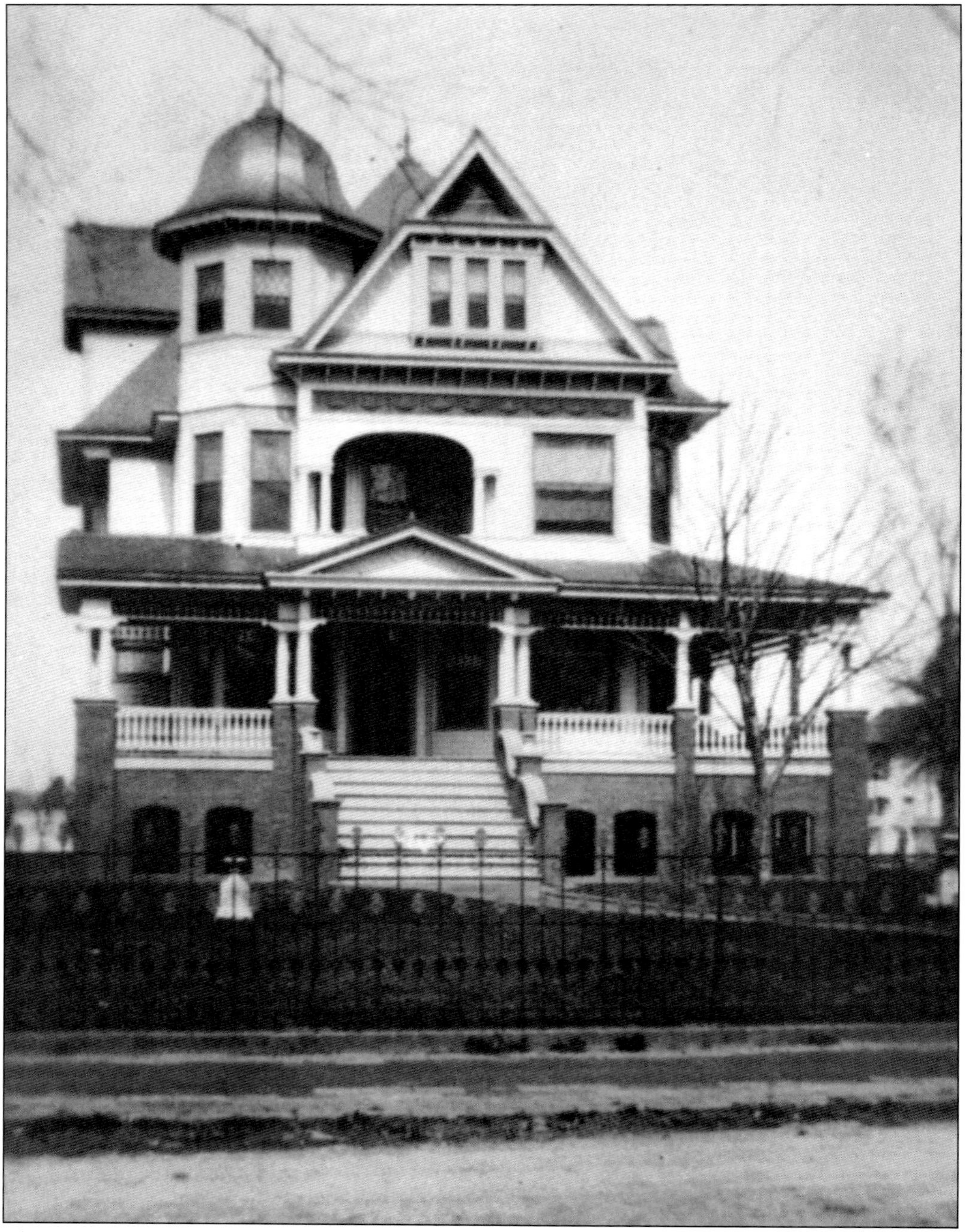

This stately home was built and owned by Albert Morris, co-owner of the Morris-Fisher fish factory. This was the largest fish-processing plant in Reedville, and its mighty stack still stands on the Great Wicomico River about half a mile north of Reedville. The stack, the last one remaining, was the focus of a community-wide restoration push during the last few years. The restoration was completed in 2012.

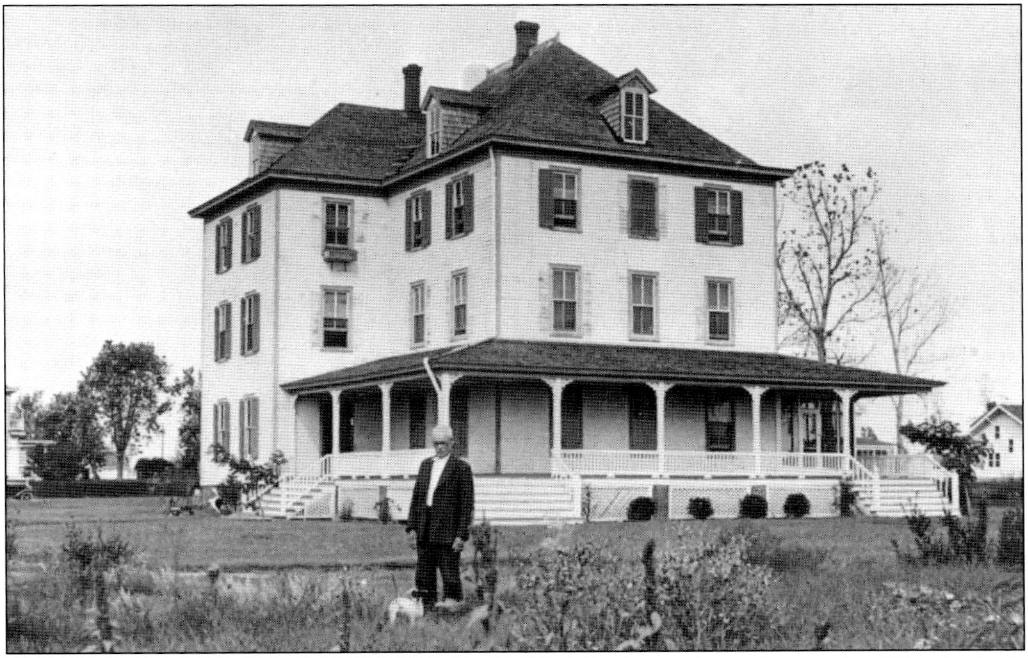

This hotel was in Fleeton, a small unincorporated settlement a few miles north of Reedville. It was established in 1903 and soon had many fancy homes built by sea captains and factory owners. Fleeton was quite exclusive, and many of the old Victorian homes still remain there. A special treat is the beautiful and still-active St. Mary's Church.

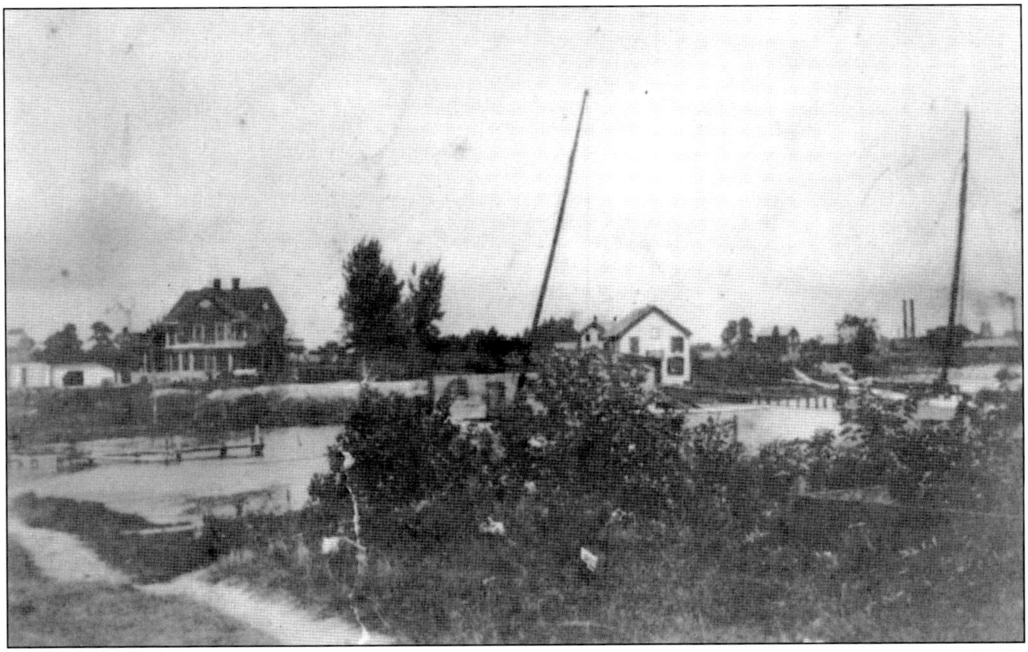

To the left is the home of Robert and Mittie Haynie in Fairport, a small town south of Reedville established a couple of decades earlier. The Haynies also ran a general mercantile store out of the white building in the center. In the background to the right, the stacks of the McNeal-Dodson fish factory are visible.

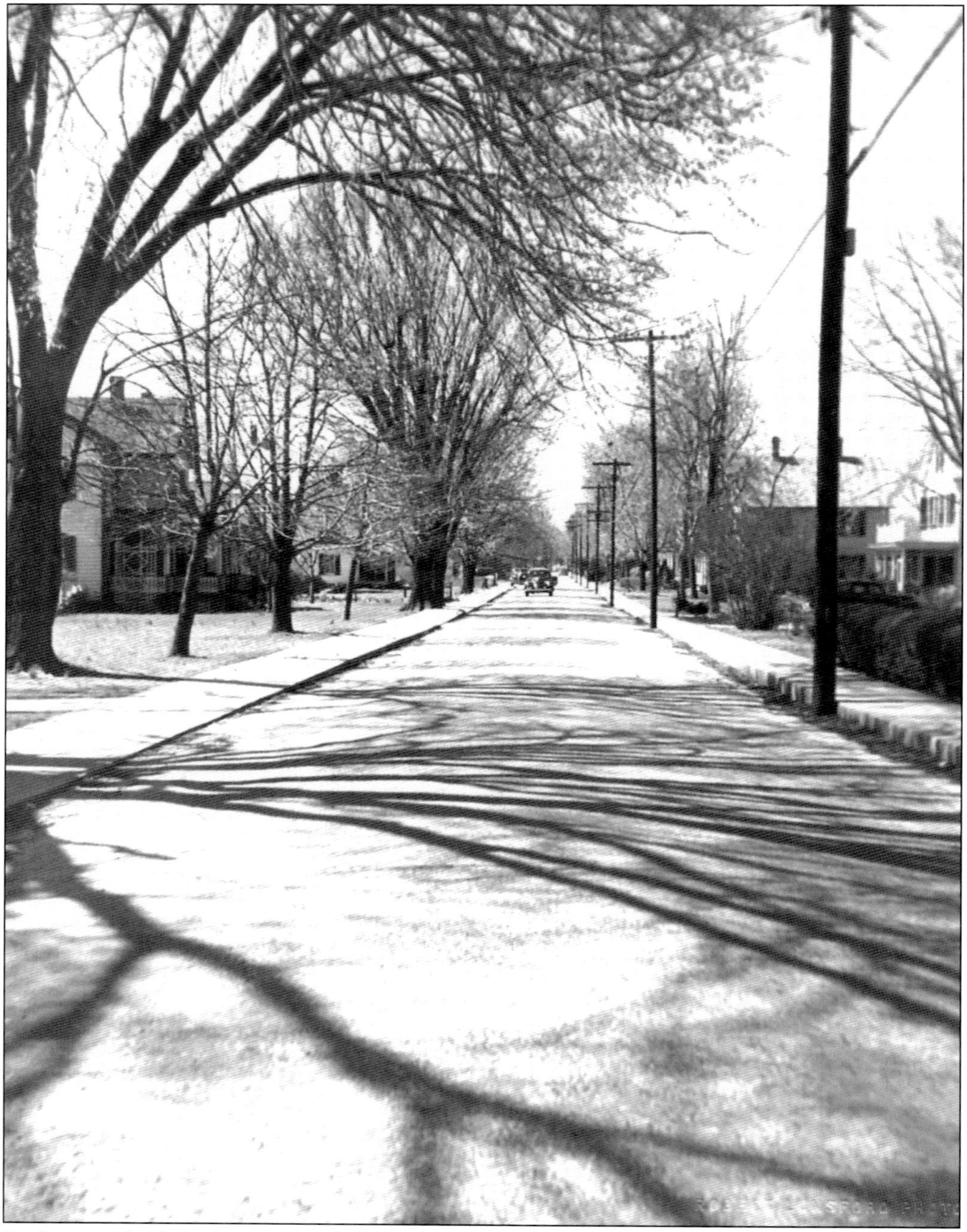

In this view looking down toward the docks, a beautiful sunny day in Reedville highlights Main Street. This photograph, taken in the 1920s, shows the road has now been paved. Since huge oyster-shell piles were prevalent in the area, many roads during that time utilized crushed shells for paving.

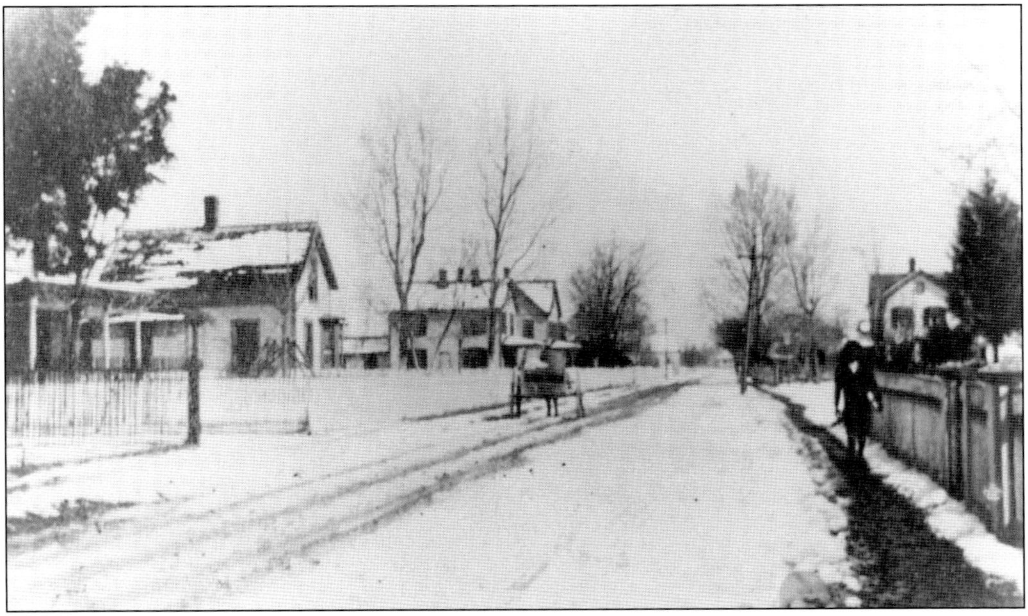

This is a serene winter view of Main Street in the 1890s. Everything slowed down during winter in town. Fishing pretty much stopped until the spring, and the factories shut down. There still was a lot of work to do. Boats were pulled onto local railways for repair, scraping, and painting, and watermen prepared nets, crab pots, and other equipment.

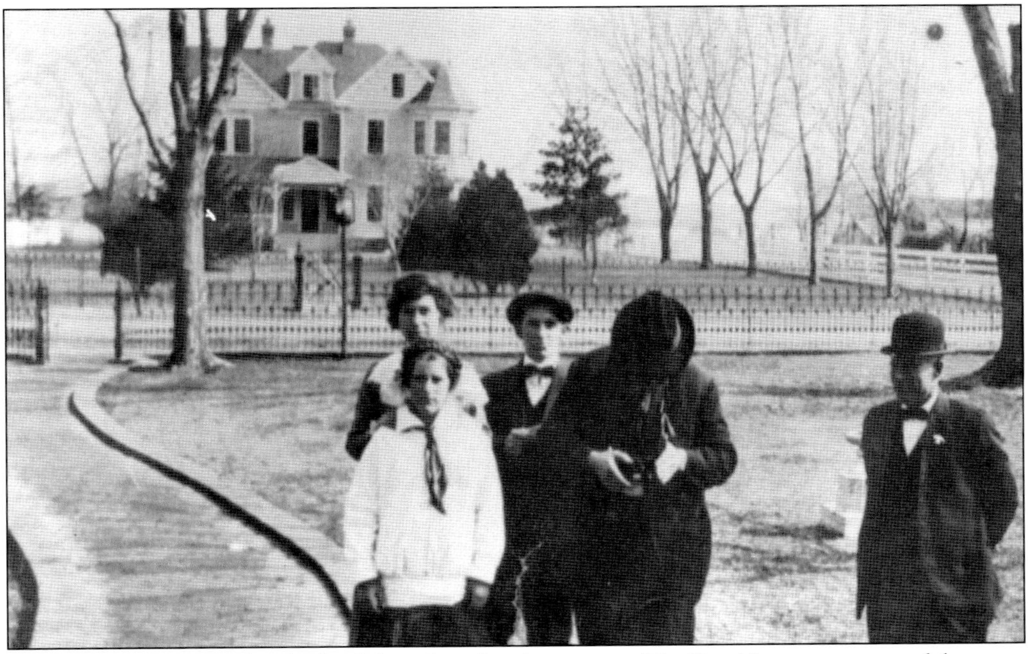

The Reed house provides the backdrop for a family portrait. The Reed house was one of the most modern and expensive homes built during the early days of Reedville. It remains one of the main attractions for visitors to the area. Pictured here are Hazel and Helda Haynie to the left and Capt. Thomas Haynie, their father, to the far right. The two men in the center are unidentified.

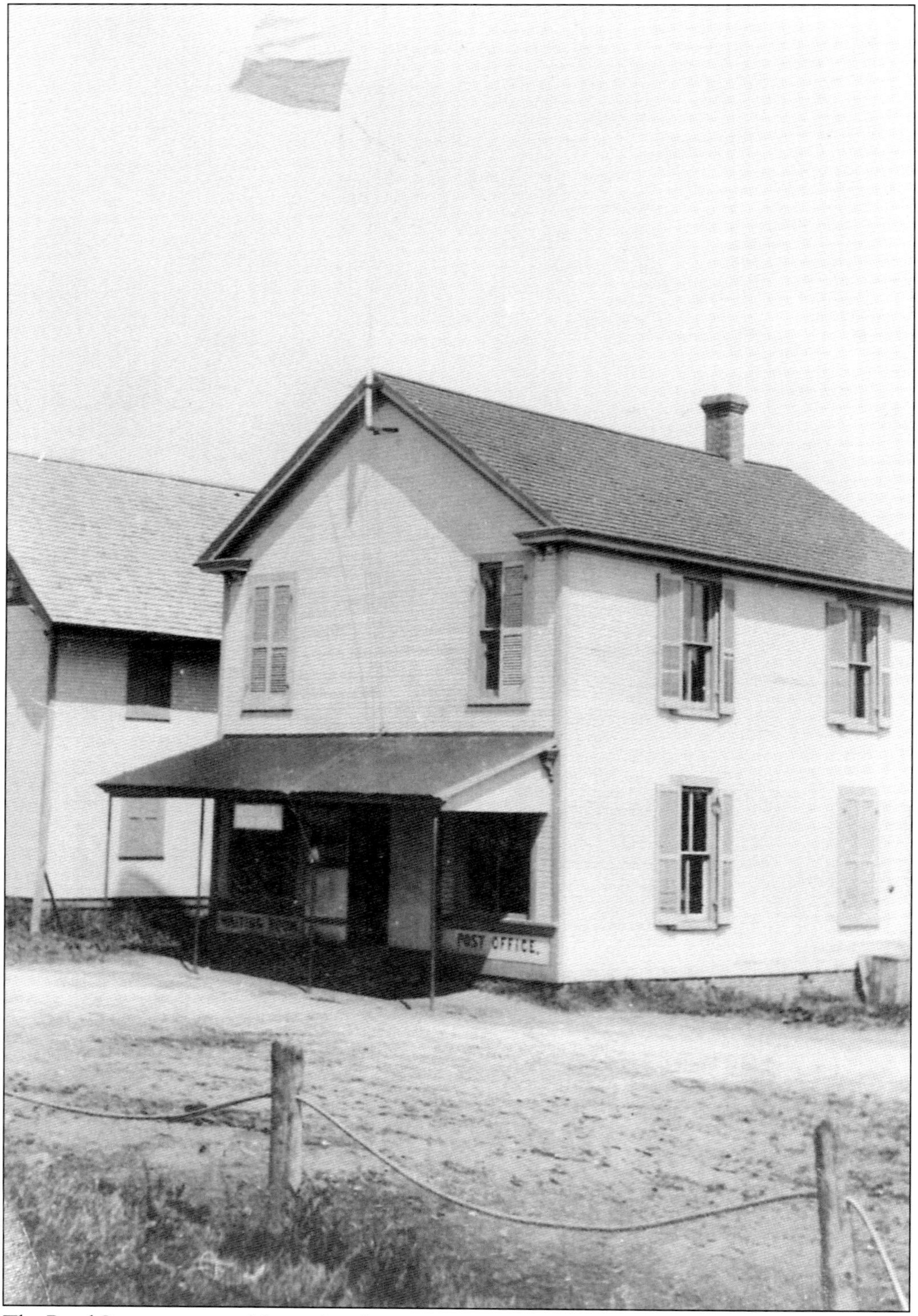

The Reed Store was one of the earliest businesses to start up in Reedville. It was run by relatives of the town founder, Elijah Reed, and conveniently located right next to the fish docks, near where the Crazy Crab is located today. The building has been gone for many years now.

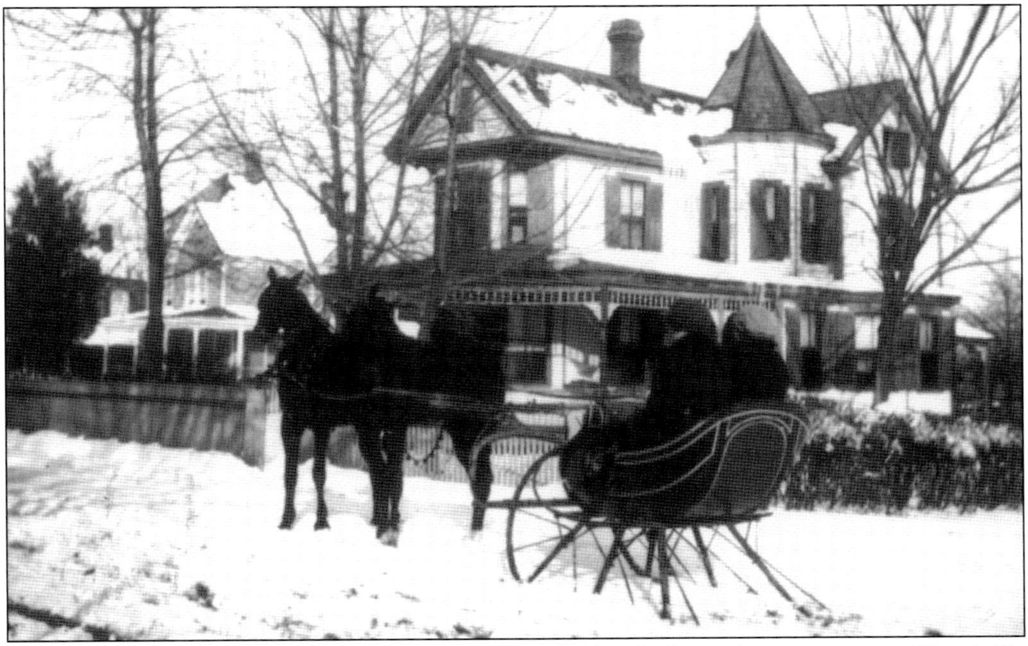

Elizabeth Reed, daughter of George Reed, enjoys a sleigh ride down the main street of Reedville around 1900. The old Bailey home is in the background. Later, the lot was used to build a Sears, Roebuck & Co. catalog home, which still stands today. That home was recently restored and is one of few remaining Sears homes in the area.

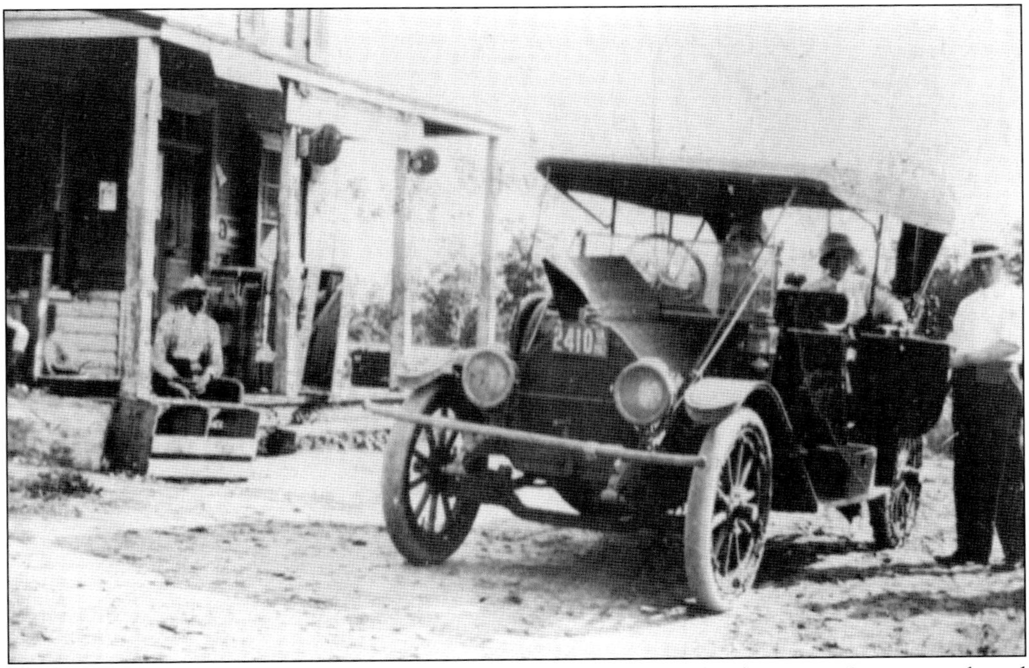

George Reed's 1912 Hudson was the first automobile in Northumberland County. George purchased the car in Richmond, and it was a two-day trip back to Reedville. He stands on the right, and in the car is Agnes Rebecca Reed Randolph, holding her son, Ward Reed Randolph, great-grandson of Elijah Reed.

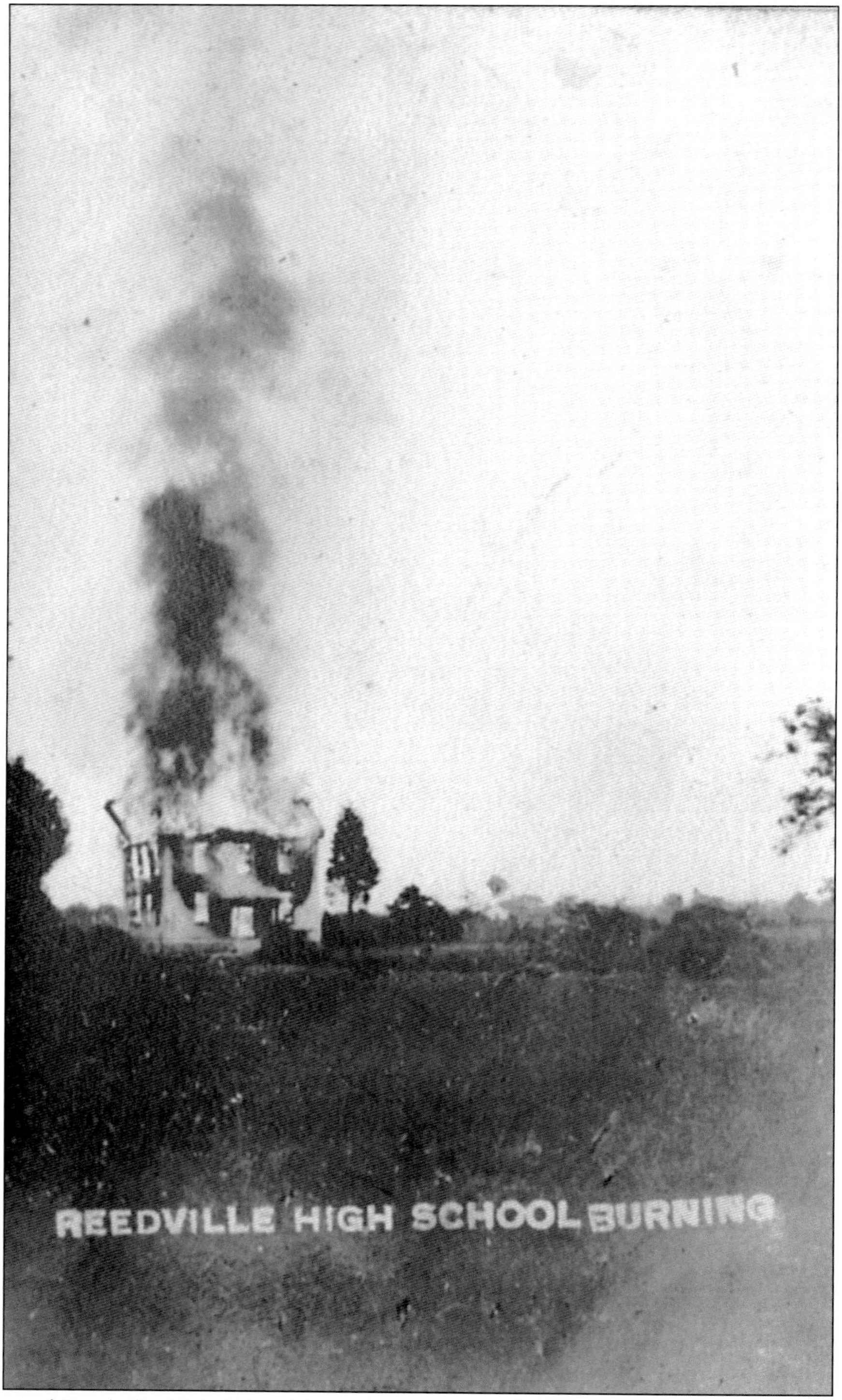

The original Reedville High School burned to the ground in June 1910. The wood structure was completely engulfed and could not be saved. It was rebuilt soon after, but with the increasing population, it was relegated to being the middle school when a new brick high school was erected in 1912.

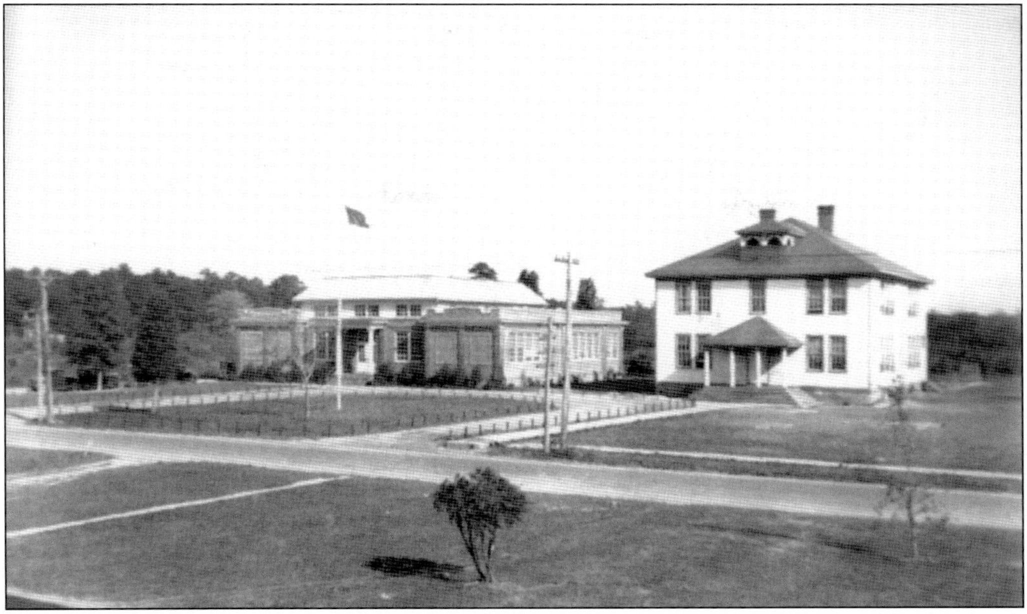

Pictured here around 1912 are the new Reedville High School (left) and original high school, which became the middle school. The middle school building was eventually torn down, and the high school has been converted into an events venue for the Reedville Fishermen's Museum.

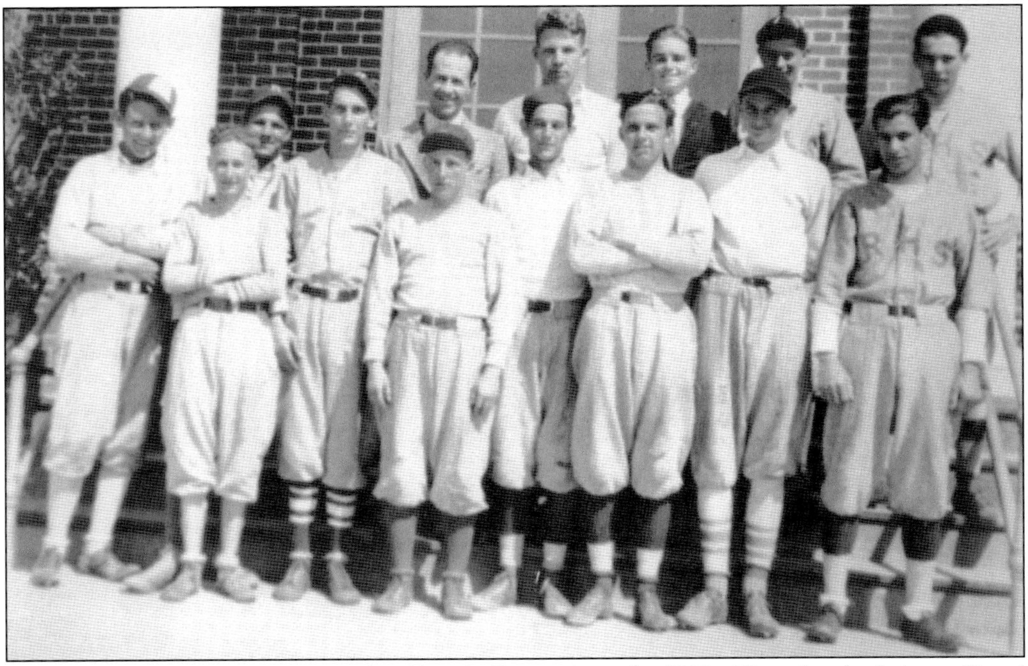

Seen here is the Reedville High School baseball team from the 1930s. The school, while small and quite poor, received great support for the baseball team from the community. It was the only major sport at the school, and the team surprised everyone when it won a statewide championship.

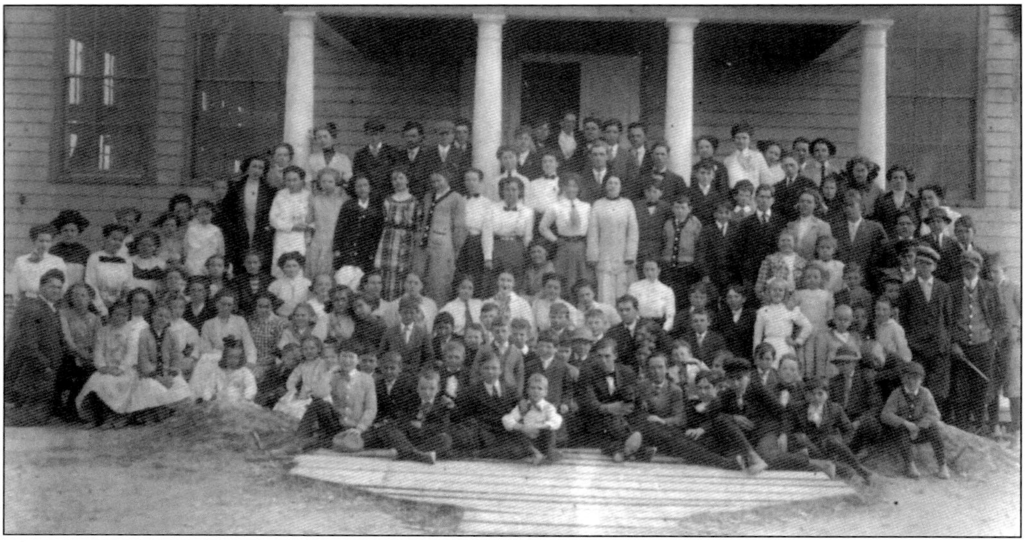

The 1907–1908 student body and staff pose on the front steps of the original Reedville High School. Note the wood plank sidewalk. This school burned in 1910 and was replaced with a two-story wood building. Overcrowding led to the construction of a new brick schoolhouse to house just the high school students.

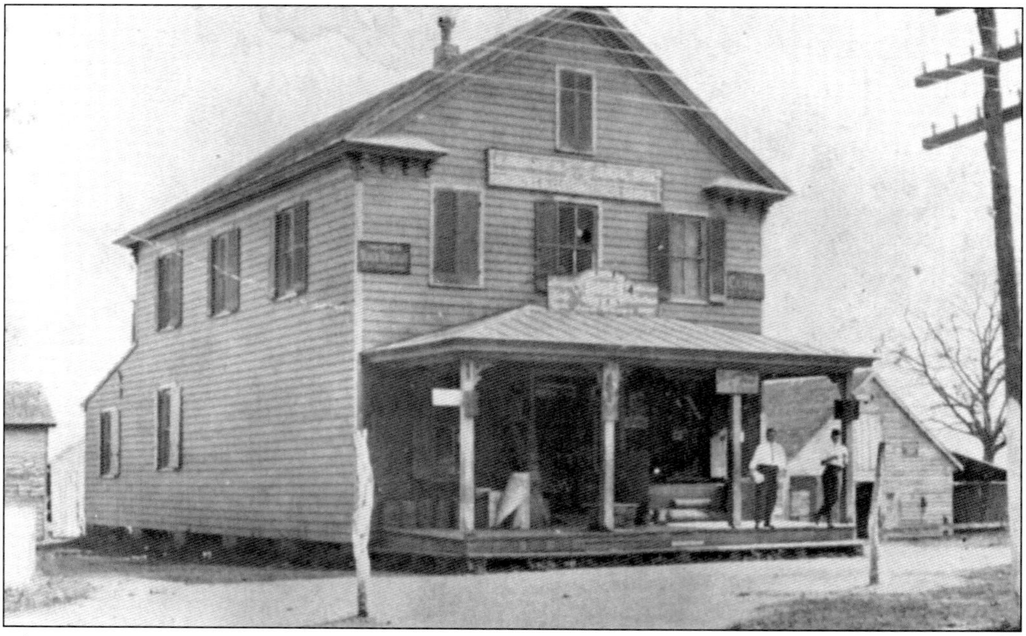

This is a view of the Blundon and Hinton's general merchandise store during the 1920s. One of the larger stores in Reedville, it tended to be the local meeting place for many years. Long after it closed, it was refurbished and converted into Tommy's Restaurant, which is still open.

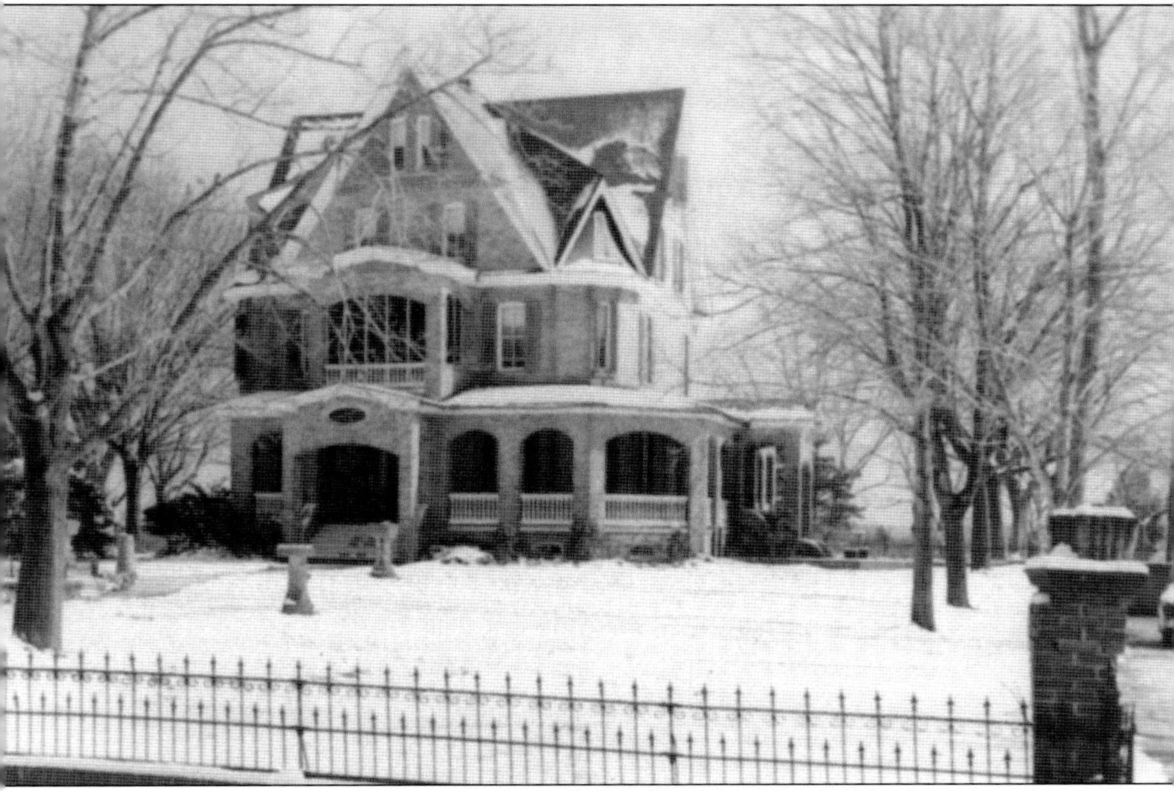

The Gables is one of many late-1800s Victorian homes located on Reedville's Main Street. This home was built by James Fisher and is one of the iconic landmarks in town. The house has been carefully restored and is now used as a stately bed-and-breakfast.

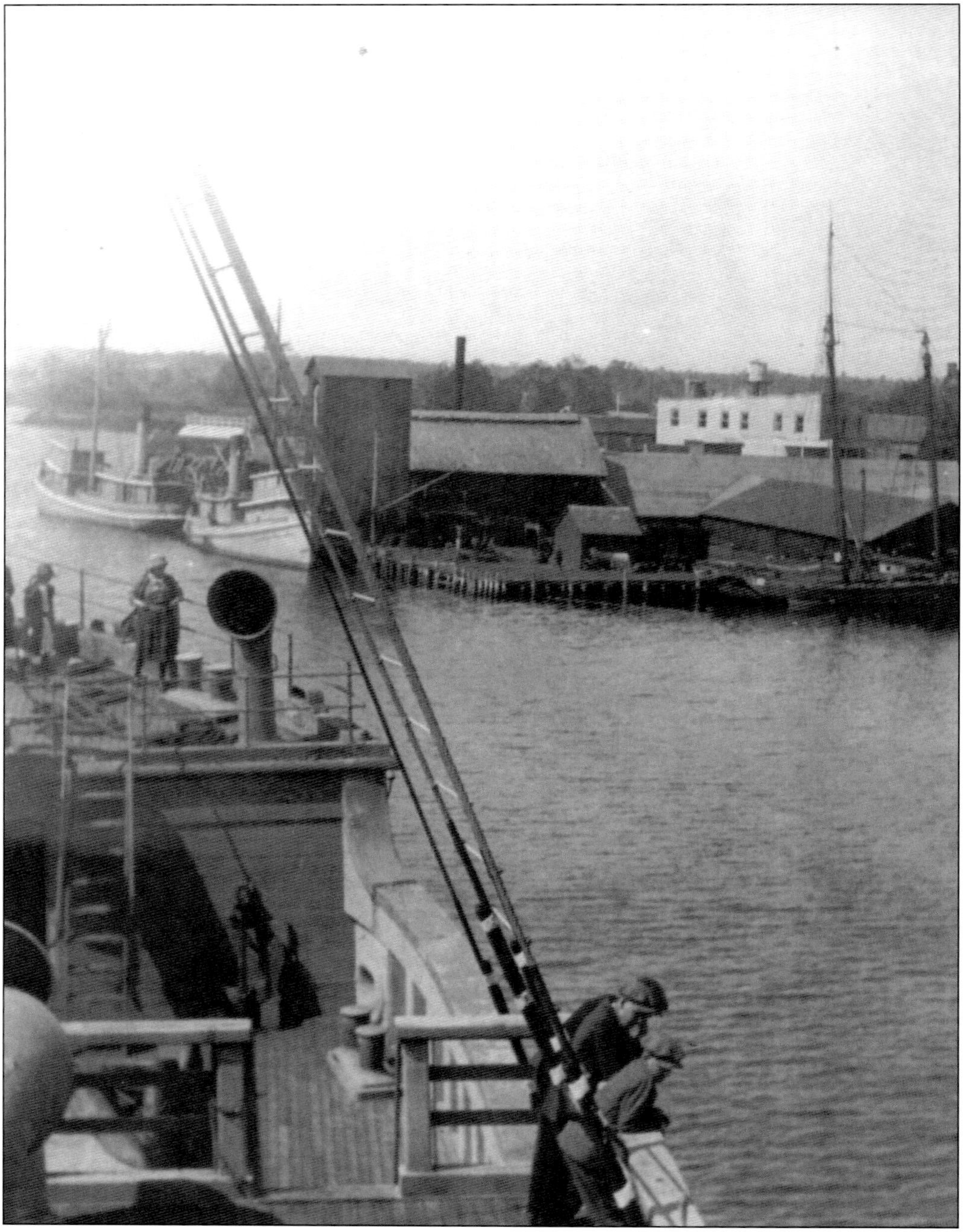

A passenger steamboat passes the Taylor and Reed fish factory on its way to docking at Reedville. The two fishing boats are the *E. Warren Reed* and *Hannah Lennen*. For many years, fish factories and canneries occupied both shores of the Great Wicomico River on the Reedville and Fairport sides. Now not much more than foundations and rusted boilers mark those sites.

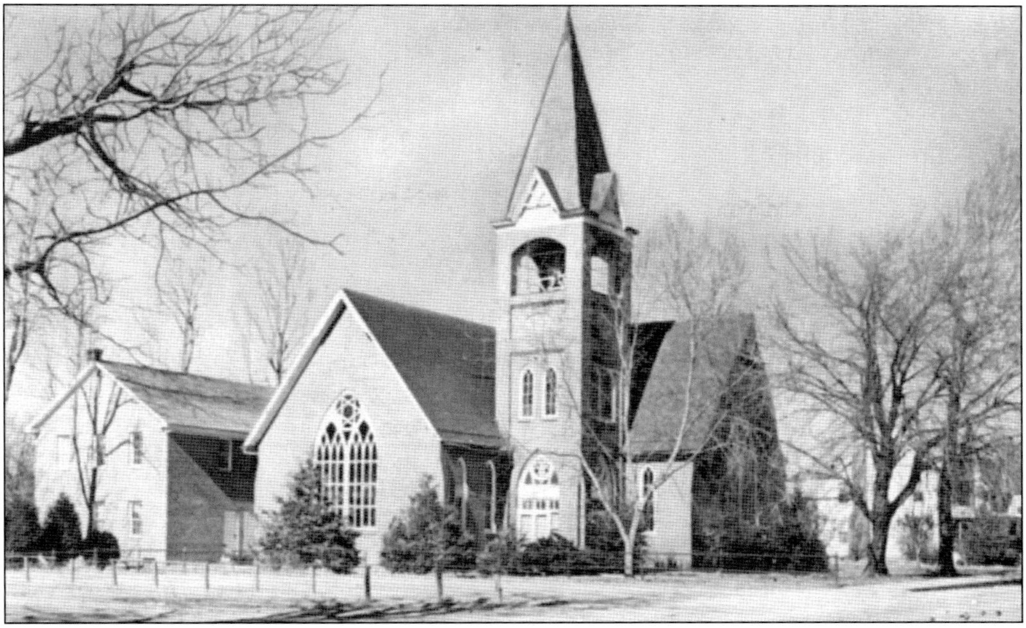

By the 1930s, the Bethany United Methodist Church had expanded by adding a fellowship hall. Later, the old town hall, adjacent to the left, was removed. Recently, that area was made into a large parking lot, which is now shared by the church and the Reedville Fishermen's Museum.

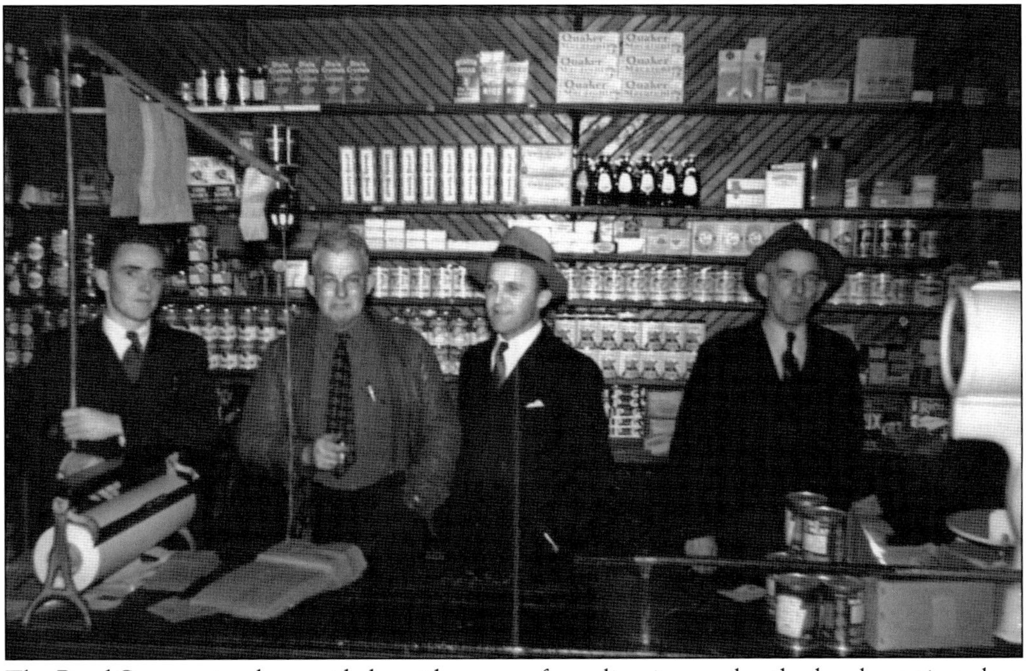

The Reed Store not only provided a wide range of supplies, it was also the local meeting place for residents. Pictured here in 1922, four men start the day catching up on the local happenings; from left to right are Robert Joseph Bowen, Howard Tankard Rice, James Olin Rice, and Carlyle Omohundro.

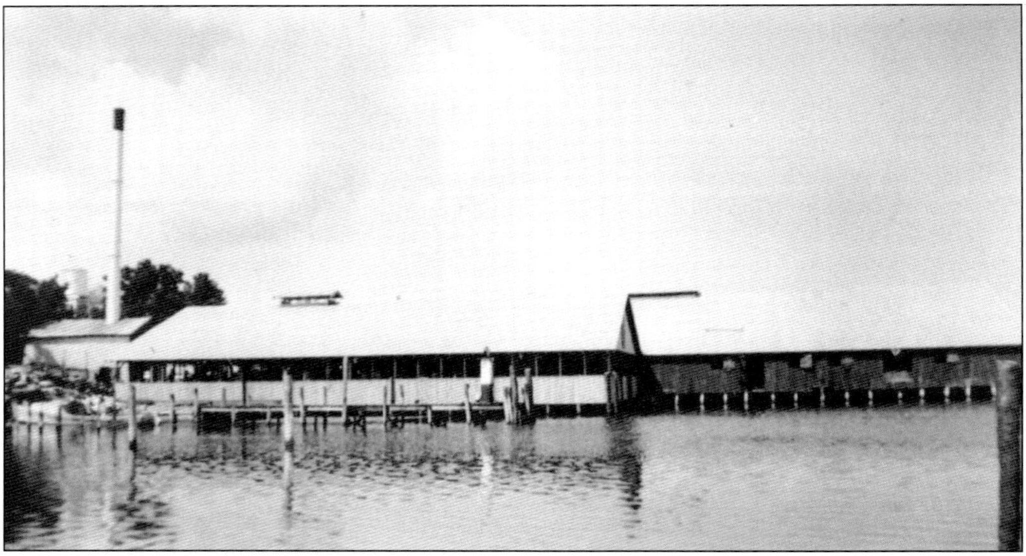

Fish factories were not the only large enterprises in and around Reedville. Because it was a main shipping port, Reedville also became prominent as a canning center. Local farms provided a large supply of tomatoes. Pictured here is the Blundon and Hinton tomato cannery on Cockrell's Creek. The buildings are stationed over the water, and any tomato waste went right into the creek, making the water completely red for long periods.

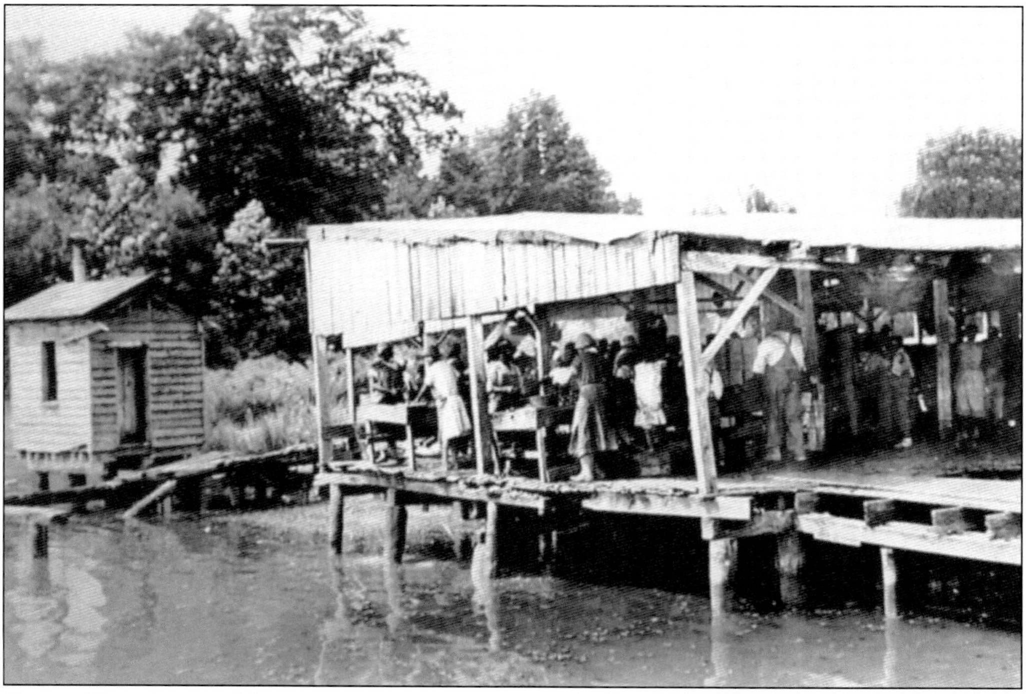

Pictured here is one of the many tomato canneries in the Reedville area during the 1930s. This is the tomato-peeling section. The peeled skins went right off the dock and into the water. Back in those days, everything went into the water, and during the summer, the waters around Reedville were most unpleasant. However, rehabilitation efforts have cleaned up the area.

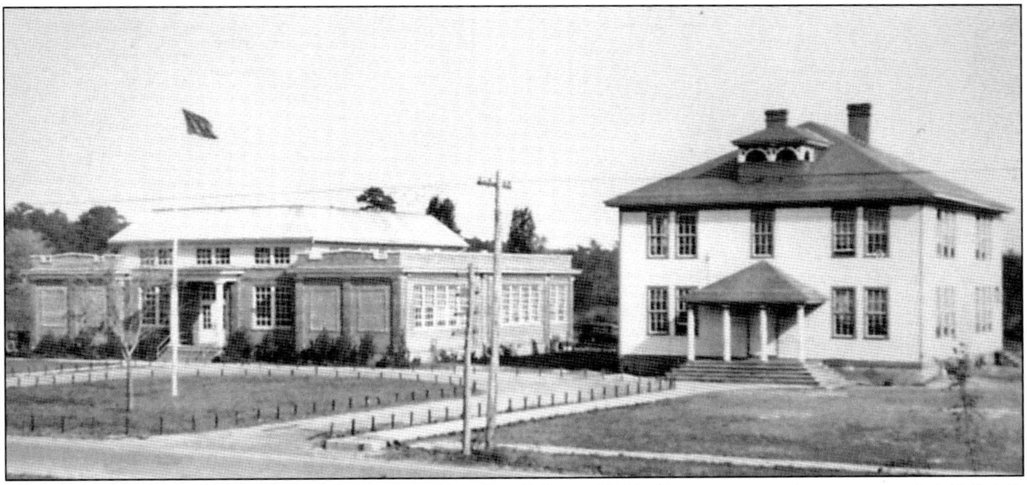

On the right is the rebuilt Reedville High School from 1911. Due to crowding, a new brick high school was erected adjacent to the original and completed in 1912. The wood school building was then designated as the middle school. While the middle school was dismantled in the 1960s, the Reedville High School still stands and has been restored. It is now part of the Reedville Fishermen's Museum and is used for all kind of events.

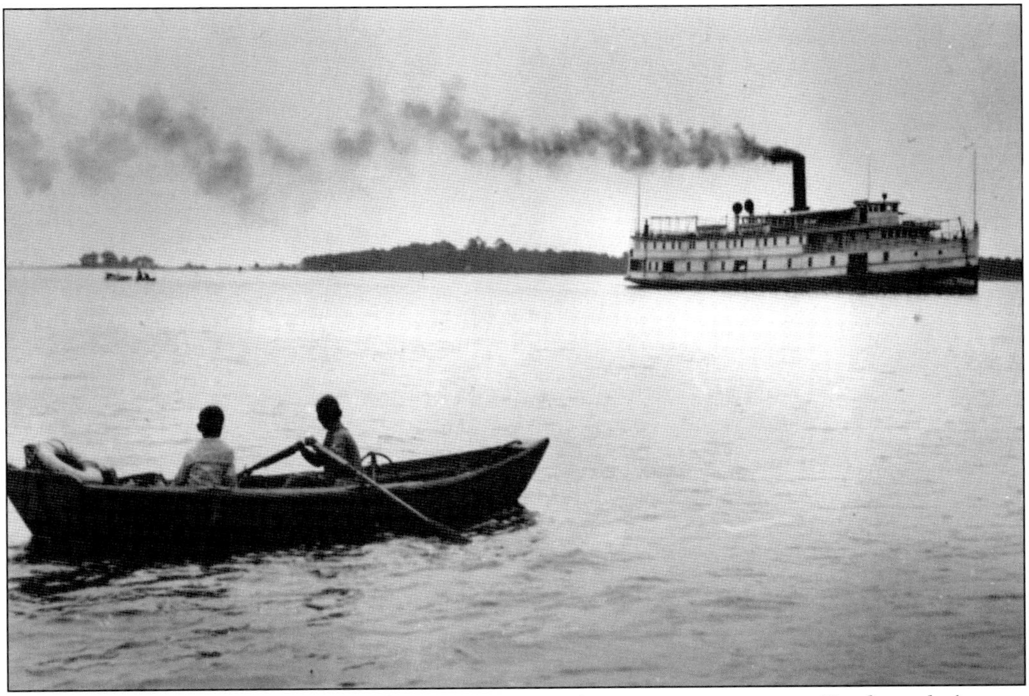

Two young boys out fishing get a front-row seat as the passenger steamer *Piankatank* departs Deltaville, passing Gwynn's Island, while on its way to Reedville. During the peak of activity during the early 1900s, there were many steamship lines connecting many small towns along the Chesapeake Bay coast. When automobiles became prevalent, the steamships slowly disappeared from the bay.

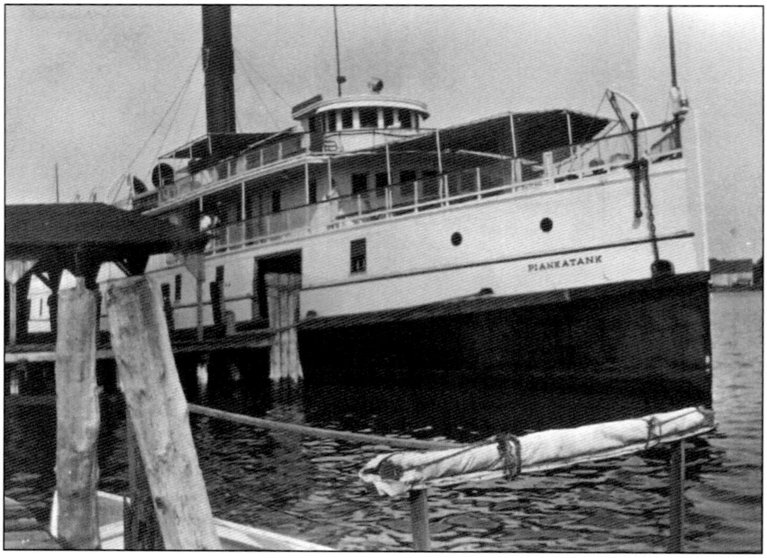

The passenger steamer *Piankatank* is pictured here docked at the Reedville wharf in 1930. A special wharf and station were built specifically to provide service to the steamships. While labeled a passenger vessel, the steamships also hauled more cargo than people most of the time. It was a much quicker way to ship than over land.

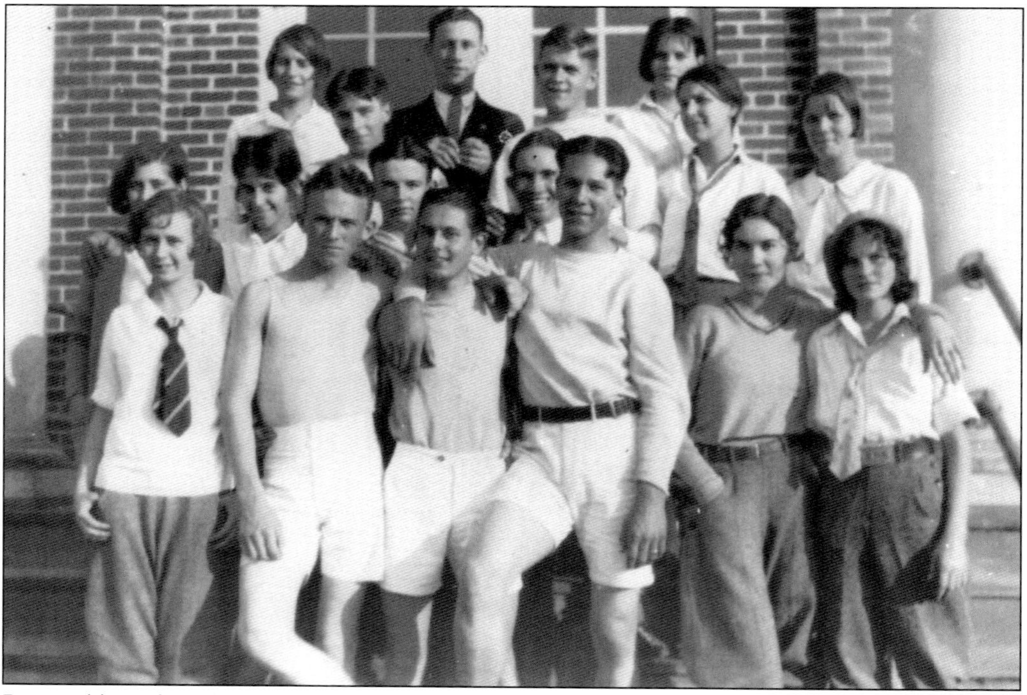

Pictured here from left to right are members of the 1928–1929 Reedville High School girls' and boys' basketball teams: (first row) Frances Booth, Walter Rice, John Robertson, Lawson Mcfarland, Flora Morrison, and Helen Sisson; (second row) Iris Williams, Thelma Williams, Walter Haynie, Franklin Powell, Evelyn Lewis, and Estelle Saunders; (third row) Lillian Lewis, Carl Haynie, Cedric Saunders, Robert Jett, and Louise Laird.

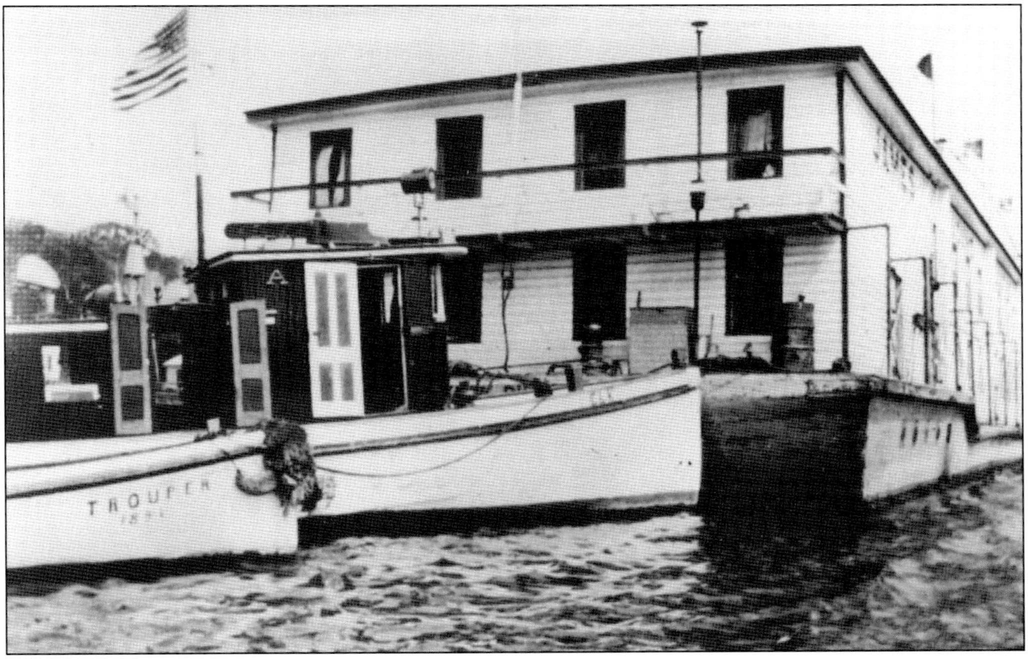

The *Elk* and *Trooper* were used for a very unique purpose in the Chesapeake Bay. These two small tugs were part of the Adams Floating Theatre Company and moved the theater and owner's quarters barges around the Chesapeake Bay. Reedville resident Teddy Haynie's father, Vernon, was one of the tug captains, and his mother, Mayo, one of the theatrical company members.

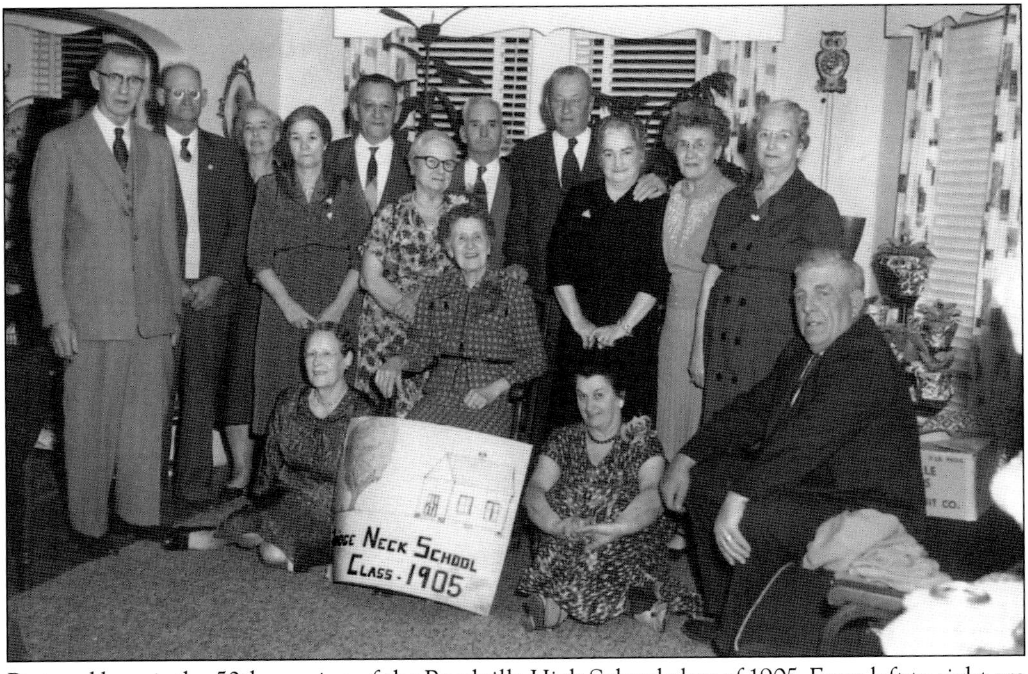

Pictured here is the 50th reunion of the Reedville High School class of 1905. From left to right are (first row, seated) unidentified, Edith Robertson, Fannie Haynie, and Russell Haynie; (second row) Tennyson Hammonds, Monroe Kenner, a Mrs. Kenner, Etta Gill, two unidentified individuals, Booth Gill, Farrell Dodson, a Mrs. Dodson, Hattie Lowry, and Julia Dish.

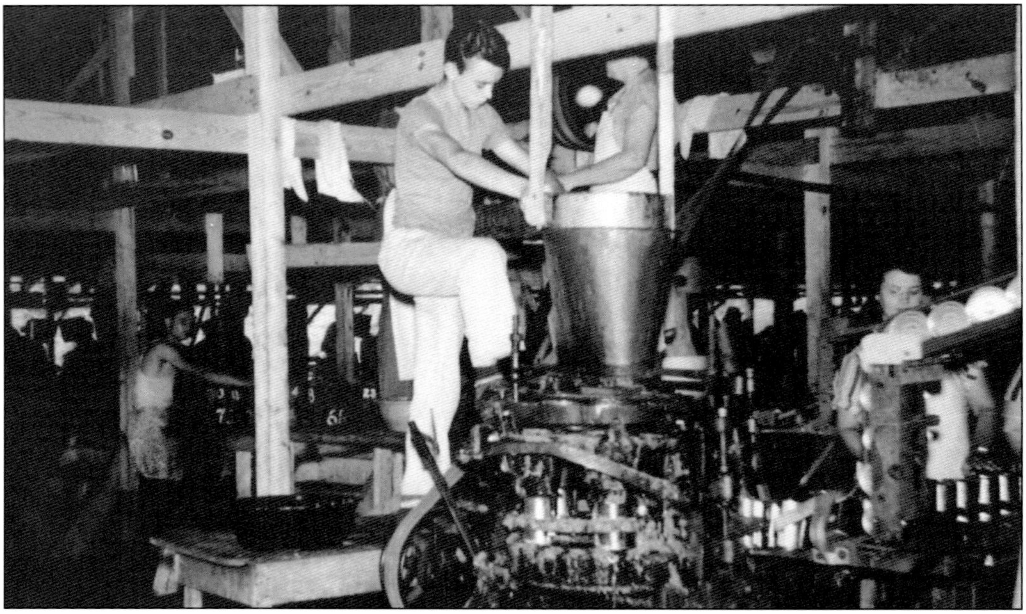

This is an interior view of one of Reedville's plentiful canneries during the 1930s. The young gentleman pictured is working on the canning machine. Many young people had their first jobs working in the canneries or fish factories. Conditions inside could be brutal, especially during the hot and muggy days of summer.

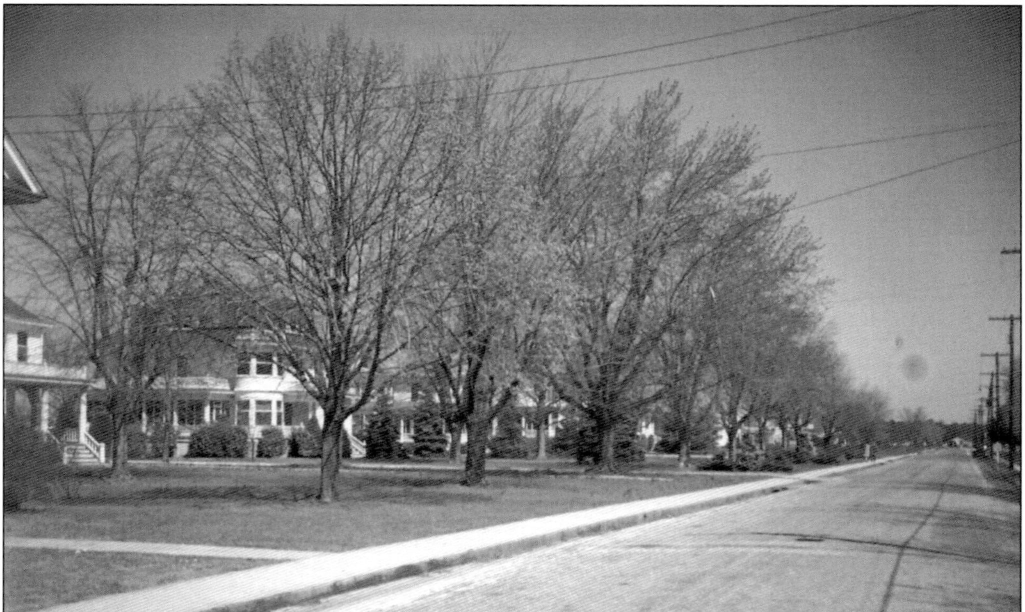

In this 1950s view looking north is Millionaires Row in Reedville. By this time, a number of factories had closed. While menhaden fishing was still the major industry, consolidations and modernization had shrunk the workforce. The glory of Millionaires Row had also faded as the owners sold their businesses and moved to other places.

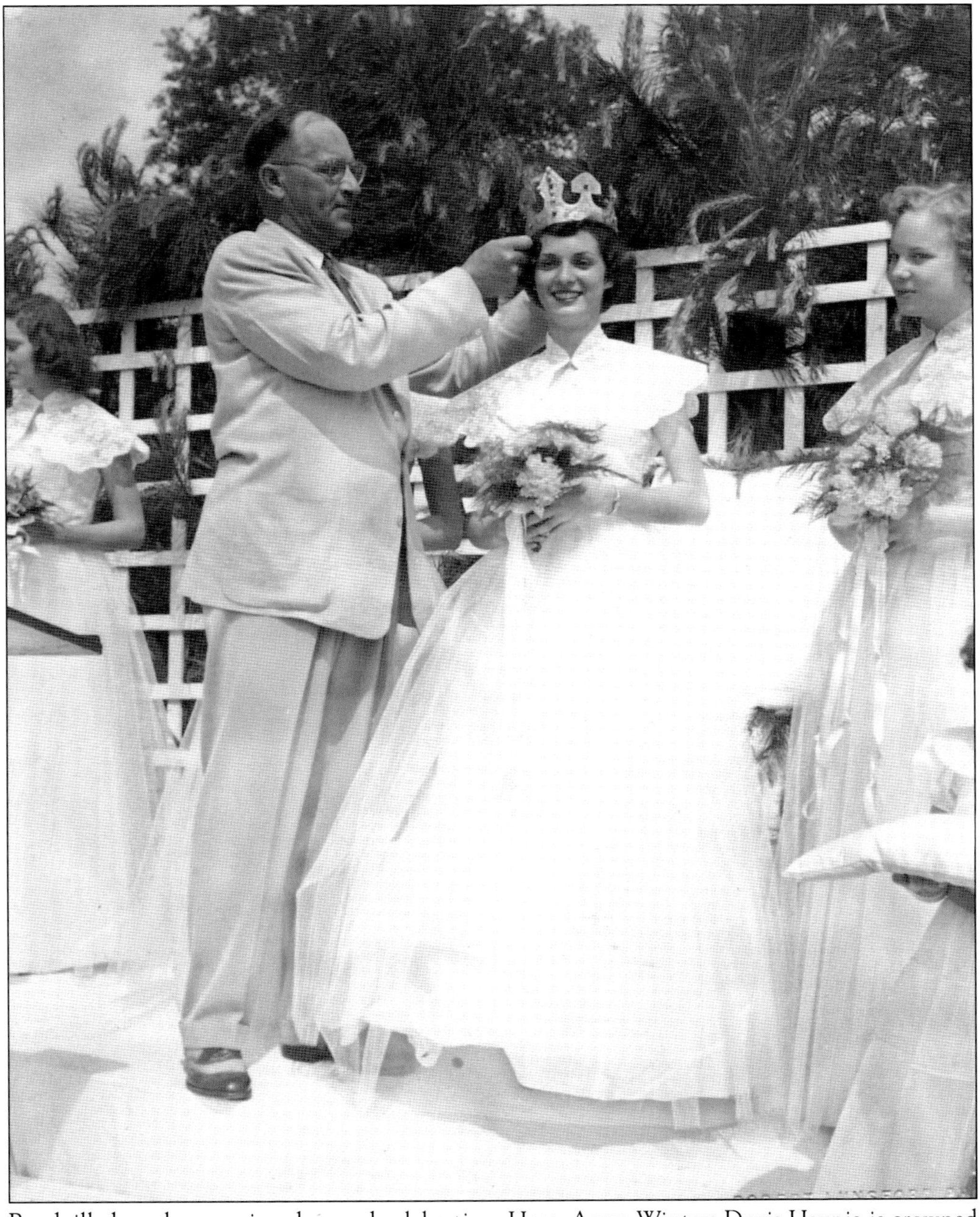

Reedville has always enjoyed a good celebration. Here, Anne Winters Davis Haynie is crowned the May Day queen for 1953. Lt. Gov. Guy Stephens crowns her while Faye Rice Pittman looks on. Anne's husband, Haynie Wendell, is one of the original founders of the Reedville Fishermen's Museum.

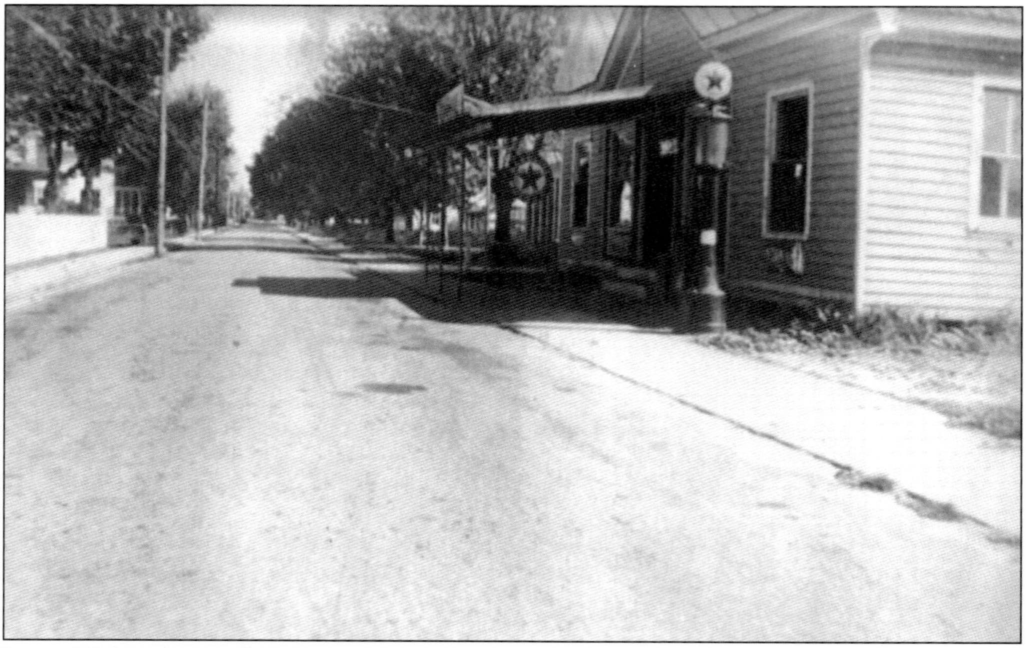

Lemuel Edward McGill ran his store and Texaco gas station for many years on the lower end of Reedville's Main Street. This photograph, taken around 1940, shows a wonderful example of the old-style gravity gas pump. The store closed many years ago, although the building still stands.

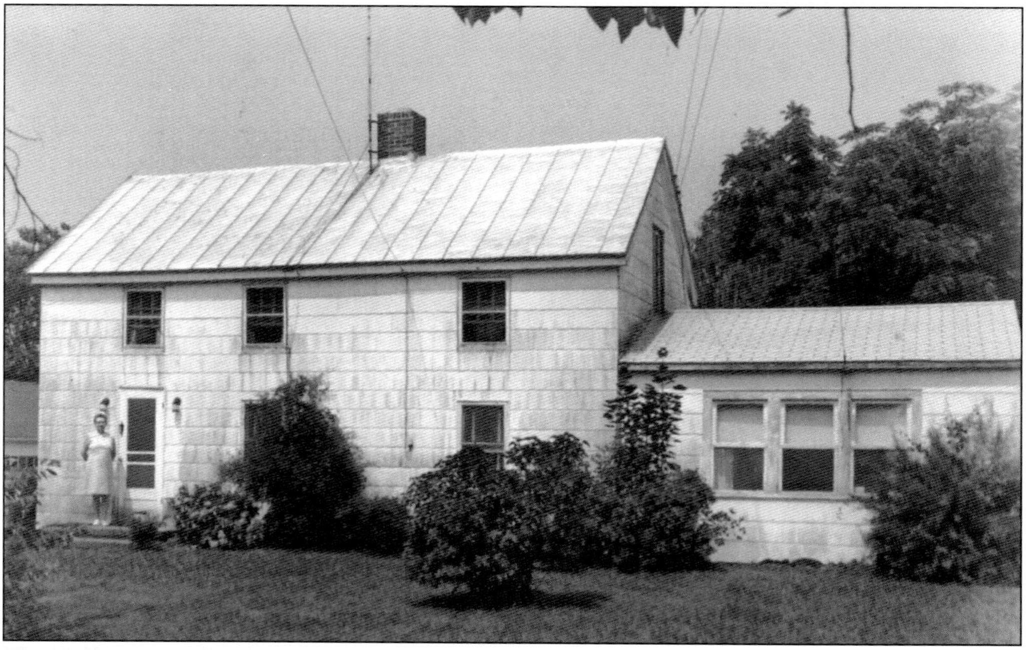

The William J. Walker house was built in 1875, making it the oldest remaining home in Reedville. The last resident, Marguerite Walker, is pictured by the front door. The Reedville Fishermen's Museum restored the home, and it became the original site of the museum. Now it is part of the museum tour. The interior is furnished in an 1800s style.

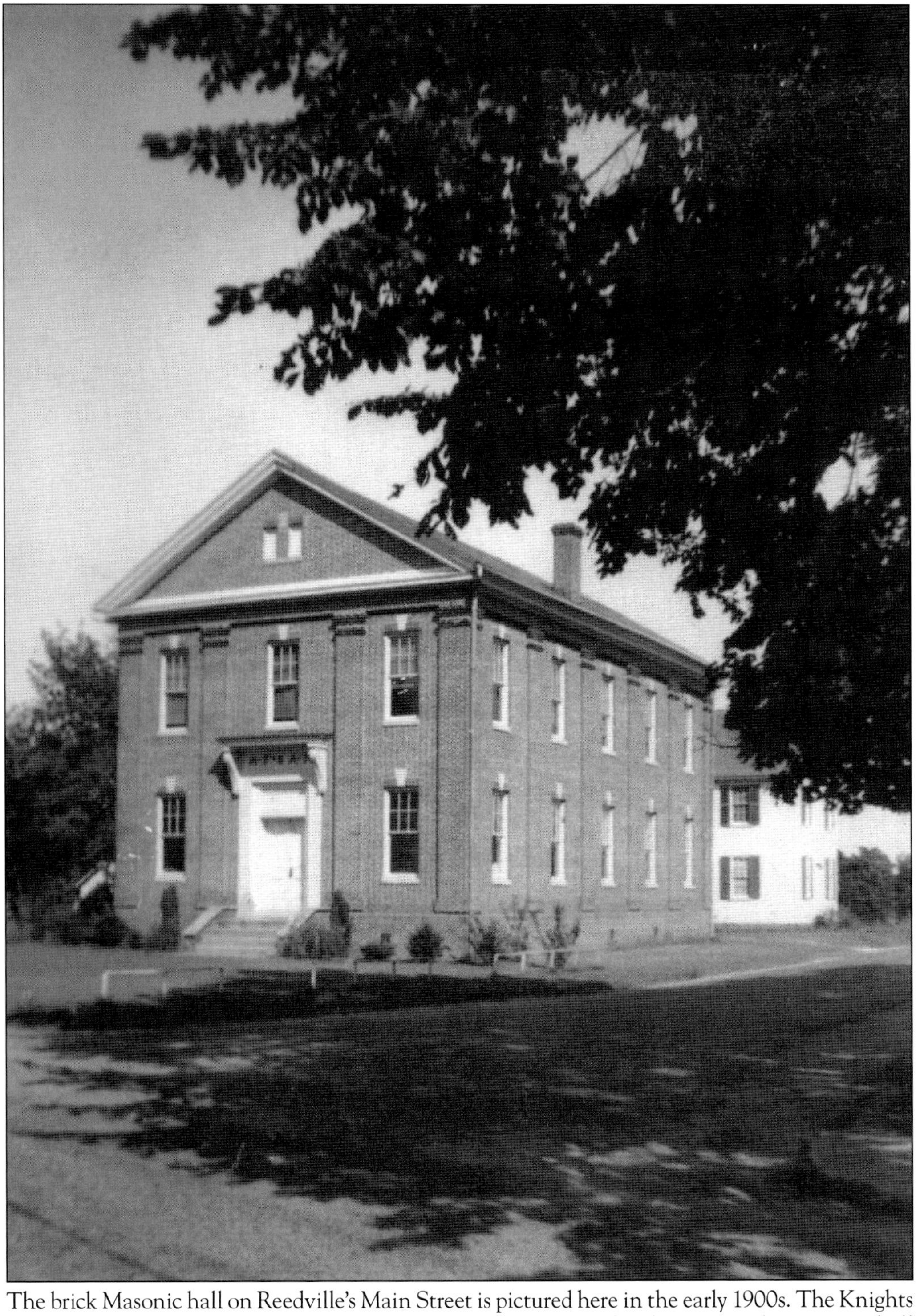

The brick Masonic hall on Reedville's Main Street is pictured here in the early 1900s. The Knights of Pythias's hall is located directly behind. While the Pythias hall is long gone, the Masonic hall remains and is still active, with a dedicated group of Masons keeping the hall well maintained.

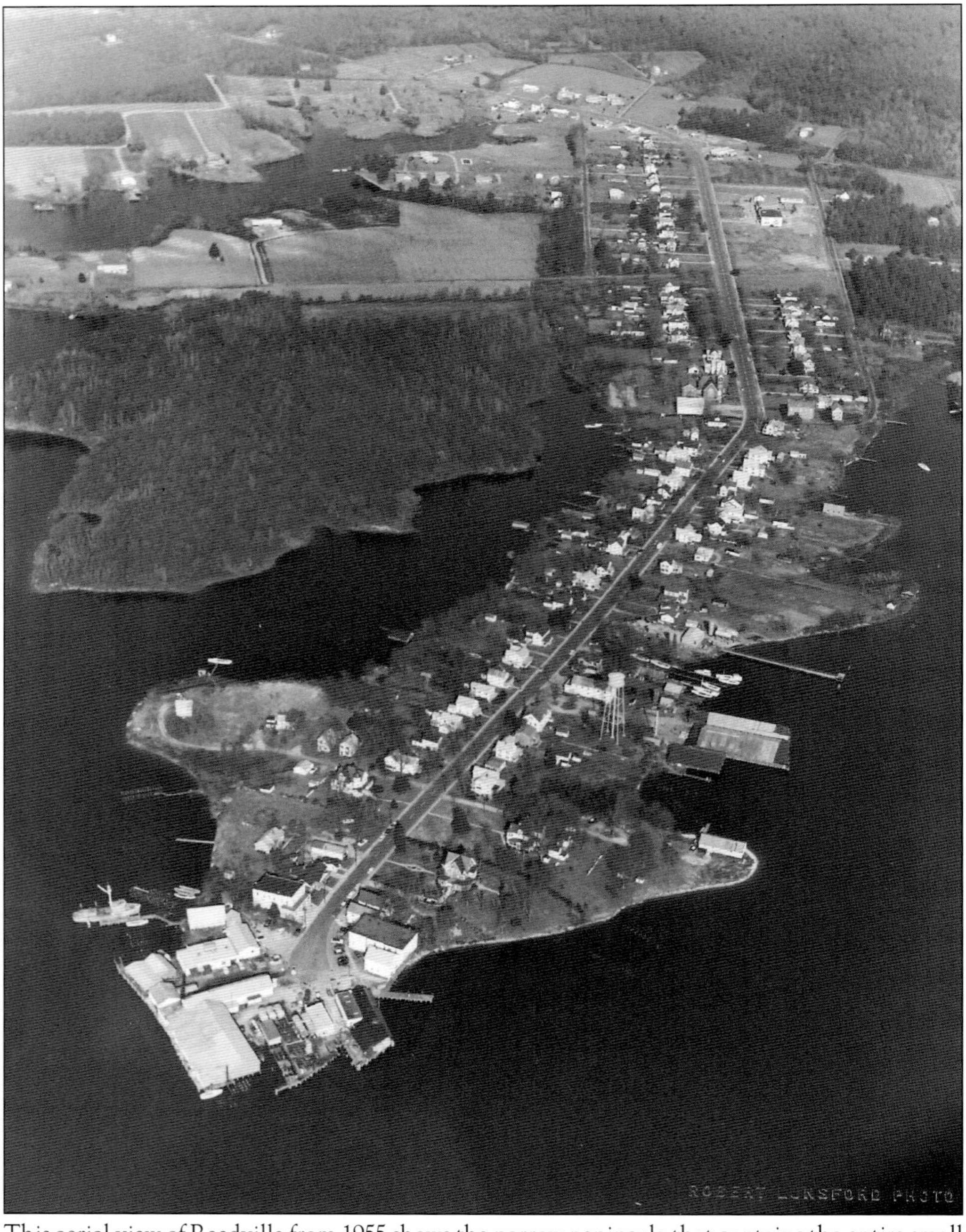

This aerial view of Reedville from 1955 shows the narrow peninsula that contains the entire small town. Only one street runs in and out. Because of all the large and stately homes built along the street, in its heyday, it was called Millionaires Row. Just beyond the bend in the road, on the left, are a long row of Victorian homes.

Six

Reedsville Fishermen's Museum

The museum is located on the banks of Cockrell's Creek on land once owned by Capt. Elijah Reed. The William Walker House was built in 1875 on land bought that year from Captain Reed. It was occupied by the family until it was purchased by the Greater Reedville Association in 1986. The association, primarily through the work of volunteers, restored the house and opened it as the Reedville Fishermen's Museum in 1988. In the spring of 1995, the home was refurbished and refurnished and now represents a waterman's home at the turn of the previous century.

A generous gift from Frank Covington enabled the museum to expand into a new structure, the Covington Building, in 1995. This facility houses both a permanent collection and changing exhibits. The Pendleton Building, which houses a boat-building shop and model shop, was added during the museum's expansion program in 2003.

In 2005, two of the museum's vessels, the skipjack *Claud W. Somers* and the deck boat *Elva C.*, were entered into the National Register of Historic Places. This action speaks to the vital role that Reedville's local heritage plays in this nation's history. Today, the museum continues to attract locals and other visitors from many states and countries to Reedville. The museum hosts a wide variety of events throughout the year and continues to preserve the heritage and history of the watermen of Reedville and the Chesapeake Bay.

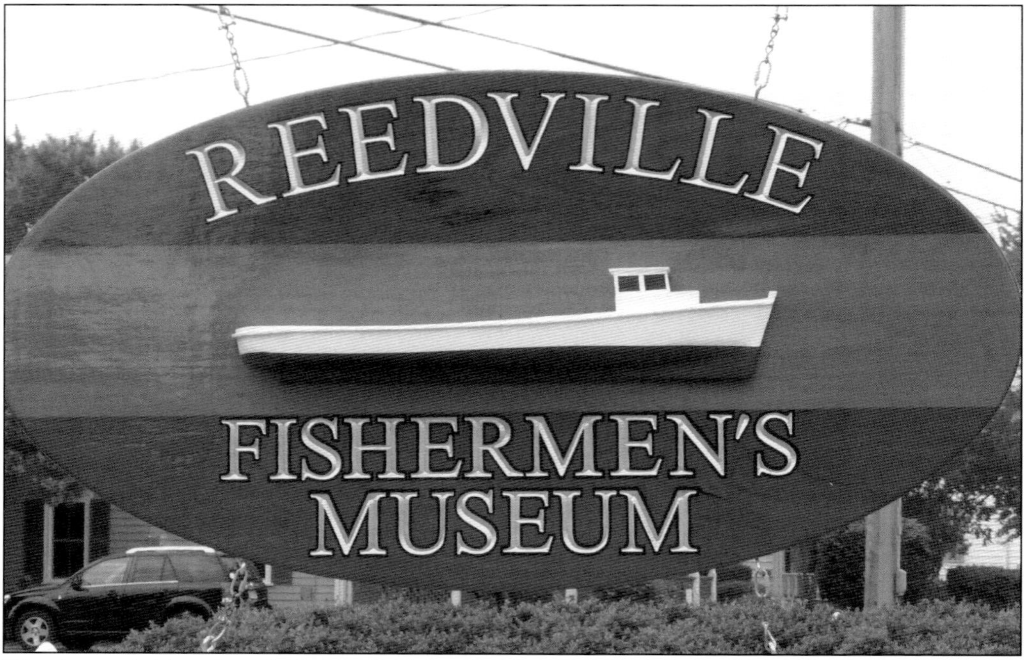

This beautiful hand-crafted sign, built by the Reedville Fishermen's Museum's dedicated boat shop volunteers, guides visitors to a hidden gem at the end of Highway 360 in Reedville, Virginia. The sign depicts one of more important styles of boats for watermen in the area: the deadrise flat-bottom boat.

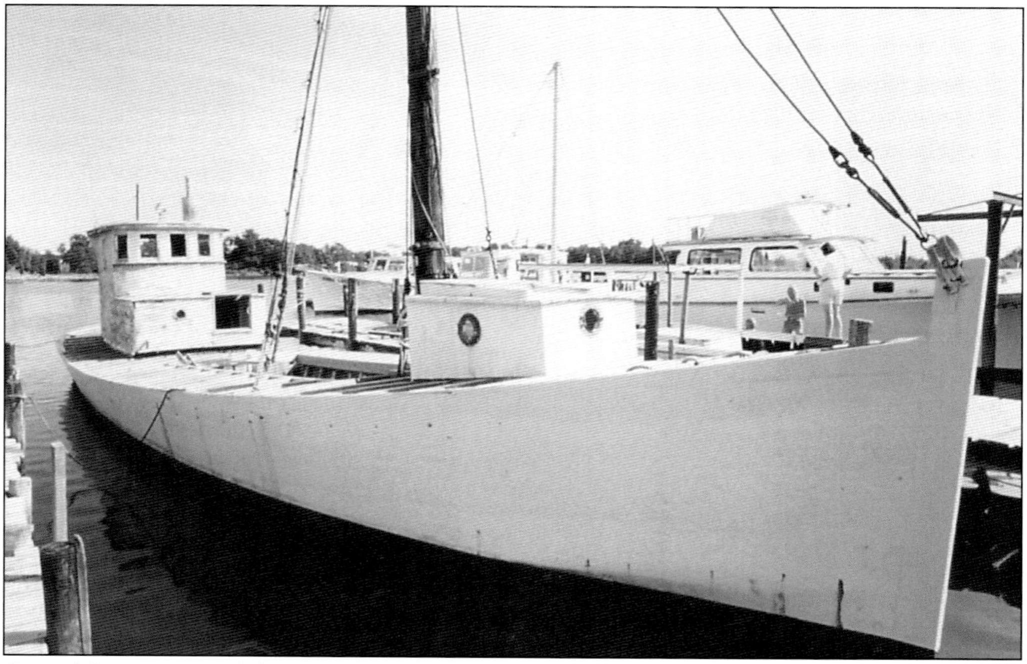

One of the missions of the museum is to preserve the legacy of the area's watermen, and one way that is achieved is the restoration of historical boats. This is what the *Elva C.* looked like when it was donated to the museum. Hard to believe at this point that the *Elva C.* would eventually be in the National Register of Historic Places.

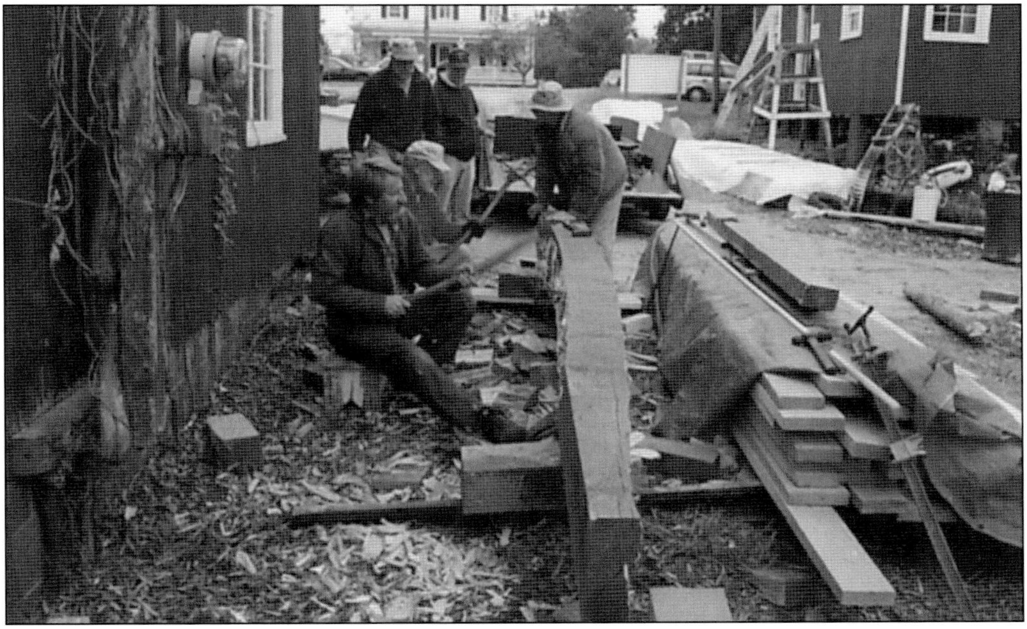

Most of the beams in the *Elva C.* had to be replaced and required a lot of hours of hewing by hand to get them to the proper size. The work was done at the Reedville Marine Railway, a long-standing business in town. Builders at the railway have constructed numerous boats of all styles over the past 80 years. Here, volunteers work on the beams. George Butler, current owner of the railway, shows them the proper method.

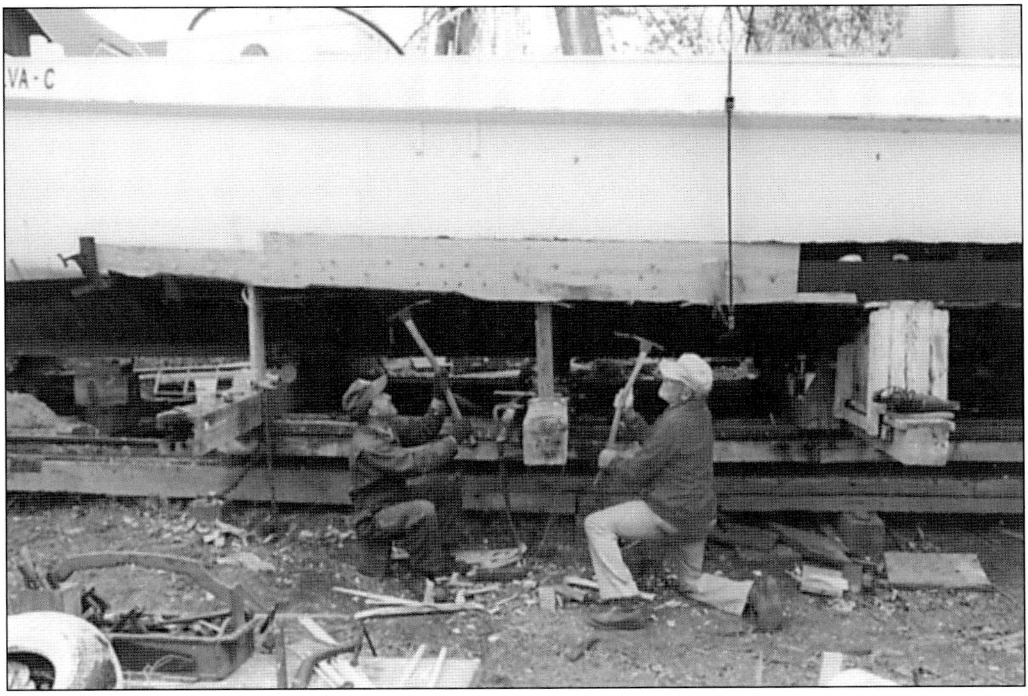

Two volunteers from the Reedville Fishermen's Museum are doing the backbreaking work of shaving down the side boards until the correct curve is achieved. A lot of planning and careful execution is required to properly rescue and preserve a classic boat like the *Elva C.*

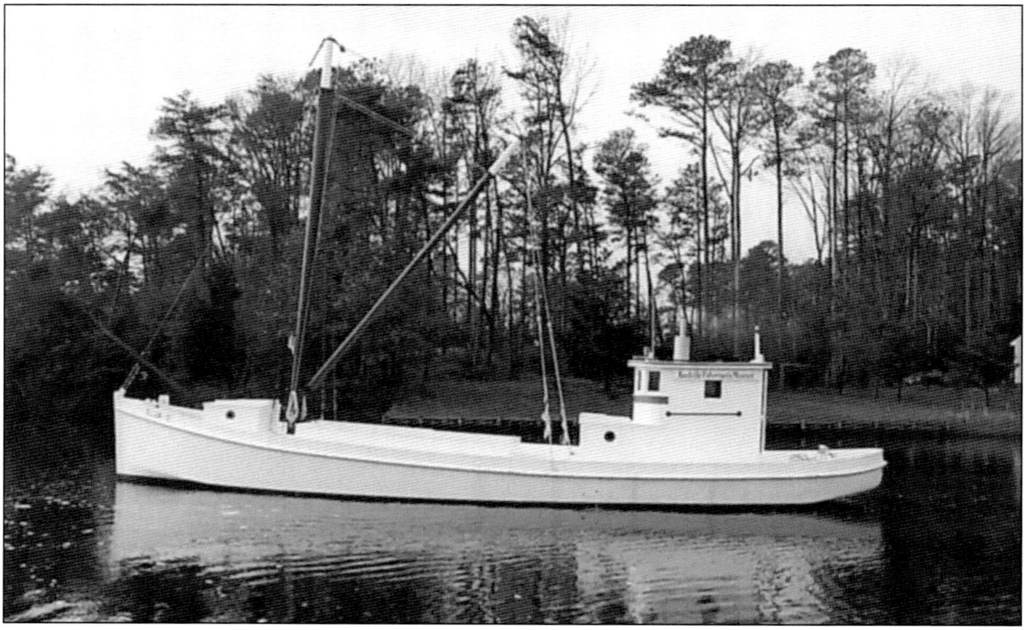

Pictured here is buyboat *Elva C.* after its complete restoration. It is one of two very special boats in the museum's collection that have been awarded a spot in the National Register of Historic Places. The *Elva C.* travels to different venues for shows and also is in constant use to take visitors to the museum on Friday evening cruises along Cockrell's Creek and the Great Wicomico River.

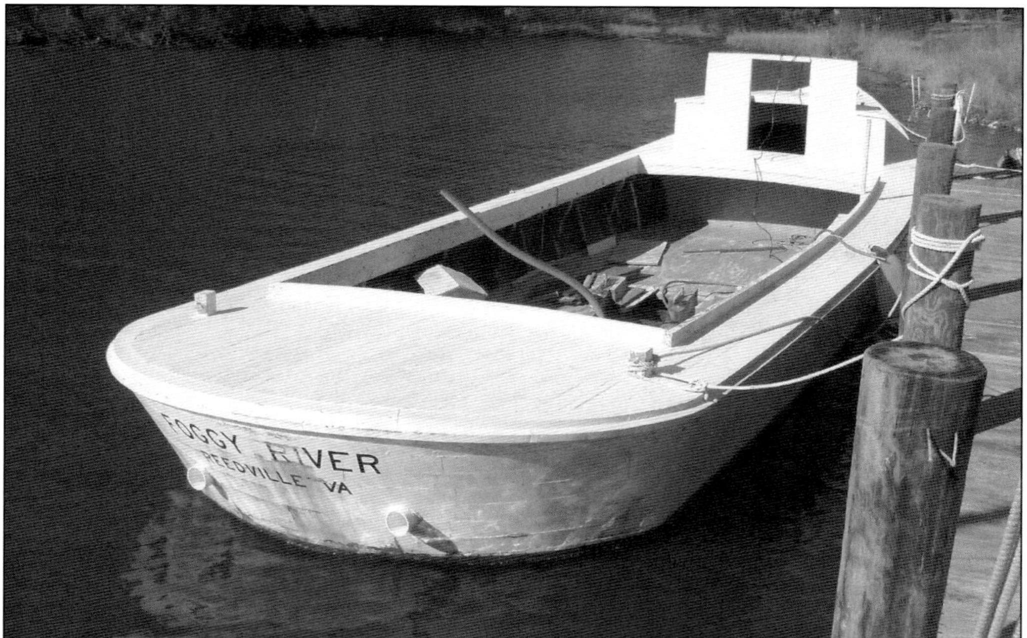

The *Foggy River* is a deadrise (V-bottom with cross planking) open boat with a small cabin forward—typical to some degree of the type still seen today. It has a distinctly graceful sheer (the upward curve of the deck from stern to bow), an unusually pronounced but attractive flare to the sides near the bow, and a round stern. Here, the *Foggy* sits at the museum's dock prior to restoration.

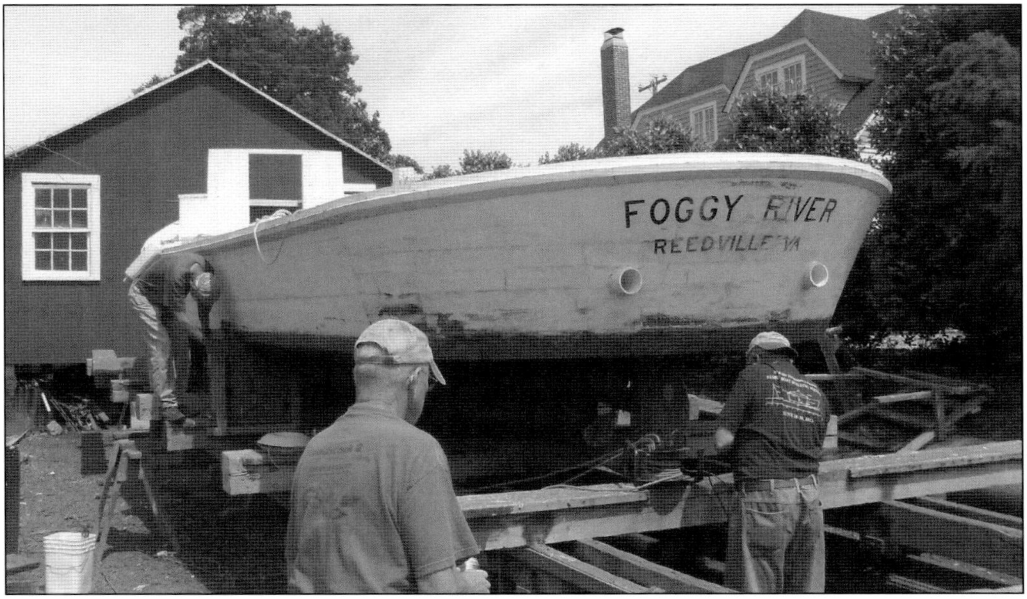

The *Foggy River* is very much a Reedville product. Its design was a collaborative effort between two local residents, owner Charles Bowles and builder George Butler, the second of the three generations of the family to own and operate the Reedville Marine Railway. Coming full circle in history, the *Foggy* returns to the same railway where it was built.

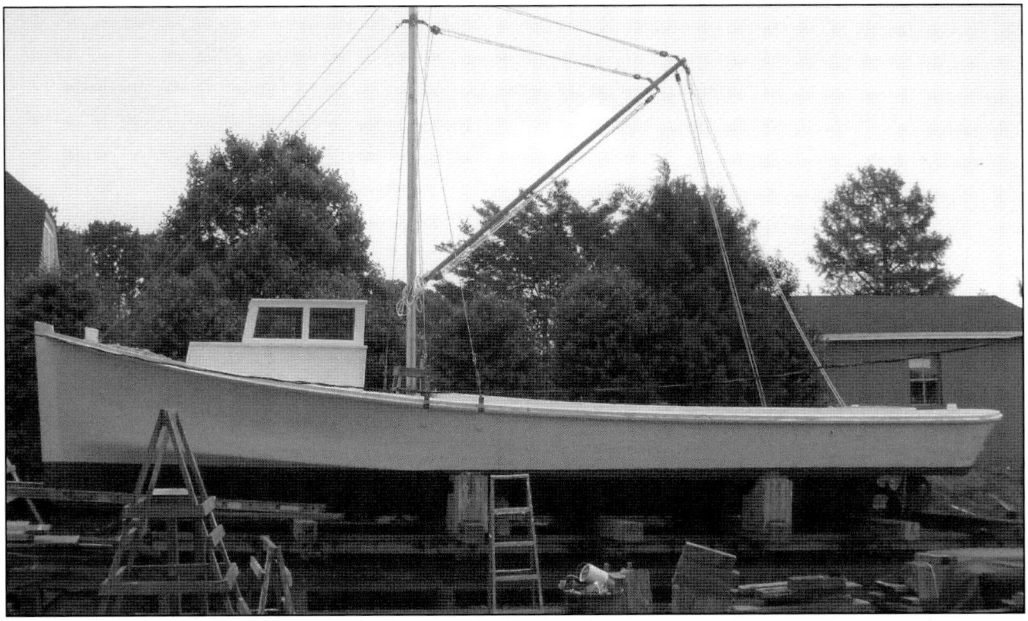

The *Foggy River* was used by Captain Bowles for a number of decades until he retired. George Verlander later discovered it lying unused near the Corrotoman River. When the engine finally failed, he donated the boat to the museum. Butler's son, also named George, helped restore the boat.

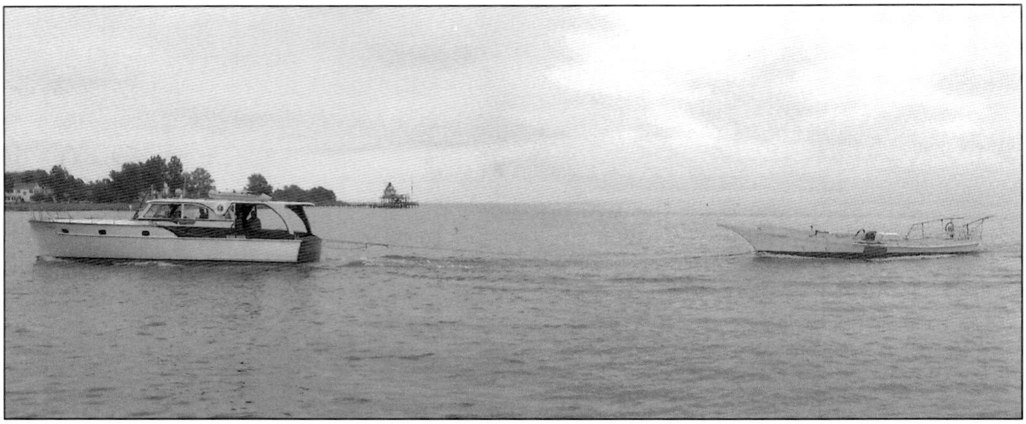

The *Claud W. Somers* was built in 1911 by Tom Young near Clam, Virginia, just north of Onantock. A two-sail bateau, or skipjack, built for oyster dredging, it is one of only a handful of skipjacks remaining on the Chesapeake Bay. This photograph shows the hulk of the *Somers* being towed by legendary local waterman Wendell Haynie to begin restoration under the guidance of the museum volunteers.

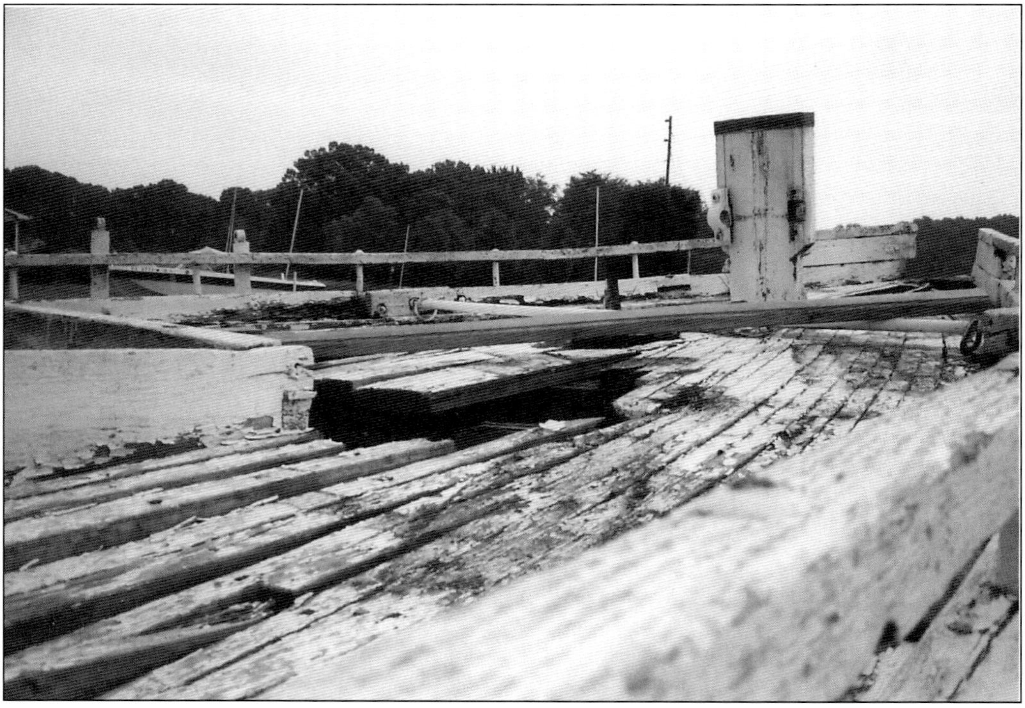

The *Claud W. Somers* continued to work the bay until 1983, when Alfred Garey Lambert purchased it and labored over the next 17 years rebuilding and restoring the vessel. Upon his death in 1999, his children selected the Reedville Fishermen's Museum as the new steward of the *Claud W. Somers*. When it was brought in, the skipjack was in desperate trouble. The deck was in terrible shape.

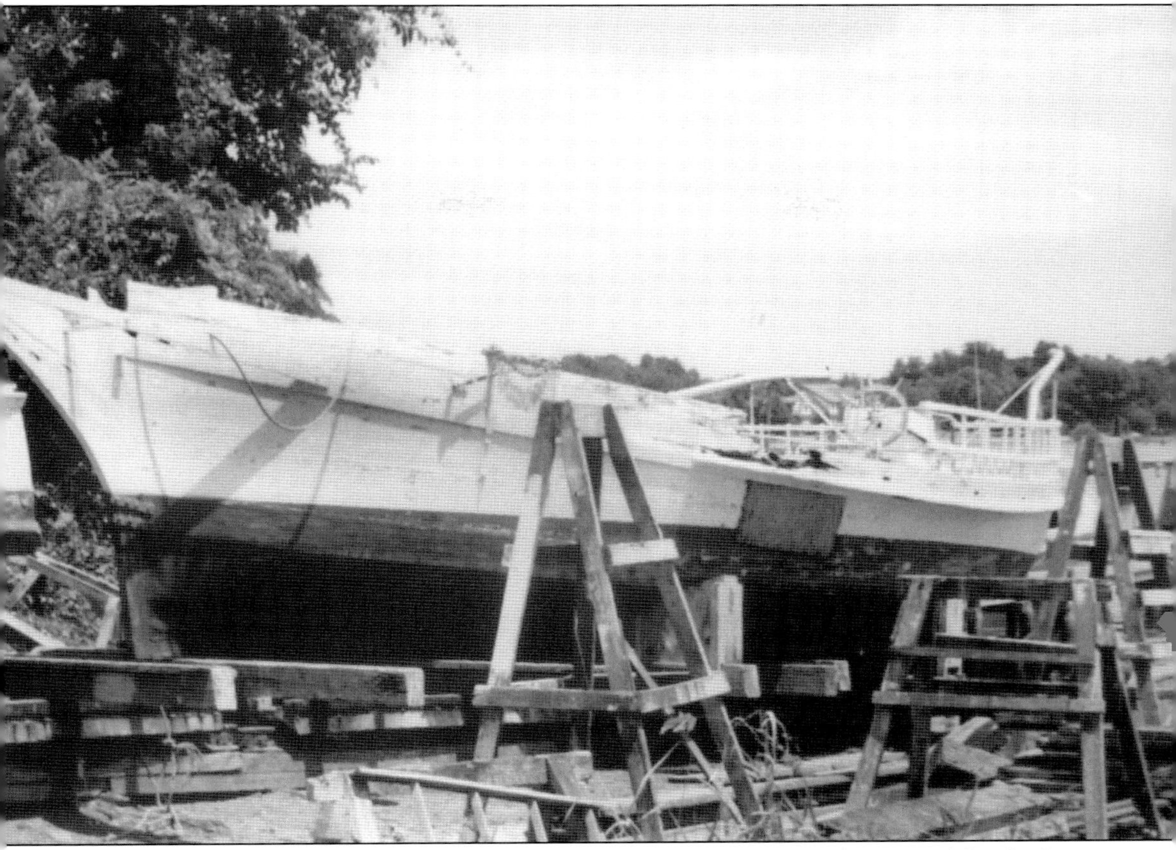

The Reedville Fishermen's Museum began restoration in the summer of 2000 and finished in October 2001. Wood from local trees was turned into lumber using the vintage sawmill at Cockrell's Marine Railway. A new keelson and horn timber were installed, the bottom was replaced, and a new oak past step was installed.

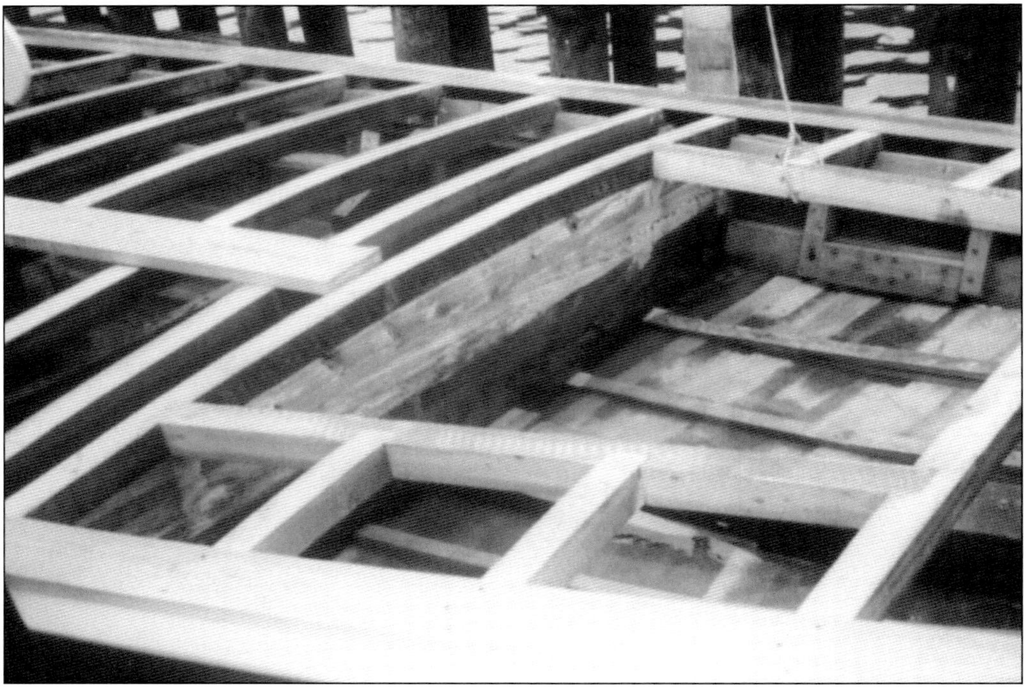

Each deck beam was replaced, and a new bowsprit was fashioned. Two-inch-wide strips were cut from pine planks and installed on their sides to make the deck two inches thick. New deckhouses were built. The volunteers were highly motivated by the desire to see this old veteran sailing on the Chesapeake Bay again.

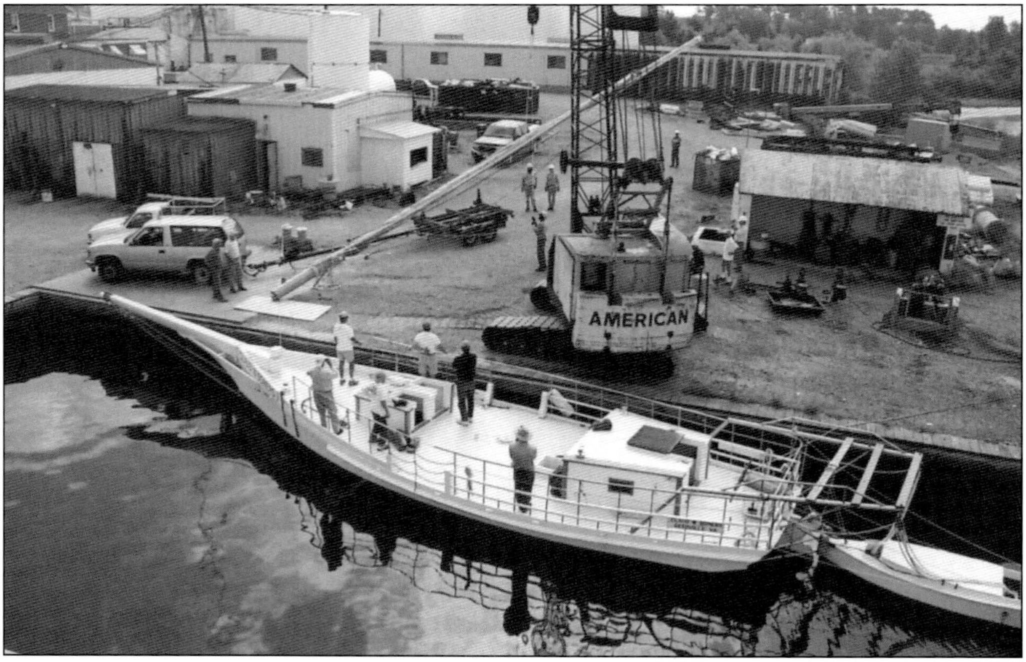

In October 2001, museum volunteers shaped a new mast and boom from Norway spruce logs donated by the State University of New York. In addition to three generations of Cockrells and Taylor Dawson, some 35 volunteers spent over 3,000 hours restoring the *Claud W. Somers*.

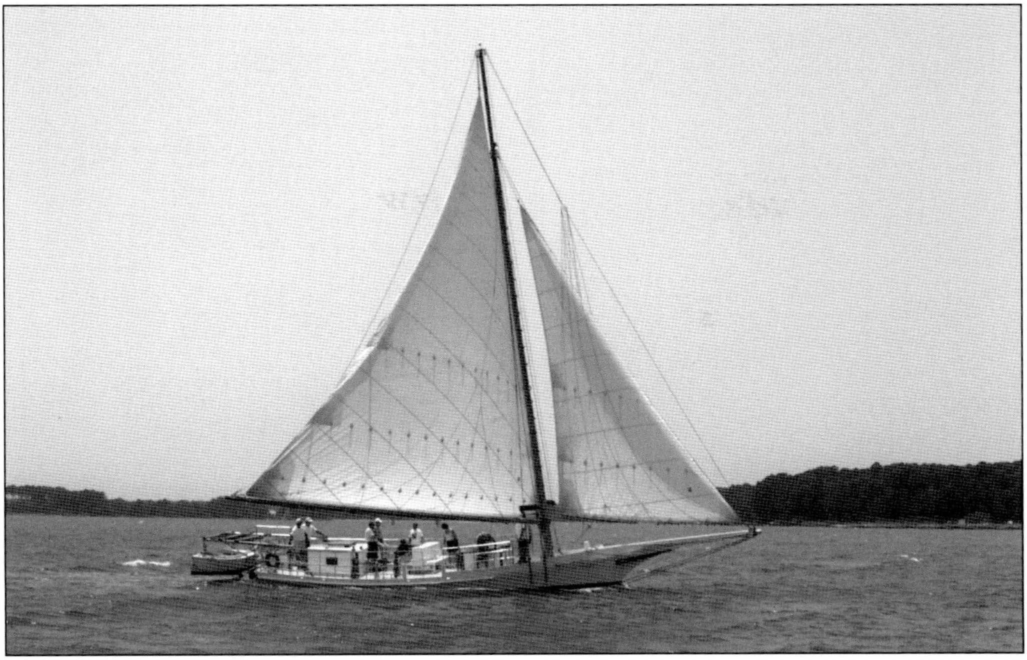

The *Claud W. Somers* is pictured here under sail once again after a successful restoration. It was later placed in the National Register of Historic Places, along with the *Elva C*. It is a very unique honor to have two active boats on the register. The *Claud* has an active crew, and it sails with passengers on special occasions.

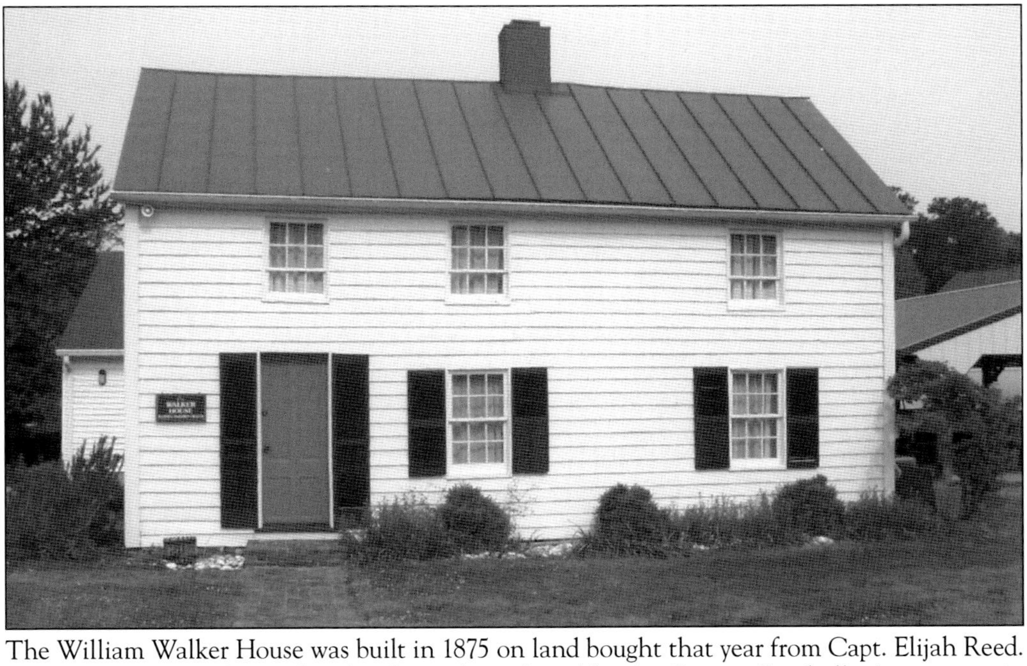

The William Walker House was built in 1875 on land bought that year from Capt. Elijah Reed. It was occupied by the Walker family until purchased by the Greater Reedville Association in 1986. It opened as the Reedville Fishermen's Museum in 1988. The Walker House served many years as the entire museum until the later construction of the Covington Building, which serves as the main museum galleries today.

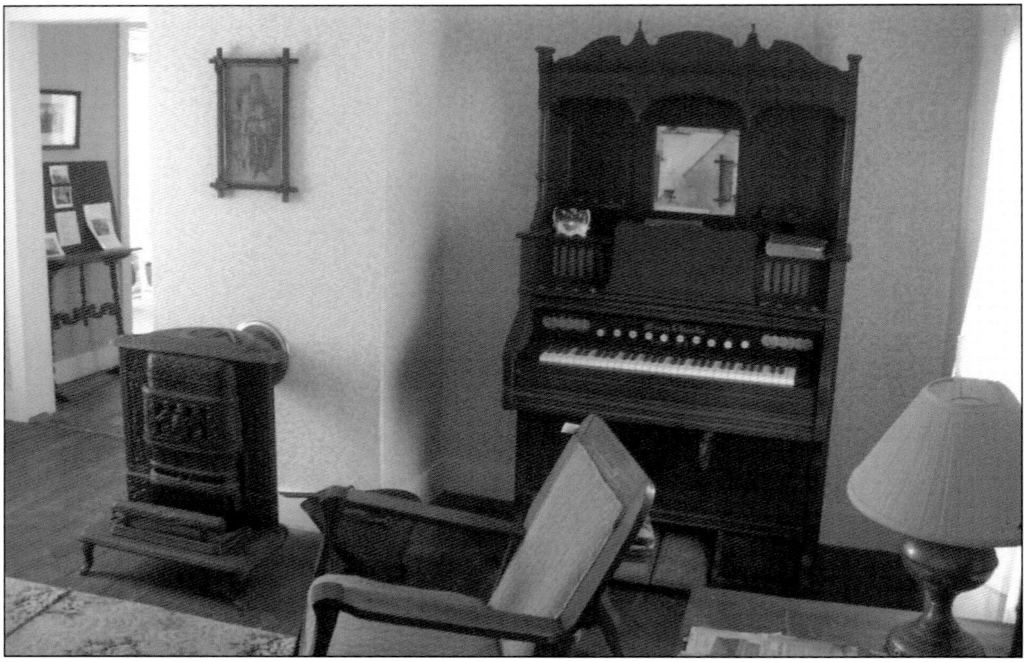

Pictured here is the living room at the Walker House. In 1995, the home was refurbished to represent a waterman's home during the late 1800s. The first floor had this room and a dining room, and the second floor had two bedrooms and the sewing room. Most of the restoration was accomplished through the efforts of local supporters of the museum.

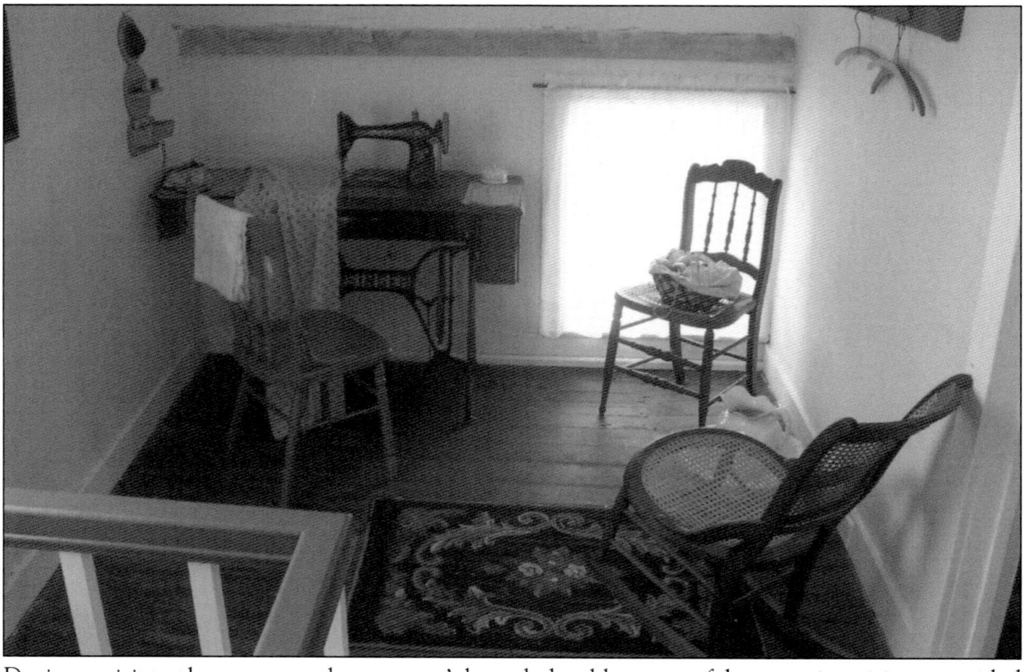

During a visit to the museum, the museum's knowledgeable group of docents give visitors a guided tour through the Walker House and its original attached kitchen. The house offers a wonderful insight into the architecture and style of the 1870s. The sewing room is one of three rooms on the second floor.

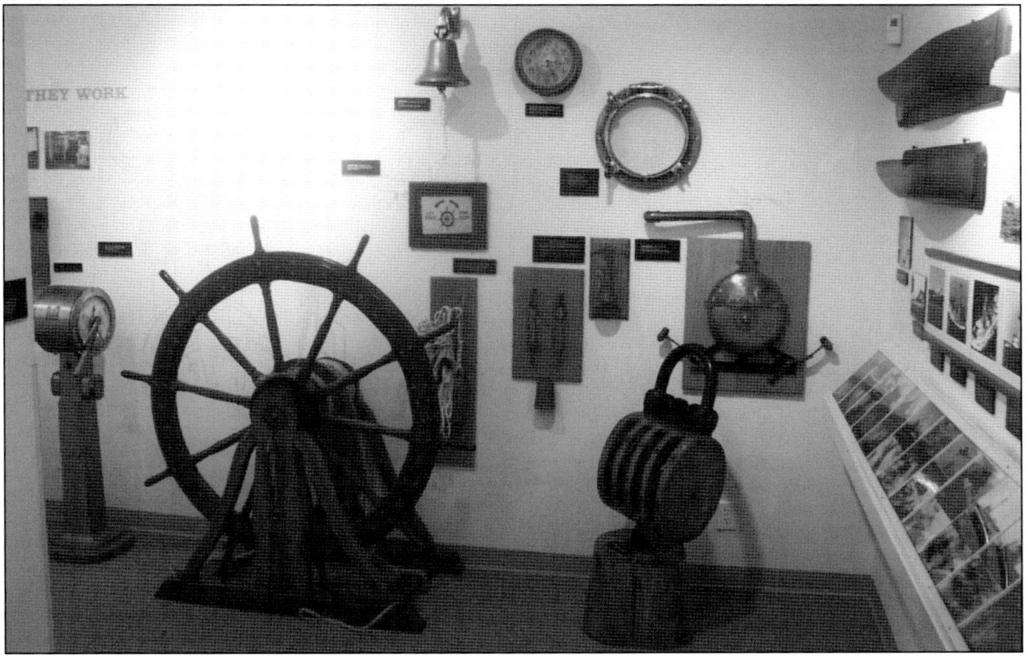

A generous gift from Frank Covington enabled the Reedville Fishermen's Museum to expand into a new building in 1995. The facility, which was significantly enlarged in 2003, houses the permanent collection in the Reed Gallery and the Frayne Gallery. The displays focus on the many different aspects of the watermen and the fishing industry.

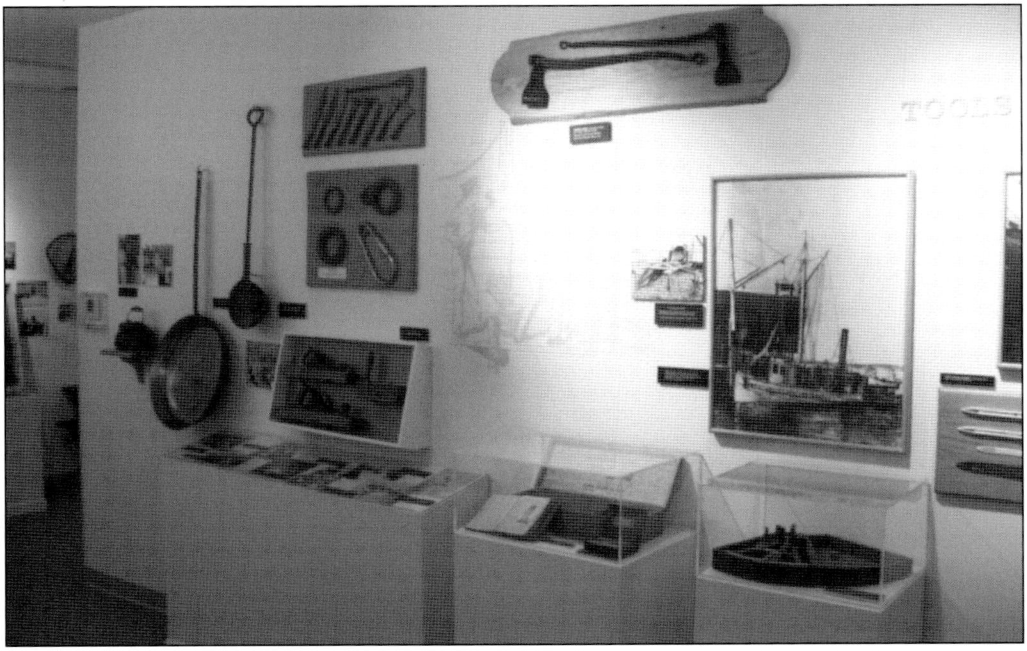

This display shows the wide variety of tools used by the watermen and provides descriptions of their purpose. Changing exhibits are displayed in the Watermen's Gallery, the most recent addition to the Covington Building. The Covington Building also houses the museum gift shop.

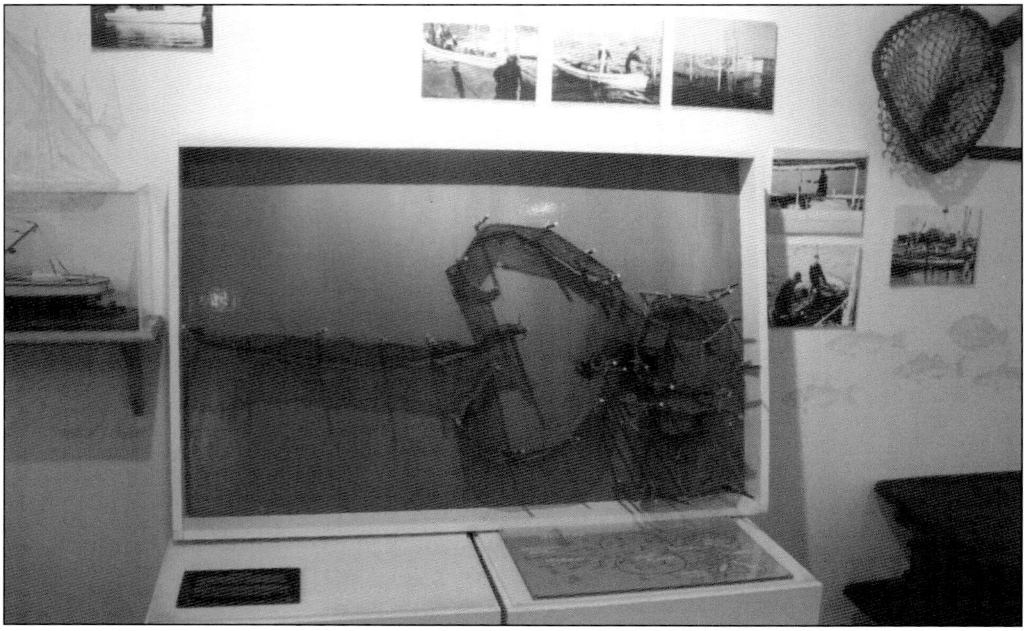

This diorama shows how pound netting is done. It is common to see an array of poles in many creeks and rivers around the Chesapeake Bay. It is a time-tested way for local fishermen to bring fresh meat to local markets. One of the most popular attractions the museum has had were the cruises out to watch the pound nets being worked. It is the hope of the organization that those trips will once again resume.

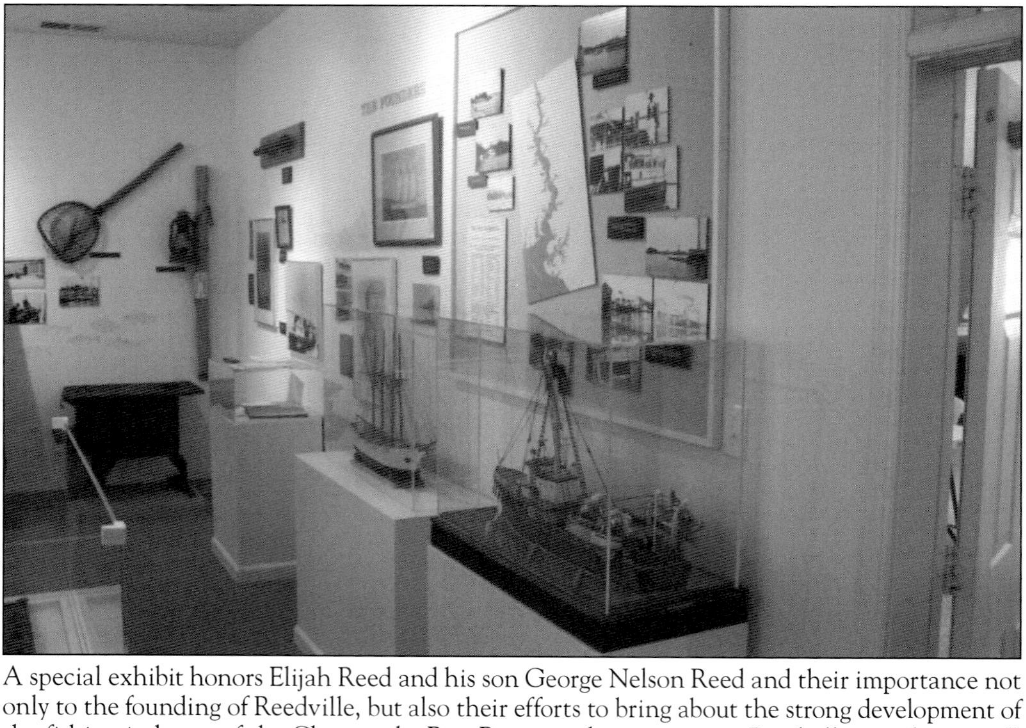

A special exhibit honors Elijah Reed and his son George Nelson Reed and their importance not only to the founding of Reedville, but also their efforts to bring about the strong development of the fishing industry of the Chesapeake Bay. Between these two men, Reedville rose from small fishing village to one of the most productive ports in the United States.

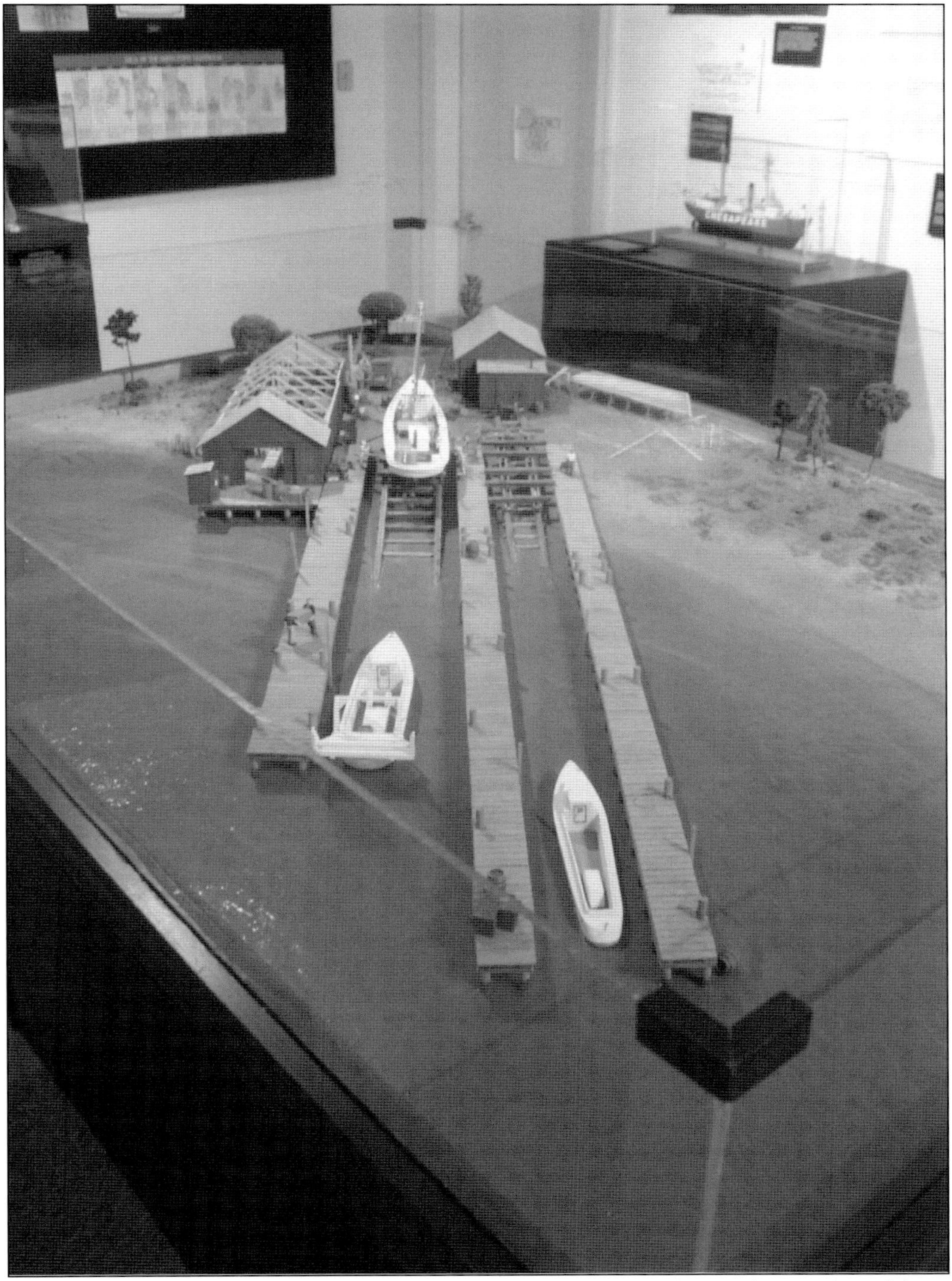

This is an extremely detailed diorama of the Reedville Marine Railway. Along with its fishing heritage, Reedville boasts a proud history of boat building, and there is no resident of Reedville more deeply steeped in this tradition than third-generation boat-builder George Butler. George has spent his entire life around the Reedville Marine Railway, the boatyard established by his grandfather.

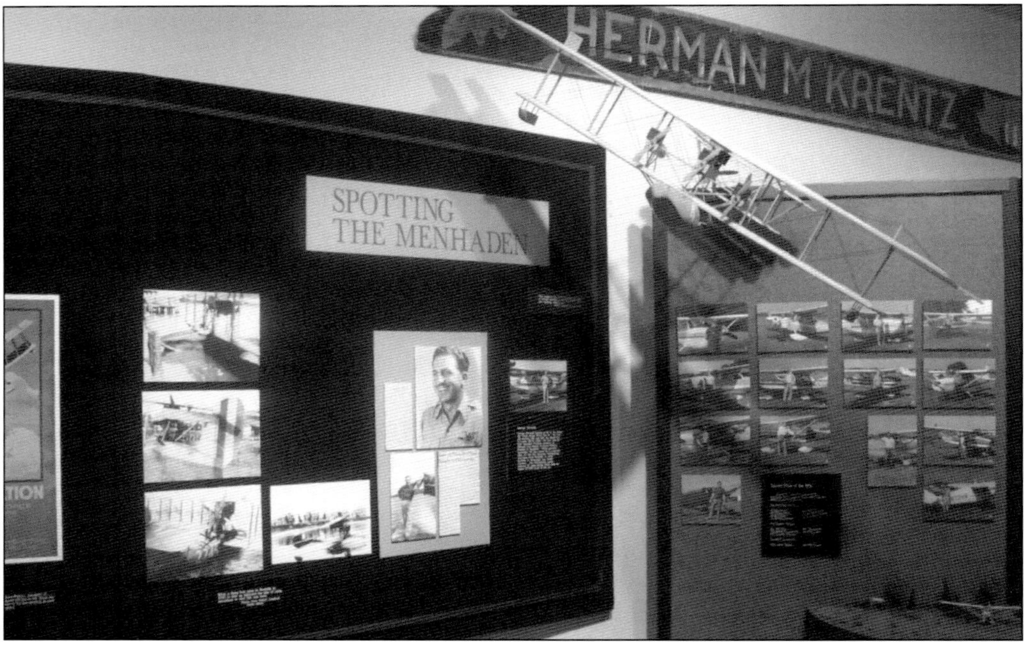

This exhibit honors the spotter pilots of the Chesapeake Bay. In the early 1920s, John Palmer conceived of the idea of using aerial spotting to find schools of menhaden. While initially unsuccessful, after improved postwar communications equipment became available, it became the preferred method. Aerial spotting has become the accepted way to track the menhaden throughout the bay.

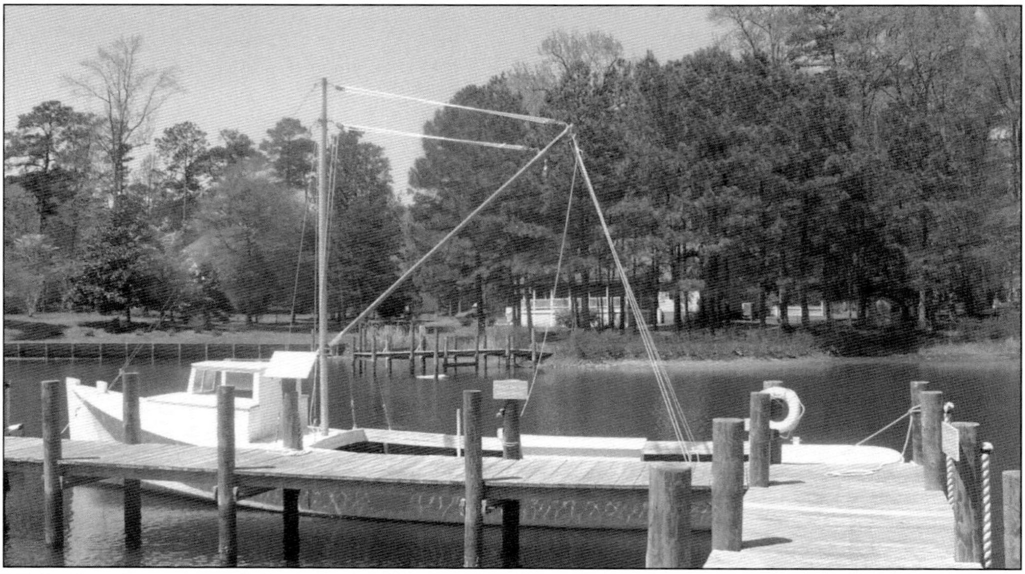

With the placement of the mast and rigging, the restoration of the *Foggy* was completed during 2015. The *Foggy River* will be used as a floating classroom, exhibiting the different equipment and rigging used in pound net fishing, crab dredging, oystering, and crab potting. A large tray sits under water next to the *Foggy* so visitors can have a hands-on experience of using authentic tongs to bring the oysters to the surface.

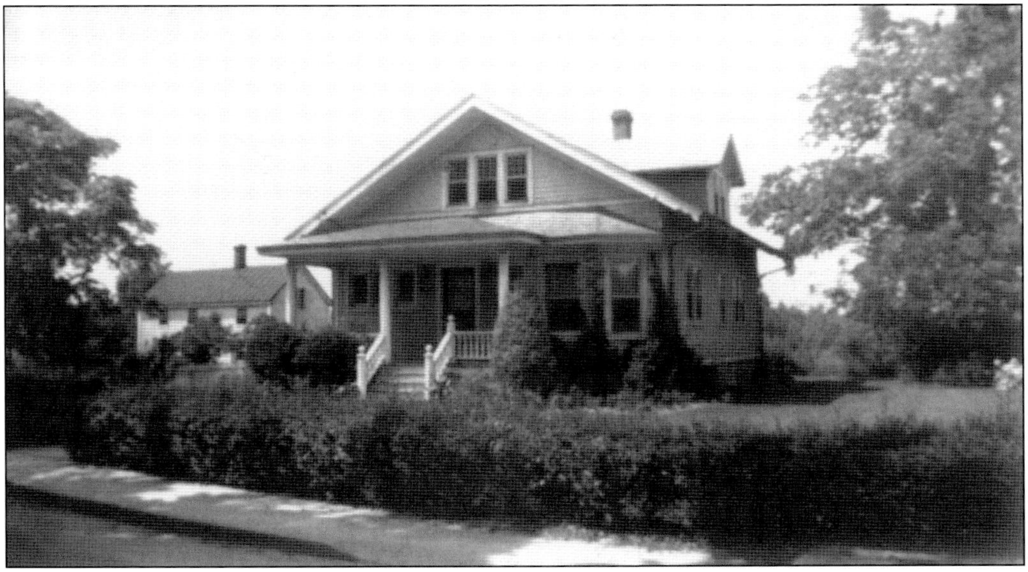

Pictured here is the Butler House, built in the late 1920s by George Butler, owner of the Reedville Marine Railway. To the left is the Walker House. Both homes were later restored and incorporated into the Reedville Fishermen's Museum. The Butler House was recently restored in 2014 and serves as the administration building for the museum.

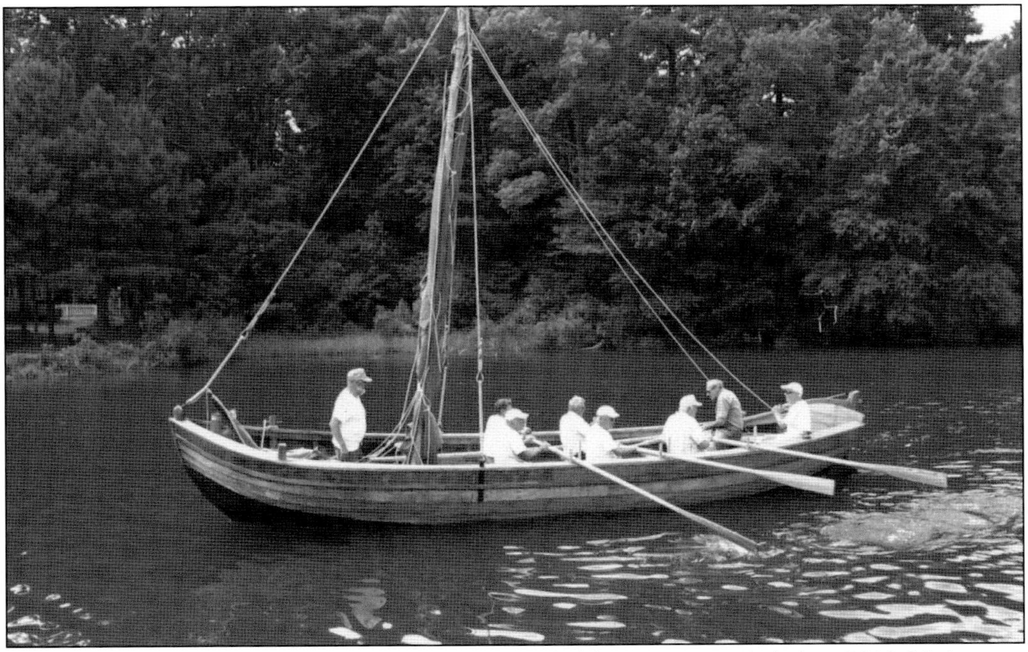

Lumber in the *Spirit of 1608* came from trees toppled by Hurricane Isabel in 2003. Utilizing a donated sawmill, 63 volunteers at the museum labored more than 4,000 hours to build the replica of John Smith's original *Barge of Discovery*. The *Spirit of 1608*'s keel was laid January 17, 2006, and the boat was christened on July 14, 2006.

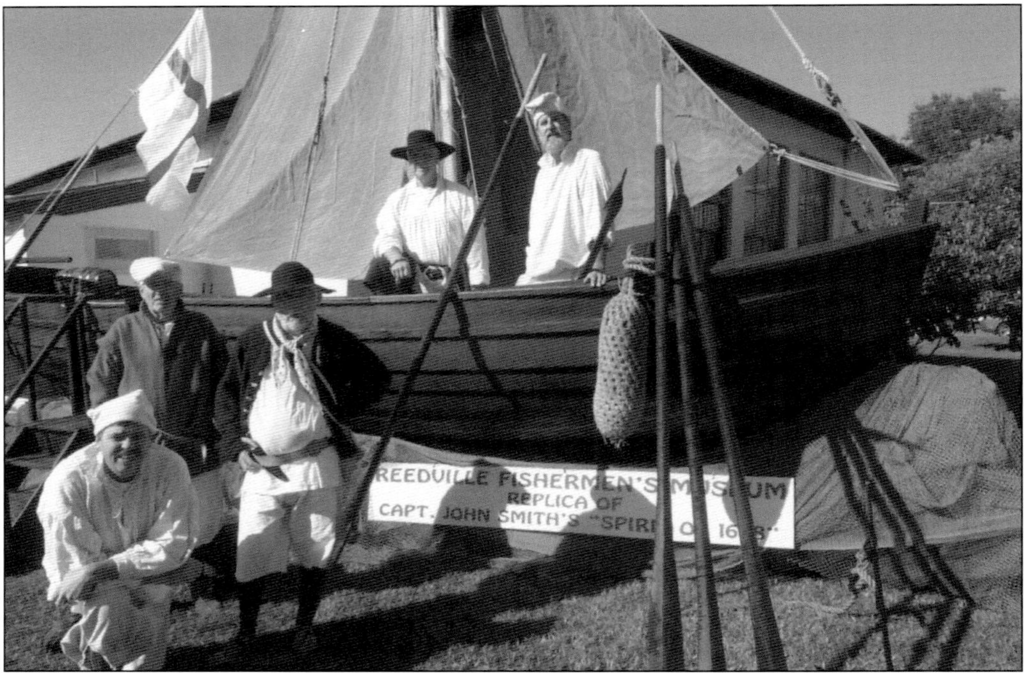

The John Smith barge is the traveling face of the museum and goes to many different types of events throughout Virginia. The crew dresses in period costumes and informs visitors of the history of John Smith's travels in the Virginia area. The *Spirit of 1608* and its crew make appearances at schools, museums, parks and many other events across the Chesapeake Bay region.

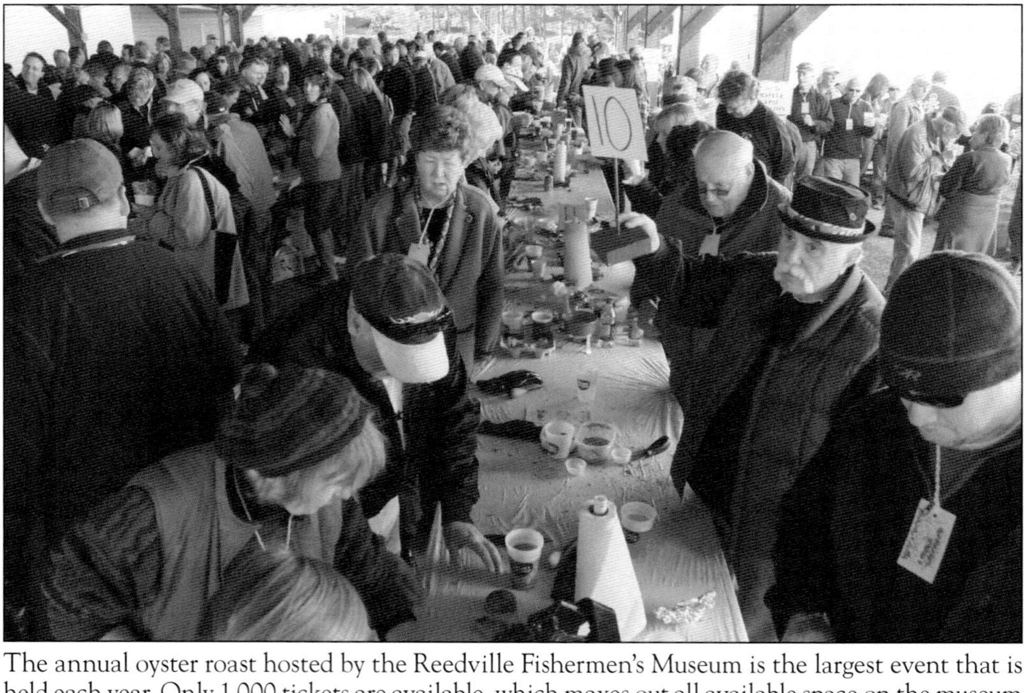

The annual oyster roast hosted by the Reedville Fishermen's Museum is the largest event that is held each year. Only 1,000 tickets are available, which maxes out all available space on the museum grounds. Ticket sales help fund the museum's many special programs throughout the year.

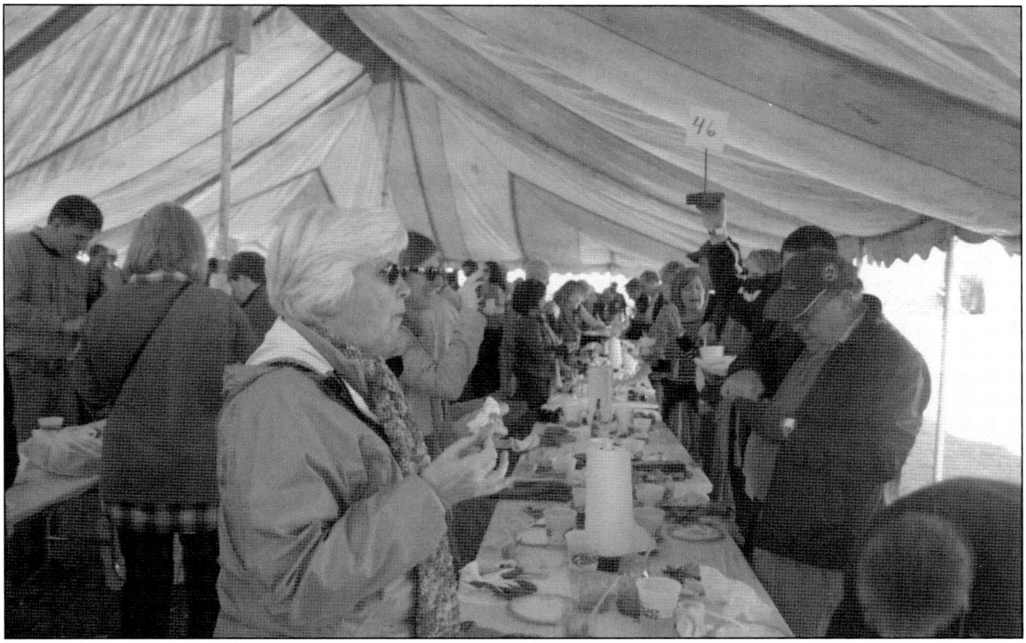

Call it "organized insanity." The oyster roast celebrated its 25th anniversary in 2014. It has proven so popular that all the tickets sell without any advertising because demand is so strong. Besides as many oysters as one can eat, other goodies available include clams, barbecue, soup, wings, beer and wine, and desserts.

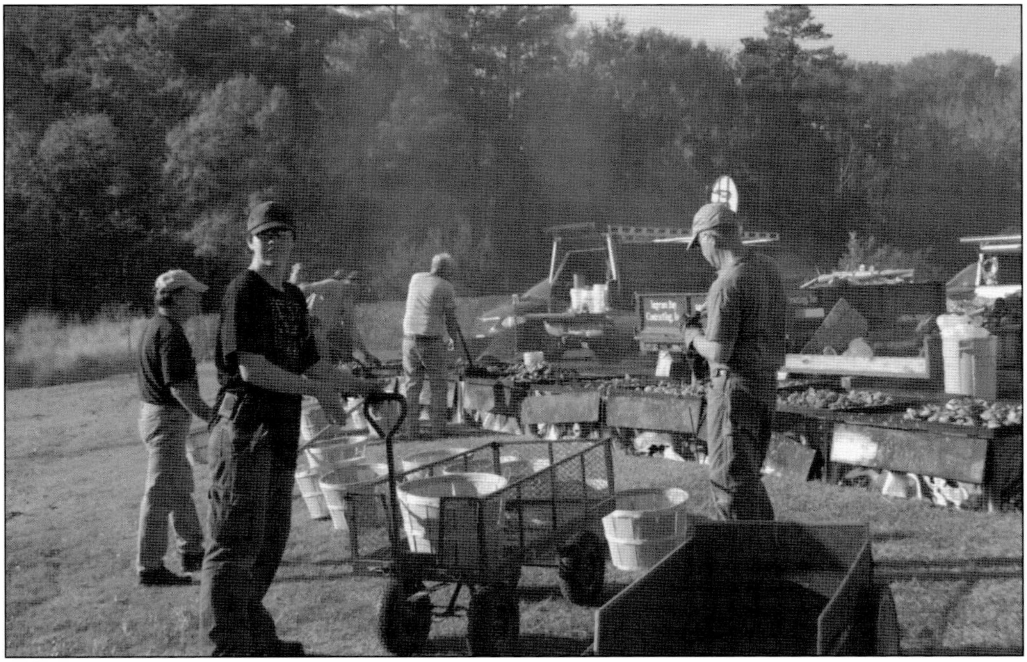

The key to any oyster roast is the skill of the oyster cookers. It is also the hottest job to do, and they are appreciative of a nice cool breeze. Most of the museum's volunteer cookers are local watermen, and the oysters used are locally harvested. It takes more than 200 volunteers to put on the oyster roast—it is truly a community effort.

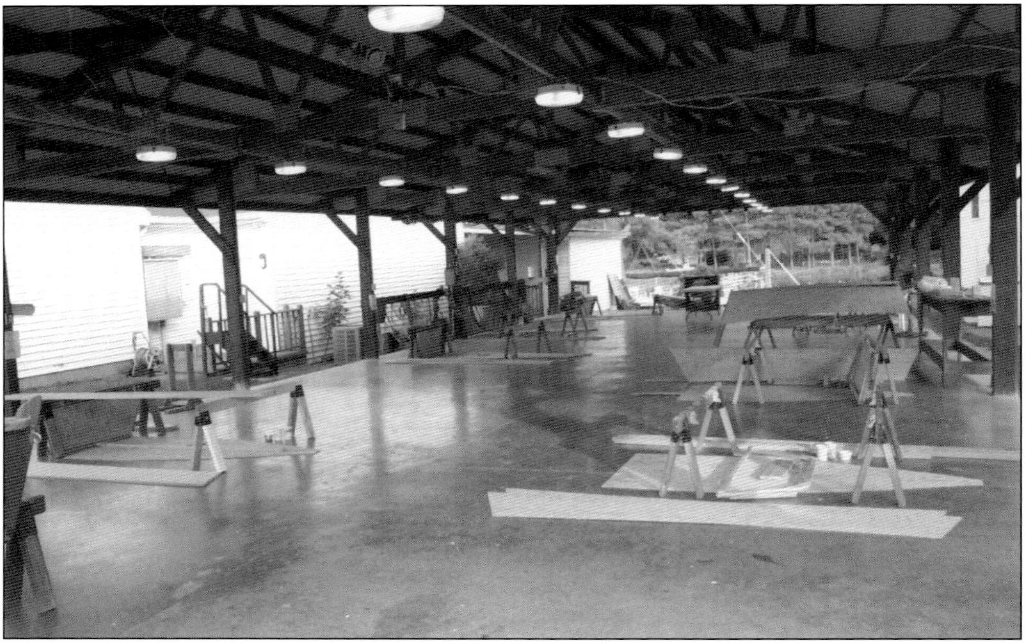

Each year, the museum also offers a family boat-building program the last weekend of June. A nine-foot-six rowing skiff is built from a kit with hand tools and basic wooden boat–building techniques that have been in use for generations on the Chesapeake Bay. It all starts with the kits, shown laid out on the museum pavilion the day before it all starts.

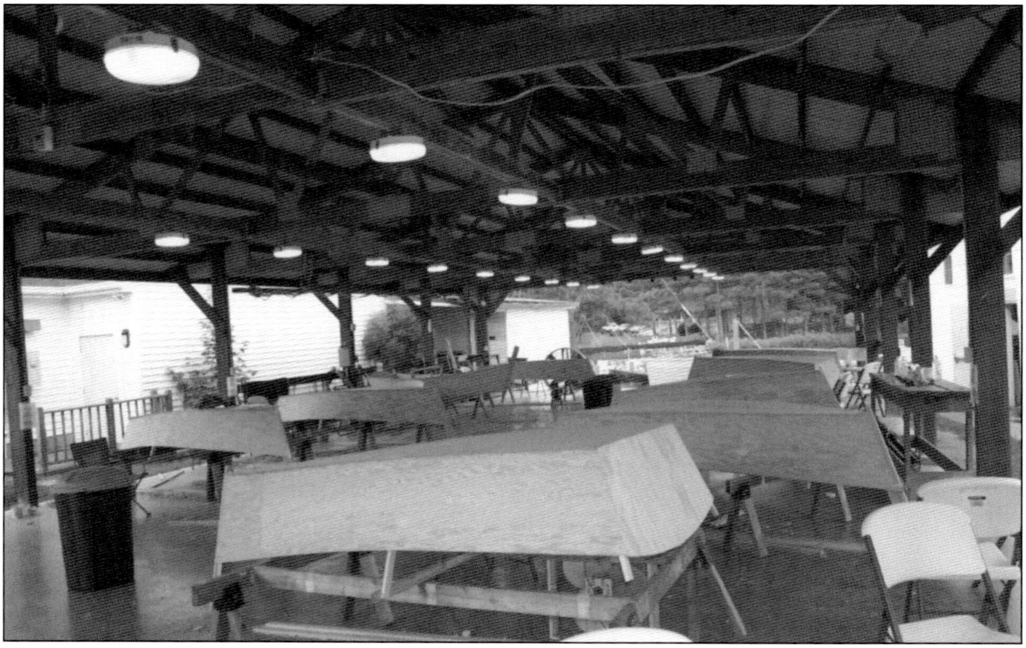

Experienced and dedicated instructors from the museum's boat shop have created the kit and will be on hand to guide teams throughout the weekend. It is a unique hands-on experience for both young and old. Teams are allowed to have up to six members involved on each boat.

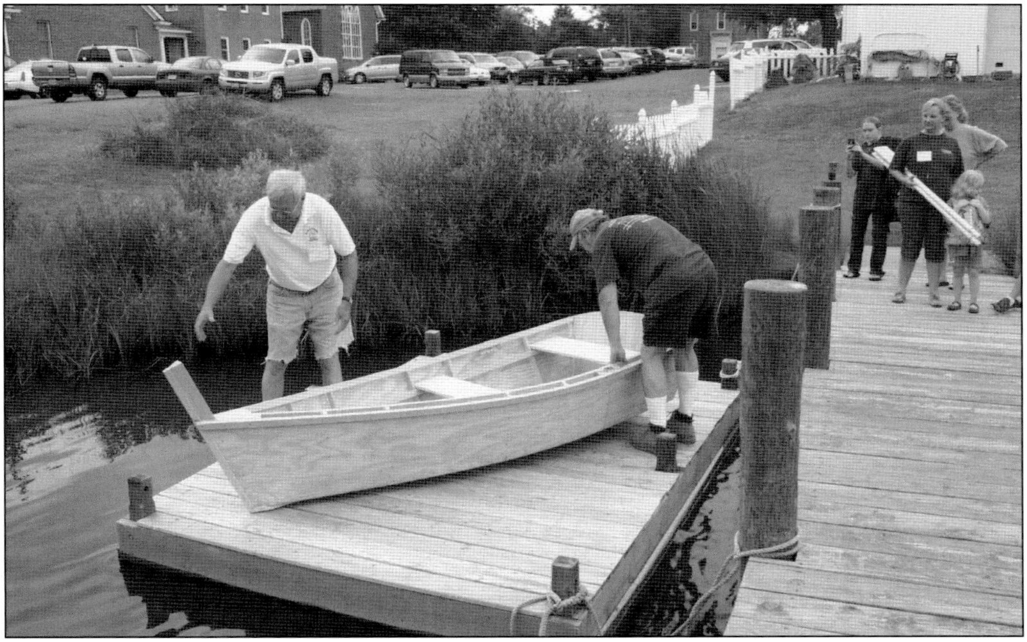

The boat is completed and ready for painting at the end of the 2.5-day adventure. This is a great opportunity to spend time with the family in the quiet rhythms of hand tools and ripples from the nearby creek. When it is time to leave on Sunday, participants will have memories of fun, knowledge of basic skills, and a nice little boat.

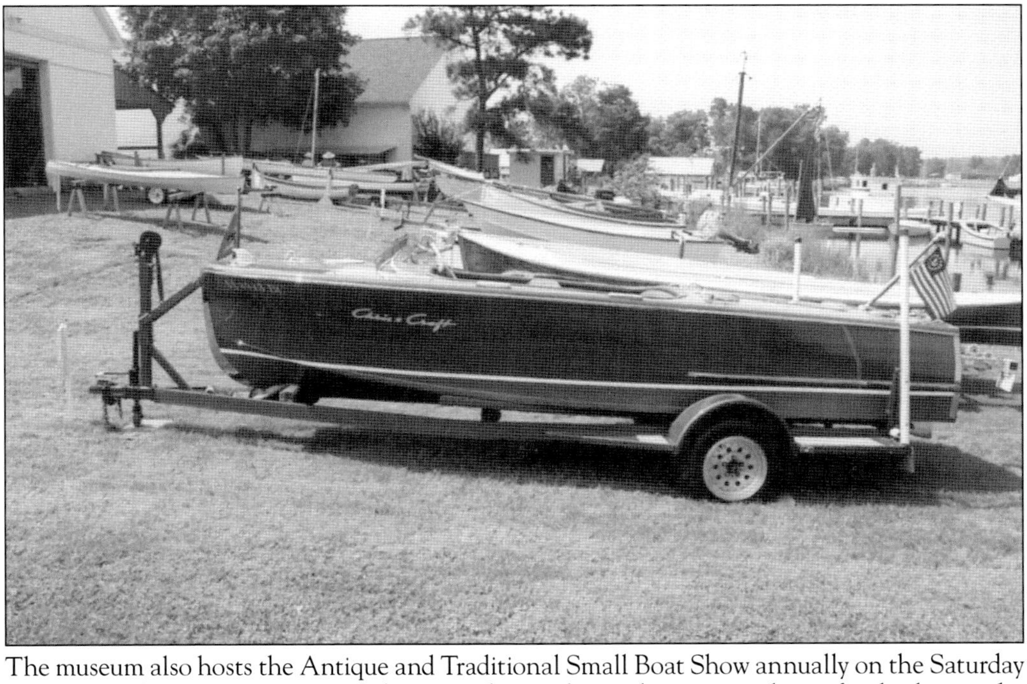

The museum also hosts the Antique and Traditional Small Boat Show annually on the Saturday following Labor Day. Boat owners from a wide area bring their unique boats for display on the museum grounds. In addition, boat rides on the *Elva C.* and tours of the rest of the museum fleet take place all day.

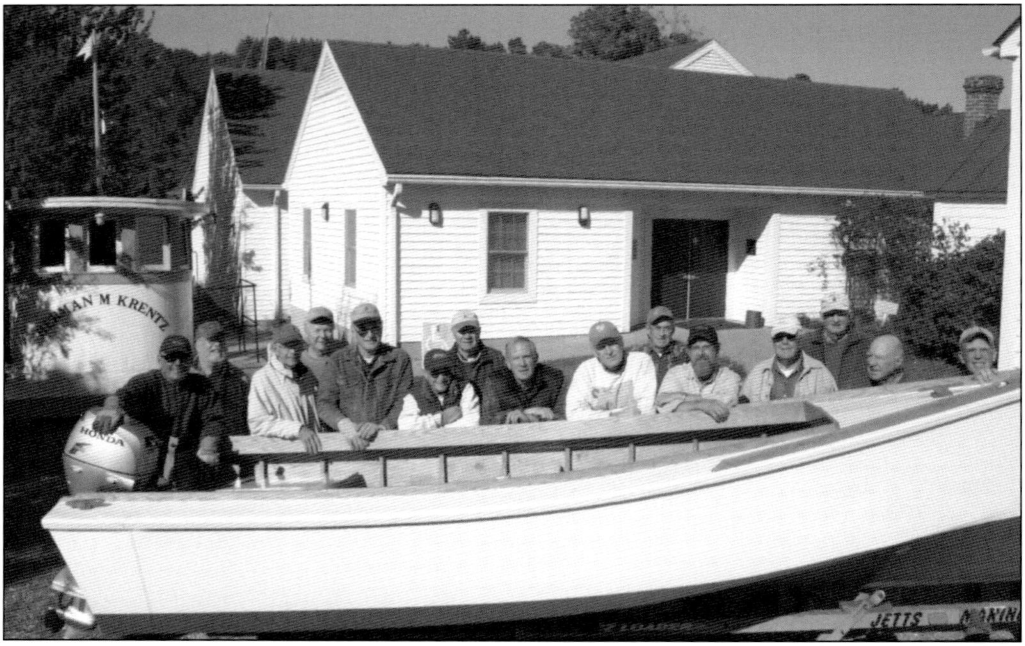

The boat shop volunteers are at the core of all boat building and repairs conducted at the museum. Besides being instrumental in the restoration of the *Elva C.*, the *Claud W. Somers*, and the *Foggy River*, these men have also restored many unique smaller boats that are part of the permanent collection at the museum. They also annually build a raffle skiff, shown here, which greatly aids in raising funds for museum projects.

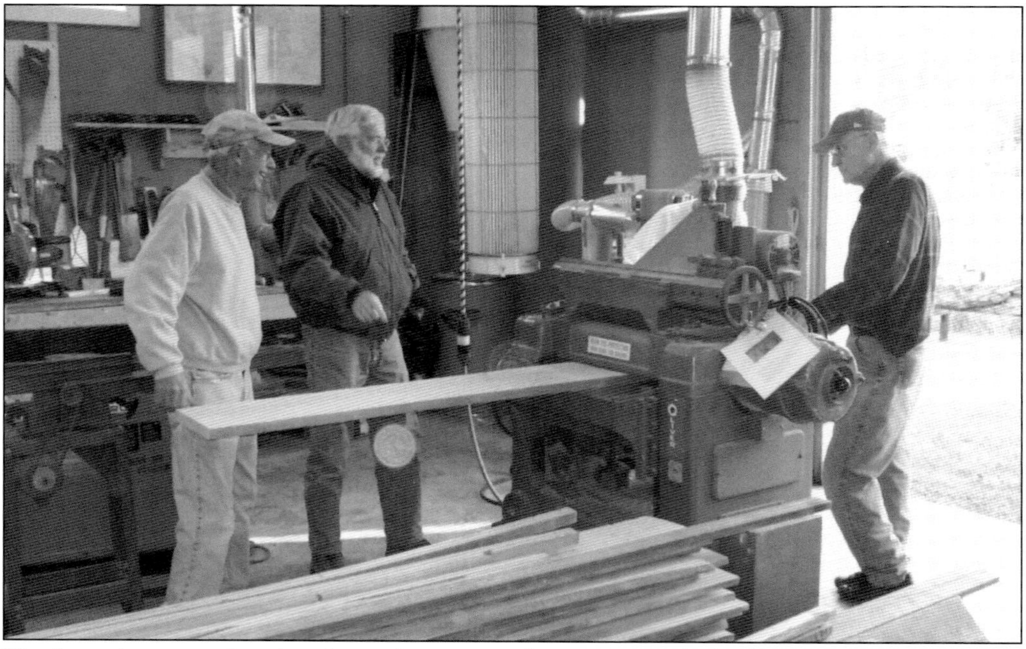

The boat shop is outfitted with a wide variety of equipment, which allows volunteers to tackle almost any restoration job. The boat shop is open and busy on Tuesday and Thursday mornings from 9:00 a.m. until 12:00 p.m., and all are welcome to visit or join in. At any given time, there are multiple projects ongoing.

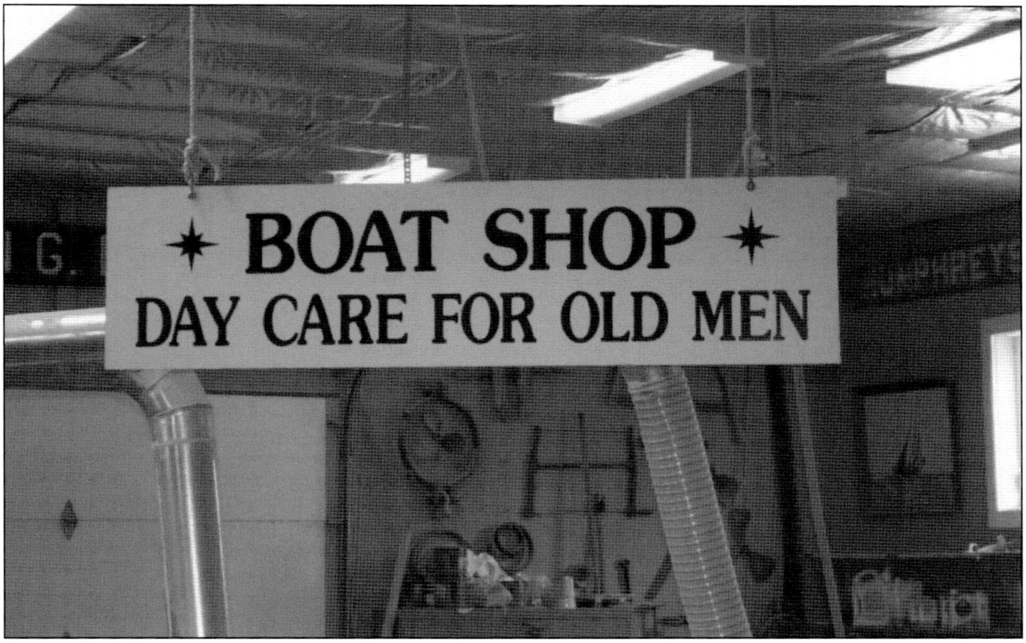

The sign says it all. The boat shop volunteers enjoy a good time, and it is often said of the shop, "Getting retired men out of the house twice a week. Wives rejoice!" The place is a carnival of personalities and good work. It is a comfortable place—a place where all pretense is left elsewhere and the guys find friendship and support while doing something that feels important.

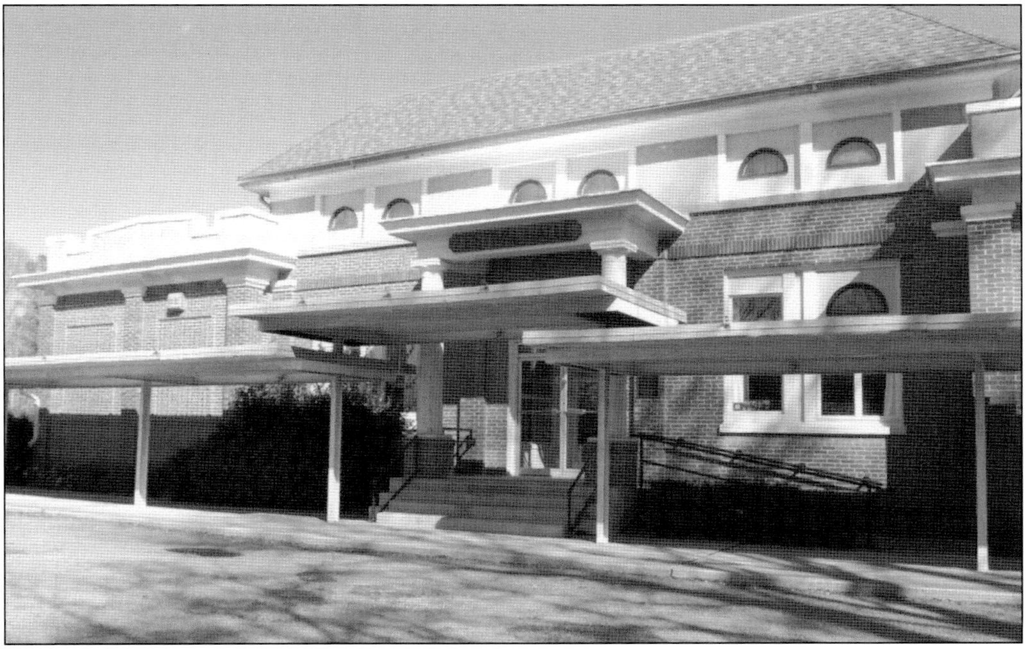

Festival Halle became part of the Reedville Fishermen's Museum and the Greater Reedville Association in 2009. The building was erected in 1912 and served as the Reedville High School and, later, a middle school until the late 1960s. Now, Festival Halle is a full-service facility that hosts events for area residents, nonprofit organizations, businesses, and other entities.

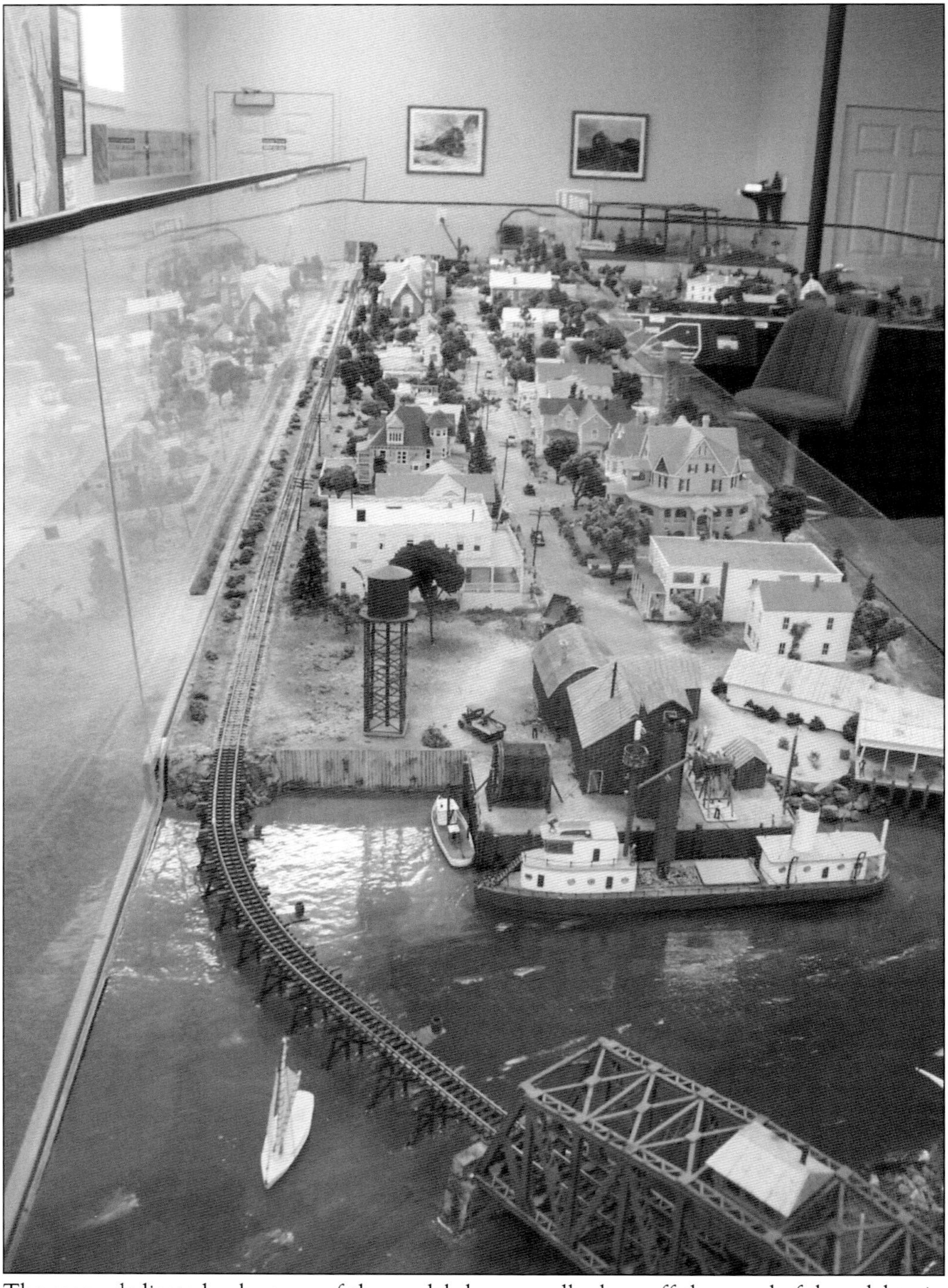

The many dedicated volunteers of the model shop proudly show off the wonderful model train layout when visitors come to the museum. The main layout is an HO scale (1:87) presentation of the Northern Neck Railway, the "Railroad That Never Was." This proposed railway was planned and designed but failed in its attempts to raise capital to make it a reality.

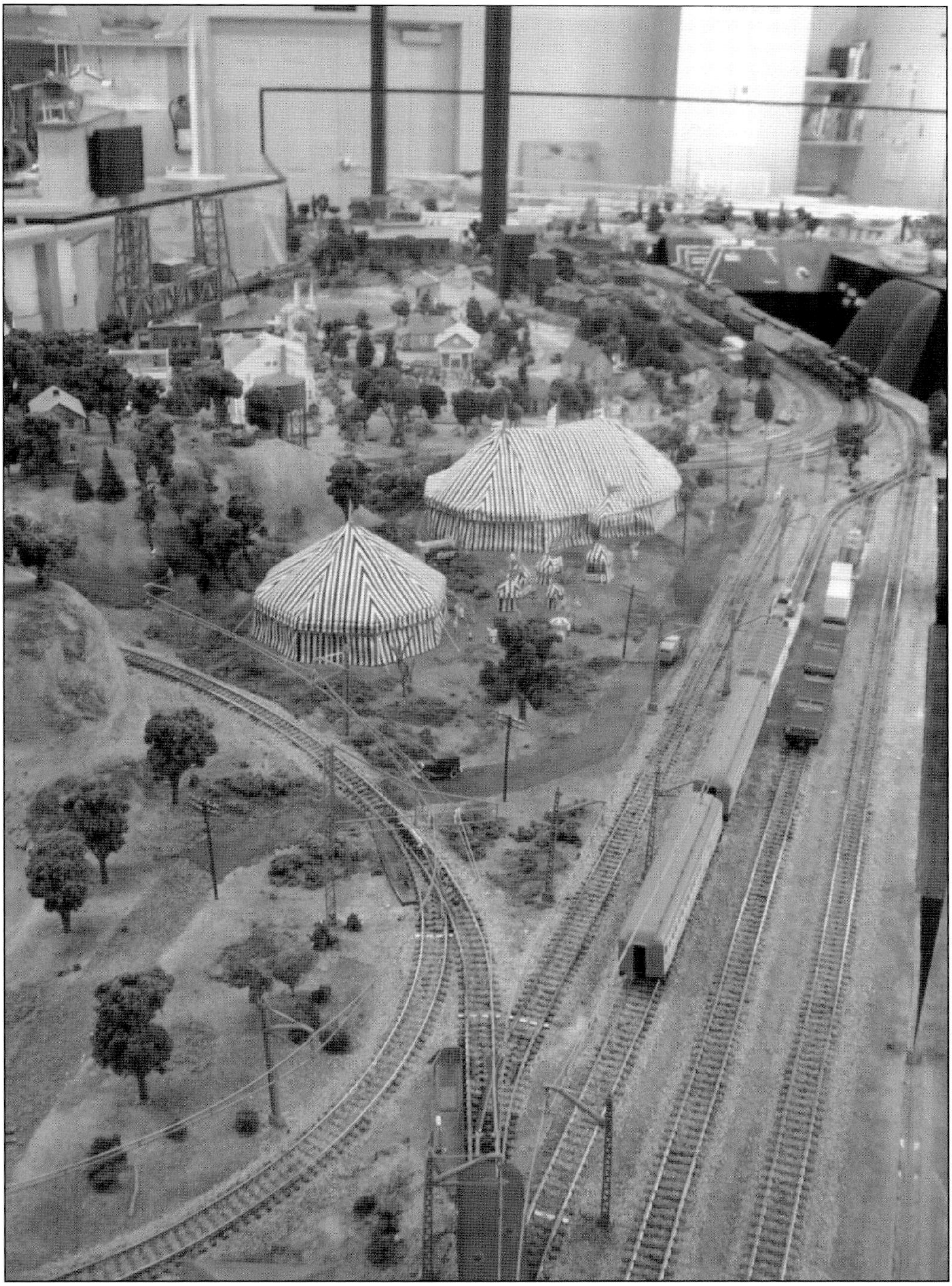

The model shop also features smaller layouts for other model railroad gauges, with hands-on items to attract the child in everyone. During the special train shows, all layouts are running, and the old sounds of the steam engines echo through the room. The model shop is also responsible for maintaining and restoring the museum's sailing vessel model collection.

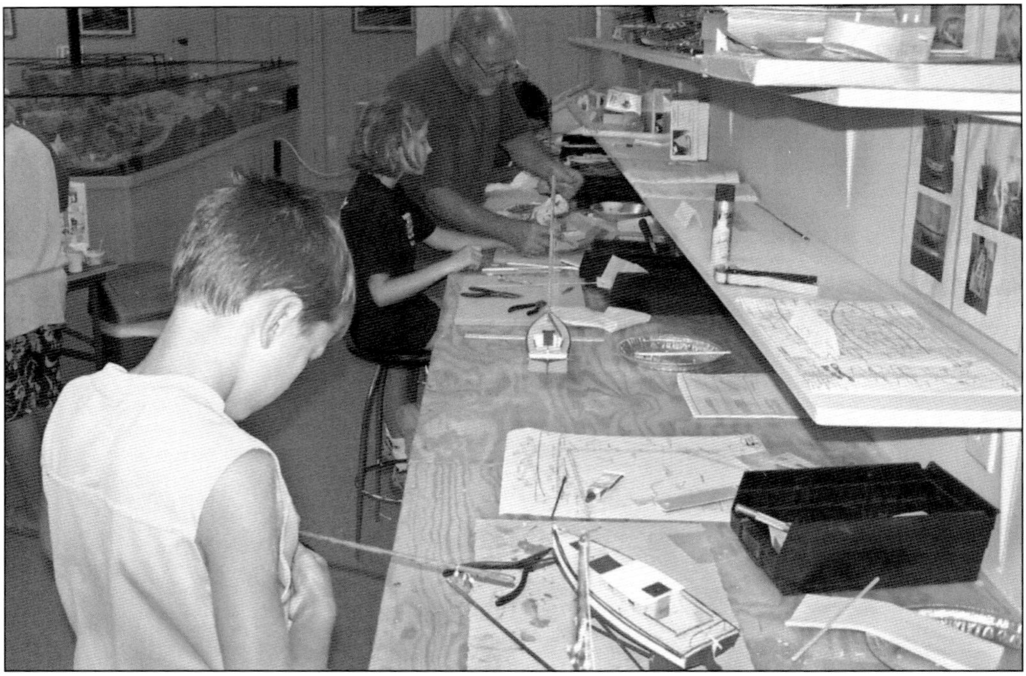

The model shop also hosts an annual model-building class for children 10 or older. This takes place in early August, and the event has always been very popular. Most participants come back for the next year. Those that return advance to make a more challenging model, which increases their skill level.

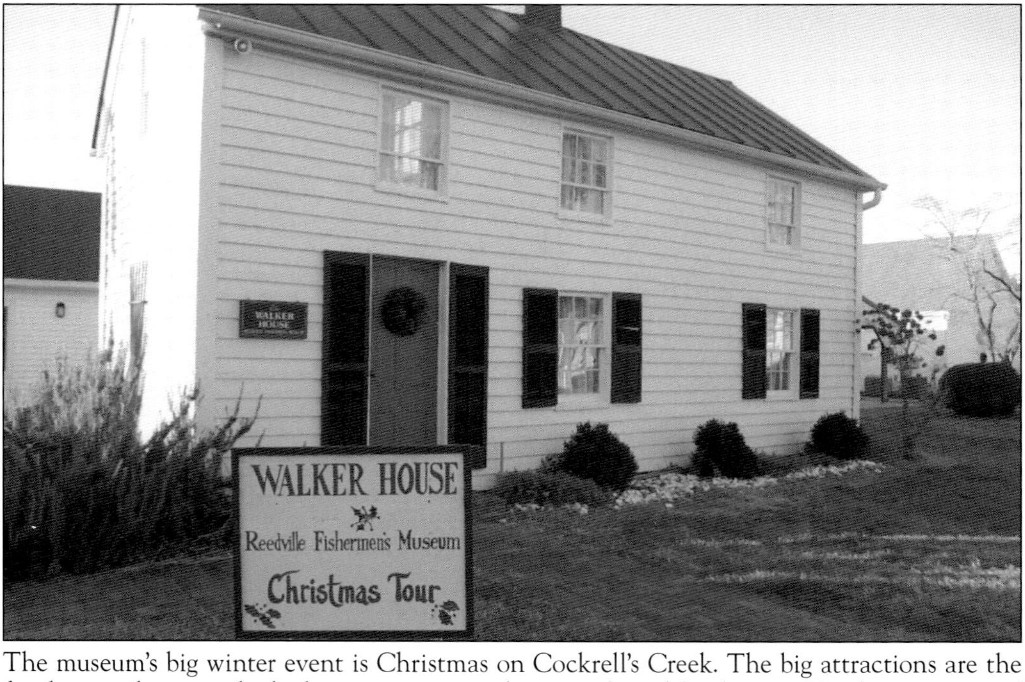

The museum's big winter event is Christmas on Cockrell's Creek. The big attractions are the five historic houses, which change every year, that are selected for the tour. Guides give tours of the decorated homes. The museum is the home base, and the Walker House comes alive with organ playing and caroling.

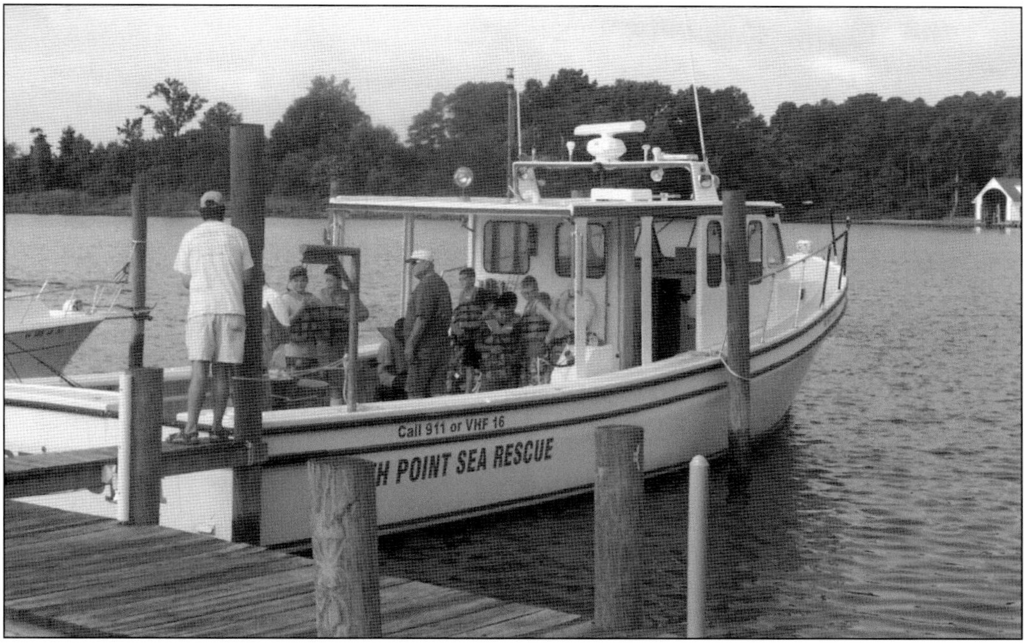

A new annual event established in 2014 in conjunction with YMCA is the Take A Kid Fishing Day. Children from the summer camp, many of whom have never fished or even been on a boat, get the opportunity to go fishing on a fleet of volunteer boats. Once done, a big fish fry is held at the museum, along with other activities. It is a fantastic community event.

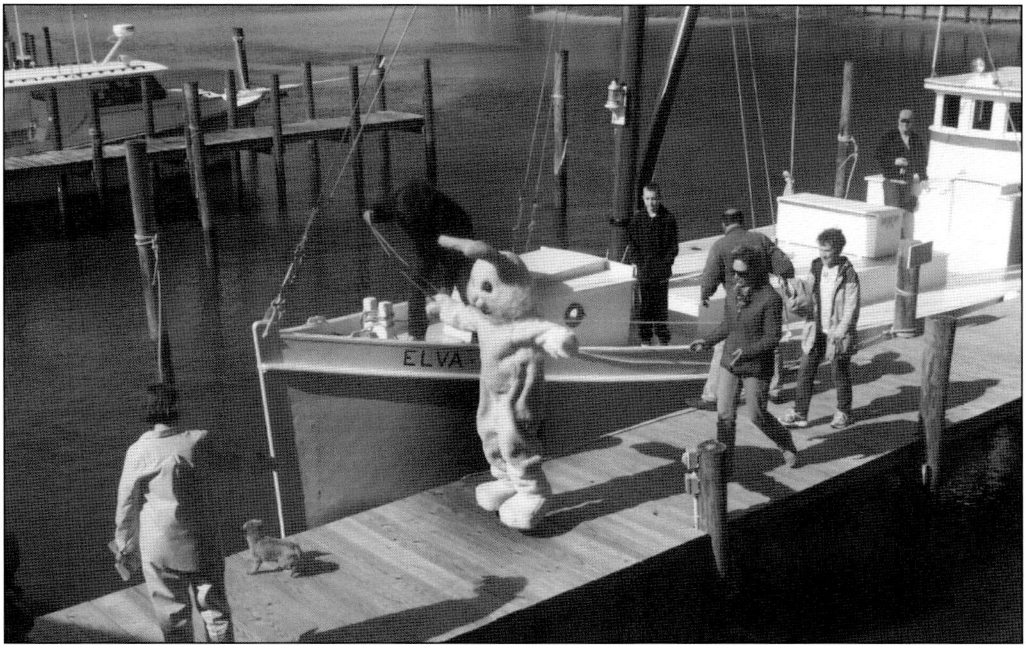

The *Elva C.* serves other purposes in addition to cruises around Cockrell's Creek. It also carries VIPs during the holidays. At Easter time, it delivers the Easter Bunny just in time for the big Easter egg hunt and other activities. For Christmas, Santa Claus uses the *Elva* for his sleigh, and his arrival kicks off Christmas on Cockrell's Creek.

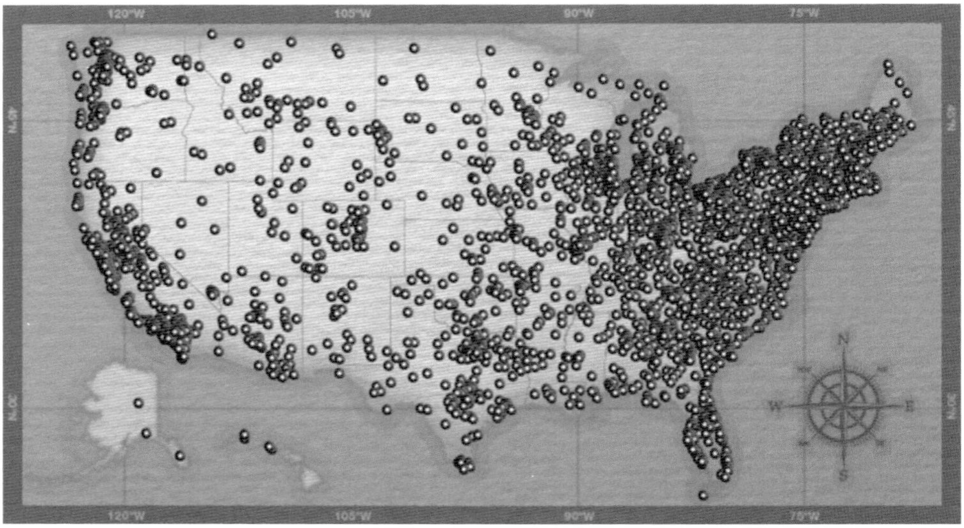